THINK AND GROW RICH:
The 21ˢᵗ-Century Edition
WORKBOOK

Based on Napoleon Hill's text for *Think and Grow Rich*

edited by Bill Hartley and Ann Hartley

with commentary by Bill Hartley

HIGHROADS MEDIA, INC.

ISBN 10: 1-932429-32-8
ISBN 13: 978-1-932429-32-9

10 9 8 7 6 5 4 3 2

CONTENTS

HOW TO USE
THIS WORKBOOK

Napoleon Hill is quoted as saying, "You can't really get *Think and Grow Rich* by reading it just once. There is just as much written between the lines as there is written in the lines themselves."

This workbook is designed to guide you through *Think and Grow Rich* and explain it so clearly that by the time you come to the last page you will know the book and understand it better than devoted students who have read it many times over. Following the format of the book, the workbook breaks down each of Napoleon Hill's principles of success, fills in the background, takes you step-by-step through his philosophical arguments, and explains how and why Hill arrived at his theories. In addition to elaborating on the information in Hill's text, the workbook also draws upon numerous outside sources to present you with related material, updated research, and new examples.

The editors of this workbook take each chapter, analyze it, explain the subtleties, point out where people often go wrong, and do everything

NOTES & COMMENTS

possible to make sure that the reader "gets" every one of the ideas Napoleon Hill was trying to convey—including those that Hill says are hiding between the lines. The result is a highly practical program of commentaries, exercises, questionnaires, and intellectual tools created specifically to make *Think and Grow Rich* the most important book you have ever read.

THE FIRST STEP IS TO READ THE BOOK

It's true that even if you have not read *Think and Grow Rich,* if you read this workbook you will still learn a good deal about Napoleon Hill's philosophy. However, if you don't read the book, you will accomplish nowhere near what this workbook is intended to do. The workbook is created to expand on each of the theories, concepts, and ideas set forth by Hill in *Think and Grow Rich,* so unless you have read the book you will not have the basics to build upon. It would be like reading a book about how to act the role of Hamlet without first having read the play. You could do it, but you won't do it as well as you should.

WHICH EDITION SHOULD YOU READ?

This workbook was developed specifically as a companion volume to *Think and Grow Rich: The 21st-Century Edition.* However, it can also be used with any of the earlier editions.

The first edition of *Think and Grow Rich* was originally published in 1937, and although it changed publishers a number of times, there were no alterations made to the text until 1960.

In 1960, Napoleon Hill and his then partner and co-author, W. Clement Stone, decided to do a minor rewrite to bring some of the references up to date. This revised edition became the official version that was used by various publishers, and the text remained unchanged until 2004.

Then in 2004 Highroads Media, in association with the Napoleon Hill Foundation, published *Think and Grow Rich: The 21st-Century Edition.* In this new edition the original text has again been preserved, but it has also been augmented with extensive annotations, commentaries, and new examples that have been added to update and elaborate on the original text.

The editors of this workbook suggest that if you have a choice, the new commentaries and updated material in *Think and Grow Rich: The 21st-Century Edition* makes it by far the preferred edition. However, if you own one of the earlier editions you will still find that the basic text correlates with the material in this workbook.

In the early publications, the book begins with introductions and prefaces that vary depending on the publisher. The actual body of the book begins with the chapter titled Thoughts are Things, which is always chapter 1 in the early editions.

In the new *21st-Century Edition,* the relevant material from the prefaces and introductions has been assembled into a new chapter 1 titled The Secret of Success. The chapter titled Thoughts are Things is renumbered as chapter 2, and the workbook chapters coordinate exactly with the *21st-Century Edition.*

If you are working with one of the earlier editions, simply disregard the chapter numbers and you will find that you can easily match the chapter titles in those early editions of *Think and Grow Rich* with the chapter titles in this workbook.

EACH WORKBOOK CHAPTER STARTS WITH A RECAP

The material in each chapter of this workbook is directly related to the material in the corresponding chapter of *Think and Grow Rich: The 21st-Century Edition,* and each chapter begins with a recap and analysis of the material that appears in the book.

> "One of the main weaknesses the average person suffers is too much familiarity with the word *impossible.* This book was written for those who seek the rules that have made others successful, and are willing to stake everything on those rules."

The recap and analysis is designed to refresh your memory about the key points in that chapter and to set the stage for the new information and exercises that follow in the workbook. If it has been some time since you read *Think and Grow Rich,* you may find that the recap can also be a warning that you are not as "up" on what Napoleon Hill had to say as you think you are.

Because you are embarking on a course of study that builds upon the material that is in the book, you will want to be sure that you have a clear idea of the concepts Hill was setting forth in each chapter. It is the editors' advice that you give the recap your full attention, and if there is anything in it that you don't clearly recall, it's time to go back and read the chapter in the book before tackling the workbook chapter. The truth is, once you get into the workbook you will probably find yourself turning to the book quite often to refresh your memory and check references.

PLEASE WRITE IN THIS BOOK

This is a workbook—and we mean that literally. This is a book that is meant to be worked in. It is designed specifically so you can make notes in the margins, and we have intentionally had the type set so that the lines are far enough apart to make it easy for you to underline the ideas and phrases that catch your fancy.

Our intention is that you will make this your own personalized version of *Think and Grow Rich.* When you have finished working your way through this workbook it should be filled with notes and reminders to yourself, it should mark the passages you find particularly relevant to your life, and it should be a record of your progress that you can go back and refer to when you can't quite recall what it was that got you so motivated and inspired.

PLEASE WRITE IN THE QUESTIONNAIRES

Throughout this book you will find lists, exercises, and questionnaires. In many cases there is a scale for you to grade yourself, followed by

> "Failure is nature's plan to prepare you for great responsibilities."

> "If it isn't your job to do it, perhaps it's your opportunity."

blank lines where you can make notes. Again, we encourage you to write down your thoughts. They don't have to be brilliant. They don't even have to be sentences and they don't have to be words if a doodle is the best way to capture what you want to convey or remember.

These are not the kind of questions that have right or wrong answers, and there is nobody but you to mark your answers anyway. These are the kind of questions that don't lead to answers so much as they lead to insights. And insights that flash into your consciousness can fade quickly if you don't write down something to capture that fleeting feeling of "ahah!"

The editors can't encourage you enough to write as you go. When an idea flashes into your mind, when you suddenly "get it," it always seems so clear that you're sure you'll be able to remember it later. However, when something comes to you like that, it's usually because a lot of things suddenly fell into place in just the right way, and the feeling of the moment that made the idea happen is hard to hold on to . . . and even harder to recall.

If you don't capture the moment in words while it's still fresh in your mind, the next time you try to recall it it's like grasping at mental straws. You know it's there somewhere but you can't quite bring it into focus, and you begin to wonder if it's really such a hot idea after all.

The editors strongly recommend that you use the spaces provided to write down key words and reminders that you can use later as a blueprint for a more detailed explanation.

THE EDITORS' MARGINAL THOUGHTS

In addition to the blank lines for your notes and comments which appear in the margins on many pages, the editors have also chosen to insert thoughts and quotes. Most of these are in quotation marks, although there are some that are not. The ones that do appear in quotes are by Hill and are taken from either *Think and Grow Rich* or

"Many philosophers have made the statement that man is the master of his own earthly destiny, but most of them have failed to say why he is the master. The reason that man may become the master of himself and of his environment is because he has the power to influence his own sub-conscious mind."

Law of Success. Those not in quotes are Napoleon Hill's ideas that have been adapted by the editors because of their relevance to material on the particular pages.

DETAILS, THE MASTER MIND, AND INFINITE INTELLIGENCE

For those readers who are sticklers for proper grammar, punctuation, and spelling, you will find that in a couple of instances we have made the seemingly peculiar decision to capitalize certain words that do not require capitalization. The following explains our decision.

As Napoleon Hill was writing his philosophy of success, he realized there were two concepts that he could not properly convey without creating his own terminology. The two new terms he created are *Master Mind* and *Infinite Intelligence.* Although the words that comprise these terms would not normally be capitalized, because they have special significance as Hill uses them, we have chosen to set them off by capitalizing them when they appear in this workbook.

We will also point out that a sans serif font has been used for anything pertaining to the workbook, and a serif font has been used for what pertains to copy from any of Napoleon Hill's books.

IS IT FAILURE OR IS IT DEFEAT?

There is one other issue of terminology that we would like to clarify before you begin this workbook, and that is the question of which is it when you totally give up: is it failure or is it defeat?

This is an issue because Napoleon Hill has used it both ways. In some of his writings he has said that even if you have temporary defeats, you have not failed until you give up in your own mind. At other times he has used the terms just the opposite, saying that everyone suffers failures but that doesn't necessarily mean they're defeated.

The editors of this workbook have concluded that the most common way the terms are used is that failures are the ones that teach us we

"It was Andrew Carnegie's idea that the magic formula, which gave him a stupendous fortune, ought to be placed within the reach of people who do not have the time to investigate how others had made their money . . .

have to make better plans, and defeat is when you give up in your own mind. So be warned, at times there will be discrepancies between the words in the book and the way the concept is stated in the workbook, but the workbook is consistent throughout: Everyone has failures and you should learn from them, but you are not defeated until you give up in your own mind.

THERE IS NO DOUBT THAT THIS BOOK WORKS

One of the great advantages in writing a workbook based on such a classic bestseller as *Think and Grow Rich* is that it teaches a system which has worked for literally millions of people all over the world. This book has inspired more successes and made more millionaires than any other book in publishing history. If it worked for them, why shouldn't it do the same for you?

The only thing standing between you and success is how prepared you are to commit yourself to the Napoleon Hill method.

Remember as you read: the people who enjoy the greatest success are those who don't just learn what Hill says, they embrace it without reservation. They don't try to second-guess Hill. They don't think that they're too smart or sophisticated to follow such simplistic rules. They just commit themselves 100 percent and persevere until they have accomplished their goals.

ABOUT THE EDITORS

For more than twenty years, the publisher/editors of this workbook, Bill Hartley and Ann Hartley, have not only been deeply involved in the study of Hill's writings, but have also been the leading publishers of his works. As publishers, producers, and editors, they have created and published more bestselling books and audiobooks by and about Napoleon Hill than any other publisher in the world.

. . . He said that if it were properly taught, it would revolutionize the entire educational system, and the time spent in school could be reduced to less than half."

THE SECRET
OF
SUCCESS

1

CHAPTER 1: OVERVIEW AND ANALYSIS

ANDREW CARNEGIE'S SECRET OF SUCCESS

This chapter begins with Napoleon Hill explaining that he first learned the money-making secret of success from one of the wealthiest men in the world—Andrew Carnegie.

EDITOR'S COMMENTARY

The Commentary that follows explains in greater detail how Hill first met Carnegie at what was supposed to have been a three-hour interview but turned into a three-day marathon meeting. It was at this meeting that Carnegie offered to introduce Hill to the most powerful people in America if he would undertake learning the secrets of their success from each of them and then turn those secrets into a philosophy of personal achievement that could be used by the common man.

In the next section Hill names some of the people who prospered from using the Carnegie secret (their stories are told in later chapters).

Andrew Carnegie told Napoleon Hill that he believed any person could achieve greatness if they understood the philosophy of success and the steps to achieve it. "It is a shame that each new generation must find the way to success by trial and error, when the principles are really clear-cut."

He also explains that although the secret appears in every chapter, it is not named or explained in detail because it works better if you discover this secret yourself.

Hill explains that in doing the research for this book, he analyzed over 500 well-known successful people who attributed their success to the Carnegie secret. This is followed by forty-five thumbnail sketches of famous men and their most recognizable accomplishments.

EDITOR'S COMMENTARY

The editors note that in the time since Napoleon Hill made that list, his philosophy of success has had a greater impact on more motivational experts than any other author, and it is estimated that Hill has inspired more millionaires than anyone in history.

This chapter of *Think and Grow Rich: The 21st-Century Edition* closes with a brief explanation of the theory behind the updated examples that appear in the book. There is also an explanation of the editorial policy regarding grammar, run-on sentences, outdated punctuation, and other matters of form.

CHAPTER 1: THE WORKBOOK

BEING READY FOR THE SECRET

The first sentence written by Napoleon Hill in *Think and Grow Rich* states that every chapter of the book contains the secret for making money. He says that the secret may come to you in a flash, or it may come as a growing awareness, but he does not tell what the secret is—only that you will recognize it when you are ready to receive it.

Hill says his own awakening to the secret came during that fateful meeting with Andrew Carnegie, when Carnegie told Hill his desire to have someone write a philosophy of success that could be used by the common person. However, if you are familiar with Napoleon Hill's past, you know that as important as this meeting may have been, Hill actually got his first lessons about success in a one-room log cabin far from Andrew Carnegie's Park Avenue mansion.

NAPOLEON HILL'S FIRST LESSON

Napoleon Hill was born and raised in the Appalachian Mountains of southwest Virginia in what he described as conditions of poverty, ignorance, and superstition: "For three generations my people had been born, lived, struggled, and died without ever having been outside the mountains of that section. There were no railroads, telephones, electric lights, or passable public highways." And there was little reason to think that anyone in the Hill clan would turn out any different.

His mother died when Napoleon Hill was barely nine years old, and with no mother to look after the family and little parental supervision, young Nap turned into the local hell-raiser. Always stubborn and hot-tempered, he began carrying a six-gun stuffed into his belt, and most of the locals expected he would follow in the footsteps of the man he proclaimed as his hero, Jesse James.

Later in life, when Hill became famous as a public speaker, he often opened his speeches by telling his audience that theoretically he should not have been there with them. Rather, he should have been with his mountain-folk kin, carrying on feuds, killing rattlesnakes, and drinking "corn likker." But that all changed when Nap's father remarried and brought his new wife to live in their backwoods cabin.

Martha Ramey Banner was well-educated, cultured, the daughter of a physician, and the widow of a school principal, and she was little prepared for hillbilly living or a pistol-toting stepson. Something was going to change, and it wasn't going to be Martha. She vowed that she would not live in poverty, and from that moment on, the Hill clan was going to change its ways. Within days of her arrival she called her new family together and, one by one, she began the process of planting the belief that they would no longer put up with living in poverty.

> "Whatever you can conceive and believe you can achieve— as long as it does not violate the laws of God, nature, or man."

James Hill, Napoleon Hill's father, responded to a three-line newspaper ad that read:

"Fill your own teeth. For fifty cents will send enough material to fill twenty teeth."

His first dental tools were made by hand in his blacksmith shop.

DEFINITENESS OF PURPOSE

It was Martha's definiteness of purpose, coupled with her enthusiasm, that would inspire each member of her new family to believe that they could become more than what they were. When she looked at her new husband, James Hill, she did not see a poor dirt farmer and part-time blacksmith. She saw a man with a genius for tinkering and an understanding of the people of the district. Soon James came to see himself that way too.

With Martha's encouragement, James left farming to become the local storekeeper and postmaster. Then one day Martha's false teeth broke and she suggested that, being as handy as he was, James could probably fix them. He carved her a temporary plate from wood that worked so well the Hills decided to send away for a do-it-yourself dentistry course. James and Martha poured over those books until James had taught himself enough to hang out his shingle as a dentist. Though he started out self-taught, he worked hard, gave more and better service than was expected, and became one of the most respected men in Wise County.

In her new stepson Martha saw not a juvenile delinquent but a boy with boundless energy, imagination, and initiative. By the time Napoleon was twelve, Martha had convinced him to give her his gun in exchange for a typewriter. By fifteen, the former troublemaker was writing stories for the regional papers. After graduation he went away to business school, and at the age of nineteen he was the youngest manager of a coal mine, supervising 350 men.

Martha's influence was just as profound on the rest of the family. It was because of Martha's vision and drive that Napoleon's brother Vivian worked his way from the local one-room school in their remote mountain village to a prestigious law practice in Washington, D.C., and Napoleon's stepbrother Paul followed the same course to become a highly respected surgeon.

CONCEIVE, BELIEVE, ACHIEVE

It's unlikely that Martha thought of what she was doing in terms of visualizing a definite chief aim and using autosuggestion to imprint it in the subconscious mind, but that is exactly what she was teaching her family to do. And she may never have defined the need to emotionalize the concepts that are to be imprinted in the subconscious, but, as Napoleon Hill often told his audiences, it was not uncommon for him to see his stepmother get so enthusiastic about an idea that she'd climb up on a chair to make sure she got his full attention.

This is not just an amusing anecdote about a mother's wisdom told by a devoted son. Martha Ramey Banner really did believe in focusing all of your enthusiasm on whatever you wanted to achieve. She systematically set out to teach the members of her family how to use their minds to better themselves—and they did. And Napoleon never forgot the methods she used.

Years later, when Andrew Carnegie began introducing Hill to the wealthy and famous men who would teach him their secrets of success, Hill was more than a little surprised to find that successful entrepreneurs, inventors, and political leaders such as Henry Ford, Thomas Edison, and President Woodrow Wilson used essentially the same method his stepmother had taught him.

THE SECRETS OF THEIR SUCCESS

Following their famous interview in 1908, Andrew Carnegie began to arrange for Napoleon Hill to meet with and study the most successful and powerful people of the day. Although Carnegie died in 1919, the seed he had planted continued to bear fruit, as the leaders of business and industry whom Hill had met through Carnegie in turn introduced Hill to other equally important figures who agreed to tell him the secrets of their success. During this time Hill also served as consultant or adviser to a number of corporations and government agencies that provided

Martha suggested Napoleon try his hand at writing. "If you will devote as much time to reading and writing as you have to causing trouble, you might live to see the time when your influence will be felt throughout the state."

LIST OF ACHIEVERS INTERVIEWED BY NAPOLEON HILL

Henry Ford

William Wrigley Jr.

John Wanamaker

James J. Hill

George S. Parker

E. M. Statler

Henry L. Doherty

Cyrus H. K. Curtis

George Eastman

Charles M. Schawb

Theodore Roosevelt

John W. Davis

Elbert Hubbard

Wilbur Wright

William Jennings Bryan

Dr. David Starr Jordan

J. Ogden Armour

Arthur Brisbane

Dr. Frank Gunsaulus

Daniel Willard

King Gillette

Ralph A. Weeks

the opportunity for him to also study large groups of working men and women in order to further his analysis of why some people succeeded while others failed.

Hill first published the results of his research in 1928 in his eight-volume bestseller, *Law of Success.* It was the culmination of twenty years of research into the habits of more than one hundred of the most successful individuals in America as well as more than 16,000 interviews with average working people, business managers, and entrepreneurs.

Nine years later, after having worked with many of the next generation's most influential people including a stint as a presidential adviser in FDR's White House, Napoleon Hill updated and reorganized his research. By this time the total number of interviews conducted by Hill had grown to more than 25,000 individuals. More than 500 of those interviews were in-depth studies of the secrets of success as explained to Hill by the richest, most influential businessmen, scientists, inventors, industrialists, and entrepreneurs who were instrumental in America's rise to greatness.

On pages 14 through 19 of *Think and Grow Rich: The 21st-Century Edition,* Hill lists the names of forty-five of those people of extraordinary achievement who assisted him in defining the principles of success. As you read through the names and their accomplishments, do not make the mistake of assuming that because you didn't see their names in this morning's *Wall Street Journal* they are not relevant to you and your success.

As is clear from the contemporary authors, educators, and motivators cited in the Editor's Commentary following Hill's list, the concepts and theories Napoleon Hill learned from his research and synthesized in his books and his lectures are the same concepts and theories that are taught in our most prestigious business schools—which are also the same concepts and theories that inspire the authors of today's bestselling motivational business books.

Study Hill's list and you will find famous inventors, scientists, and successful businessmen in every industry including communications and media, advertising and marketing, hospitality and service industries, manufacturing and merchandising, and automotive and transportation. These are exactly the same kind of people who are also the biggest successes today. In fact, if you go to a bookstore, a library, or log on to the Internet and look up business biographies, you will find the story of a modern-day counterpart to every one of the people mentioned by Hill.

BUSINESS BIOGRAPHY ASSIGNMENT

Your assignment is to do just as is suggested in the preceding paragraph: go to a bookstore, a library, or log on to the Internet and compile a list of modern business biographies that parallel the men named in Hill's list. To illustrate, and to get you started, the editors suggest that the following books would be appropriate choices:

- Napoleon Hill's first entry is Henry Ford. A book about a more contemporary figure in the automobile industry might be *Iacocca: An Autobiography,* or perhaps *My Years with General Motors* by Alfred Sloan.

- William Wrigley, the second man named, created an empire built on a pack of chewing gum; *Pour Your Heart Into It* tells how Howard Schultz created the Starbucks empire with a cup of coffee.

- An obvious parallel to the Merchant Prince, John Wanamaker, would be the autobiography of the founder of Wal-Mart, *Sam Walton: Made In America.*

- James J. Hill built railroads. A modern transportation counterpart might be found in *Nuts,* the story of Herb Kelleher, president of Southwest Airlines, or maybe *Flying High,* the story of how JetBlue founder David Neeleman beats the competition.

Judge Daniel T. Wright

John D. Rockefeller

Thomas A. Edison

Frank A. Vanderlip

F. W. Woolworth

Col. Robert A. Dollar

Edward A. Filene

Edwin C. Barnes

Arthur Nash

Clarence Darrow

Woodrow Wilson

William Howard Taft

Luther Burbank

Edward W. Bok

Frank A. Munsey

Elbert H. Gary

Dr. Alexander Graham Bell

John H. Patterson

Julius Rosenwald

Stuart Austin Wier

Dr. Frank Crane

J. G. Chapline

Jennings Randolph

You may choose to disregard certain of the lesser known, non-business names such as John W. David, Dr. David Starr Jordan, Ralph A. Weeks, Judge Daniel T. Wright, Stuart Austin Wier, and J. G. Chapline. And there are so many biographies and autobiographies about every American president written from every political point of view, that for this exercise your time will be better spent researching contemporary entrepreneurial successes rather than trying to select appropriate modern counterparts to Theodore Roosevelt and William Howard Taft.

However, Hill names some other well-known figures of the era, such as William Jennings Bryan, Arthur Brisbane, Dr. Frank Gunsaulas, and Clarence Darrow, who are not associated with business but about whom it may be interesting to try to identify modern counterparts.

As you compile your list of business biographies, watch for those that focus on the industry you work in or are about businesses you find especially interesting. Buy or borrow at least one of those books that resonate with you, and begin your outside reading.

The editors of this workbook are confident that no matter what book you have chosen, as you get into it you will find that the basic theories and concepts will be the same as the theories and concepts that Napoleon Hill explains in *Think and Grow Rich.* In fact, don't be surprised if the author of the book you have selected mentions Hill or *Think and Grow Rich* as an influence in their own success.

Basics are just that: basic. They don't change. Styles may change, and technology might get better or faster, but the significance of specialized knowledge or organized planning, the need for networking, the importance of a clear and focused objective—all these and Hill's other principles of success are just as important in launching Bill Gates' next line of computer software as they were in marketing Thomas Edison's dictating machine.

MOTIVATIONAL BOOKS, AUDIOBOOKS, AND VIDEOS

The editors of *Think and Grow Rich: The 21st-Century Edition Workbook* strongly encourage you to make business biographies a regular part of your plan to succeed. They are entertaining, inspirational, and they offer an opportunity to see examples of Hill's principles of success at work in the real world. They are filled with ideas that you can adapt and use.

Napoleon Hill's friend, partner, and co-author, W. Clement Stone, said his lifelong passion for success literature began when, as a boy of twelve, he spent the summer living on a farm. One day while rummaging in the attic of an old farmhouse, he discovered a collection of about fifty books by Horatio Alger. That summer he read every one of them and developed a habit that stayed with him for the rest of his life.

Over the years, Stone read so many motivational and self-help books that he developed his own system for getting the most out of inspirational literature. His system worked so well that the Napoleon Hill Foundation began to include it in most of their publications, and then adopted it as a part of their home-study programs. The following is an explanation of W. Clement Stone's system as explained in his bestseller *The Success System That Never Fails*:

> In order to attain any goal in life, you must first learn to recognize, relate, assimilate, and apply principles from what you see, hear, read, think, or experience. [W. Clement Stone calls this his R2/A2 Formula.]
>
> When you read an inspirational self-help book, for example, you will not receive any benefit from the words unless you study, understand, comprehend, and *apply* the principles it sets forth.
>
> There is an art to reading such a book. The first thing you must do is concentrate. Read as if the author is a close personal friend and is writing to you and you alone.

Horatio Alger Jr. (1832–1899) became one of America's most successful authors, whose sales rivaled Mark Twain's and whose name has become synonomous with stories of people who succeed by pulling themselves up by their own bootstraps. After studying poetry at Harvard, and an ill-fated attempt at the clergy, in 1866 Alger moved to New York and began writing his distinctive style of novel. In his career he wrote 135 "dime novels" that almost always followed the same format, about a young boy born into poverty who struggles to get ahead. Through some act of honesty or bravery, the boy comes to the attention of someone who sees the qualities in the boy and who is in a position to step in and help him achieve success.

NOTES & COMMENTS

It is wise to *know what you are looking for.* If you really want to relate and assimilate into your own life the ideas that are contained between the covers of an inspirational book . . . *work at it.* A self-help book is not to be skimmed through the same way you might read a detective novel.

Dr. Billy B. Sharp, a widely respected educator and author of *Choose Success,* wrote: "In a novel the author usually controls the conclusion. In a self-help book the reader writes the conclusion." This means action on your part.

Since ideas often come from unexpected places, it is important to read with a notepad at hand. Anything of interest (a flash of inspiration or an answer to a problem) should be jotted down immediately.

The reader should read by asking the question: *What does this mean to me?*

The reader will want to be alert for the How-to's. A good self-help book will have How-to information as well as What-to. Be alert for both, and for the relationship between the two.

Here are some other suggestions I have always found helpful when reading an inspirational self-help book:

Read the dedication, the index, and each page in sequence. Read the entire book. If you own the book, *underscore what you feel is important,* especially anything you would like to memorize. Put a question mark next to a statement you question or don't understand. You can even write short notes in the margins of a page. Write on your notepad any inspiring ideas or potential solutions to any problem that flashes into your mind. Complete a chapter before you stop reading.

After you have completed your first reading, read the book again for the purpose of *studying*, so that you understand and comprehend the information in each paragraph. Identify and *memorize* self-motivators in the text. Again, underscore additional words and phrases that are important to you.

At some future date, read the book again. I remember that Napoleon Hill once had a problem and seemed unable to come up with an answer. How did he finally find the answer? By rereading his own book, *Think and Grow Rich.*

NOTES & COMMENTS

THOUGHTS
ARE
THINGS

2

CHAPTER 2: OVERVIEW AND ANALYSIS

THE MAN WHO "THOUGHT" HIS WAY INTO PARTNERSHIP WITH THOMAS A. EDISON

This chapter opens with Napoleon Hill setting up the story of how Edwin C. Barnes planted in his mind the burning desire to become the partner of Thomas Edison.

THE INVENTOR AND THE TRAMP

In the main body of this section, Hill makes the point that Barnes did not want to work *for* Edison, he wanted to work *with* him. His opportunity came when Edison introduced a dictating machine that received a less than enthusiastic response from his salesmen. Barnes stepped up and offered to take over the sales of the machine on a partnership basis. The deal was done and Barnes became the only partner Edison ever had—and a very wealthy man. Barnes had accomplished his burning desire and turned his thoughts into reality.

Barnes literally thought himself into a partnership with the great Thomas Edison.

He had nothing to start with, except knowing what he wanted, and he had the determination to stand by that desire until he realized it.

THREE FEET FROM GOLD

Hill tells about R. U. Darby who got gold fever and went out West with his uncle to try his luck during the Colorado gold rush. At first they struck it rich, but the vein of gold petered out, they lost their nerve, sold their equipment to a junk dealer, and hopped a train back home.

The junk dealer hired a geologist, drilled where the expert advised, and struck the mother lode just three feet from where Darby and his uncle stopped digging.

R. U. Darby attributed his later success in the insurance business to the lesson he learned from his failed gold mine. He said he could accept that sometimes he would lose, but he would never, ever give up again.

EDITOR'S COMMENTARY

The editors cite Napoleon Hill's creed, "Every failure brings with it the seed of an equivalent success." They cite *The Joy of Failure*, which documents famous successful people who learned from their failures.

The editors also note that inventor Charles F. Kettering says our school system discourages creativity because students are afraid to fail.

A FIFTY-CENT LESSON IN PERSISTENCE

Hill again quotes R. U. Darby, who told Hill about the little girl who came to collect some money that Darby's uncle owed to the girl's mother. When the uncle told her to run along, she stood her ground in the face of daunting odds and demanded to be taken seriously. So determined was the little girl, she overcame a grown man.

This time the lesson for Darby was the importance of being so convinced in your own mind that you are doing the right thing that there is no question of abandoning your principles or your goal.

SUCCESS CONSCIOUSNESS

Hill says that to follow his philosophy means that you must stop measuring the world by your old thought-habits steeped in poverty and defeat. You must learn that the limitations you were taught to live by are not necessarily the right way to see the world.

THE IMPOSSIBLE FORD V-8 MOTOR

Henry Ford's engineers told him it was impossible to make a solid block V-8 motor. Ford told them to try anyway. They insisted it was impossible. Ford told them to keep trying. If the engineers had their way they would have given up, but Ford persevered and they finally did what they said was impossible: they cast a solid block V-8 motor.

EDITOR'S COMMENTARY

The editors note that it is now common to start on a project even though there may be problems that do not yet have solutions. Today's strategic planners just assume a solution will be found when needed.

WHY YOU ARE THE MASTER OF YOUR FATE

This is a statement of Hill's basic principle—that you are the master of your fate because you can control what you think, and that whatever you can conceive and believe, you can achieve.

PRINCIPLES THAT CAN CHANGE YOUR DESTINY

Hill tells about a university commencement address he delivered in which he was so convincing in his explanation of the need to have a burning desire that one of the graduating students, Jennings Randolph, made it the cornerstone of his lifelong philosophy. Randolph went on to become a senator from West Virginia, a close confidant of President Franklin D. Roosevelt, and a pioneering airline executive. The section closes with a letter from Jennings Randolph to Napoleon Hill extolling the importance of a burning desire, and thanking Hill for providing his original inspiration.

EDITOR'S COMMENTARY

The chapter closes with the reminder that Hill has made millions of people successful, but only because they trusted that he knew what he was talking about and they did exactly as he advised. Either you commit to Hill's program, or you take the chance that you know better than the man who made more millionaires than any other person in history.

"More than 500 of the most successful people this country has ever known told me that their greatest success came just one step beyond the point at which failure had overtaken them."

The New Thought Movement began in America in the late 1800s, inspired by the teachings of Phineas Quimby. It was rooted in traditional Christianity, but also incorporated aspects of metaphysical traditions. Central to its beliefs was the power of thought to affect change in the real world.

New Thought was back in the news again in 2006 with the release of the best-selling motivational video and book titled *The Secret.* According to its creator, Rhonda Byrne, *The Secret* was inspired by New Thought author Wallace Wattles' 1906 book, *The Science of Getting Rich.*

The secret that the book and video reveal is summed up as the law of attraction, which, as it is presented in *The Secret,* is a rather simplistic variation on creative visualization: If you think it, it will manifest itself in your life.

CHAPTER 2: THE WORKBOOK

THOUGHTS ARE THINGS

To authors of Napoleon Hill's generation, poetry and literary references were an essential part of a well-rounded education, and often in their own works they would turn to a favorite quote or verse to help illuminate a thought. During Hill's formative years there was widespread interest in the New Thought Movement, a philosophy that focused on the power of the mind. One of the influential books in the movement was titled *Thoughts are Things,* by Prentice Mumford. At roughly the same time, Henry Van Dyke wrote a poem which he also titled *Thoughts are Things,* the first four lines of which are:

> I hold it true that thoughts are things
> Endowed with bodies, breath, and wings,
> And that we send them forth to fill
> The world with good results—or ill.

Either the book or the poem would have been perfect inspiration for the title of this chapter dealing with a positive mental attitude.

NEVER GIVE UP

This chapter is basically four stories that illustrate Hill's first principle of success: the story of Edwin Barnes becoming the partner of Edison, the story of R. U. Darby's failure as a gold prospector, the tale of the little girl who needed the money for her mother, and the story of Henry Ford and the impossible V-8 motor. Those four stories, and the letter from Jennings Randolph that closes the chapter, are all variations on the same point: all success begins with knowing clearly what you want and having the definiteness of purpose to turn it into a burning desire.

The secondary message is that you must not only firmly set your burning desire, but you must then stick with your burning desire until you either achieve your goal or—by failing—you prove to yourself that it couldn't be done the way you planned to accomplish it. That of course raises the question, "How will I know when it is finally time to give up?"

The answer is: never.

You never give up. It is possible that you may fail, but you must never give up.

You begin with the burning desire to win, to achieve, to accomplish. You pursue that desire with unwavering focus until it is yours. Even though you never deviate from your goal, you know going into anything that there is always a possibility you may fail to achieve your desire. You know that, and you also know that failure does not mean defeat.

Failure is only learning that the plan you made was not good enough to accomplish your goal. The answer to failure is to review what you did, analyze why you failed, learn from your mistakes, select a new goal, make a new plan, and go after it with a burning desire.

Giving up because something is too hard, takes too long, because you're frustrated, you've lost interest, or it's not as good as you thought it would be is not failure—it's you admitting defeat. Failure is something that happens to you. Giving up is what you do to yourself.

SUCCESS CONSCIOUSNESS

After telling the stories to set up the concept of a burning desire and definiteness of purpose, Hill introduces a related concept that he calls *success consciousness.* Success consciousness is Hill's term for a particular attitude and way of looking at things that can affect your ability to develop a burning desire.

At other points in the book he also refers to this concept as *money consciousness* and *prosperity consciousness,* but for the most part in this workbook we use the term *success consciousness.*

IT'S ALL IN HOW YOU LOOK AT IT

The classic illustration of success consciousness is the example of a glass that contains water to the halfway point. Is the glass half-full or is it half-empty? Quite clearly it is both or either. It all depends on how you look at it.

The person who has developed success consciousness looks at the glass and immediately sees it half-full. It is Hill's contention that if you are going to succeed with the *Think and Grow Rich* program, it will only work if you decide to become a person who sees the glass as half-full.

FAILING YOUR WAY TO SUCCESS

Closely related to the concept of the half-full glass is Hill's creed that every failure or misfortune holds the seed of an equal or greater success. Once again this deals with how you see things, but here it is whether you see failure as a defeat or as an opportunity to learn a lesson that will help you succeed the next time.

In *Think and Grow Rich: The 21st-Century Edition,* the idea of using failure as a positive motivator is clearly illustrated by the examples in the commentary from Wayne Allyn Root's book *The Joy of Failure* and in Hill's quotes from inventor Charles F. Kettering.

The important point about both the half-full glass and the failure-as-opportunity is not just that it depends on how you see it, but that how you see it is up to you. It is entirely within your power to control the way in which you respond to things.

POSITIVE MENTAL ATTITUDE

Napoleon Hill's concept of success consciousness is the precursor of the theory behind the bestseller *Success Through a Positive Mental Attitude,* which Hill co-authored with W. Clement Stone. In their book they use the acronym PMA to refer to the state of mind that results from approaching life with a positive mental attitude. W. Clement Stone practiced that philosophy every day of his life, and he believed that this, combined with Hill's principles of success, was the reason he had achieved so much in life. As Stone defines it, PMA is much more than what we usually consider to be positive thinking.

Starting with only one hundred dollars and a burning desire to succeed, W. Clement Stone turned himself into a master salesman and built a multibillion-dollar insurance empire. As his success grew, he made a point of analyzing his achievements and identifying each technique that worked for him. He would then formalize it into a written theory and it would become part of his personal PMA philosophy.

W. Clement Stone was an avid reader, an inveterate memo writer, and an inspirational motivator who loved to share the lessons he had learned as he built his empire. He made sure that every person he hired learned the PMA method, and he gave each new employee a free copy of the book that had been the greatest inspiration to him—*Think and Grow Rich.* By doing so, he changed their mindset and helped make many of them successful and wealthy beyond their wildest dreams.

HAVING ENTHUSIASM OR BEING ENTHUSIASTIC?

Anyone who ever experienced W. Clement Stone's upbeat, larger-than-life personality has witnessed PMA in action. No moment in his presence was ordinary, no subject got less than his full attention, and every idea was approached as though it had at least the possibility to be wonderful. PMA is not just giving something the benefit of the doubt; PMA is *active enthusiasm* for its possibilities.

Is it really possible for you to emulate W. Clement Stone and have honest enthusiasm for everything that comes your way? According to Stone's philosophy, to do so you must first understand the difference between having enthusiasm and being enthusiastic. The difference between the two is that enthusiasm is an inward mental attitude, while

"Some of you will have trouble believing that you really can think and grow rich, because your thought habits have been steeped in poverty, misery, failure, and defeat.

If you have formed the habit of seeing life only from your own perspective, you may make the mistake of believing that your limitations are in fact the proper measure of limitations."

Every failure brings with it the seed of an equivalent success.

Jack Welsh, Charles Schwab, Sylvester Stalone, Bruce Willis, Oprah Winfrey, Bill Clinton, Steven Jobs, Donald Trump

. . . every one of them was a failure but none of them was defeated.

acting enthusiastically is the outward expression. According to Stone, either one can create the other.

We all know that acting enthusiastic comes naturally if you have inner enthusiasm. But Stone says it can also work the other way and be just as genuine. Even if you don't feel enthusiasm for something to begin with, if you intentionally give it the benefit of the doubt and *act* enthusiastically anyway, your outward actions will influence your inner attitude. It is a fact, acting "as if" really does work. You cannot be positive and negative at the same time, and it is entirely within your power to control the way in which you respond to things.

Now, does everything deserve your enthusiasm?

Probably not, but isn't it better to at least start from the point of view that it does? If it proves to be less than you'd hoped, you can always change your mind. That way you are less likely to be the person who doesn't listen to F. W. Woolworth's idea about cheap prices, who turns down the script for *Star Wars* because sci-fi is dead, the person who fired Steven Jobs, the person who . . . well, you get the idea. It's always easier to say no than to say yes. And that brings us back to success consciousness.

Success consciousness means that in every way and in everything you do, you enthusiastically expect the best and look for the possibility of success. Simply stated, you consciously make the decision that you will see the glass half-full instead of half-empty. You decide for yourself that the next time you fail at something you will not see it as a defeat but as an opportunity to learn a lesson that will help you succeed the next time.

A WORD OF CAUTION

There is a certain kind of person who will belittle your glass-half-full attitude and look down on you as being naïve. We all know at least a few of those people. They are the ones who pride themselves on being realistic and facing facts. They will tell you that they don't want to burst your balloon, but by converting you to their half-empty point of view, they are doing it for your own good and to keep you from being hurt.

The next time someone tells you that, you should stop and ask yourself a few questions. What will it gain you to view life from their cynical point of view? Will cautious suspicion and guarded optimism inspire anyone you know? Does moderation and sober reserve fling open any doors for you? In what way will your chance of success be made better by filtering everything through the lens of the worst-case scenario?

The next time someone tells you to face facts or to see things as they really are, here's the fact you should face: the fact is that the glass is just as much half-full as it is half-empty. If it's a choice, why not go for the one that could make you a winner? The chances of you taking a half-full glass and making something of it are a lot better than if you are trying to build on something you see as half-empty.

As was mentioned previously, Napoleon Hill warns that you will not succeed with the *Think and Grow Rich* program unless you make success consciousness your natural habit.

In later chapters you will learn a number of techniques to help you do so, but as you start this workbook and read these first few chapters, you can set the right tone by firmly deciding that as you go forward you will view things in the positive light of success consciousness.

DESIRE

3

CHAPTER 3: OVERVIEW AND ANALYSIS

THE STARTING POINT OF ALL ACHIEVEMENT

This chapter opens with Napoleon Hill recapping the story of how Edwin Barnes had such a burning desire to make himself the partner of Thomas Edison that he gave up everything to be in a position to sell himself to Edison. And when that time finally came, Barnes pitched his idea, got the deal, and made himself rich and Edison even richer.

ALLOW YOURSELF NO RETREAT

Hill tells of the warrior who burned his boats so that his soldiers would have to win because there was no way to retreat.

Hill then tells how Marshall Field vowed to rebuild his store after the devastation of the Chicago fire. Once Field declared himself and gave his word that he would do it, he was just as committed as Barnes without a penny to catch a train back home, or the warrior without a boat to sail to safety.

Successful people think their way into realizing their goals.

Thoughts become powerful when combined with a definite purpose.

Riches begin with a state of mind and definiteness of purpose.

EDITOR'S COMMENTARY

If you have a burning desire, you will become success conscious and begin to view everything from the perspective of whether it will help you achieve your desire.

SIX WAYS TO TURN DESIRE INTO GOLD

Hill explains how your aim or desire can be transmuted into financial success by following a six-step formula that spells out exactly what you want, when you want it, how you plan to get it, and instructs you how to write out your statement and use it as a visualization.

EDITOR'S COMMENTARY

The editors note that modern research supports Hill's methods; those methods are also used by today's most successful motivational experts. Even if you don't understand his methods, remember that it's the people who follow Hill's advice to the letter who have had the greatest success.

THE POWER OF GREAT DREAMS

The greatest leaders and biggest successes are those people who dream big dreams. Never mind what "they" say; remember that failing is just a way of telling you that you have to improve your plan.

HILL'S STORIES AND RELATED EDITOR'S COMMENTARY

This section comments on the concept of the "other self," defining it as the "you" that would rather fail than give up.

The majority of this section is devoted to stories about people who changed the world when they discovered their other self, such as the famed short-story writer O. Henry and his modern country-music counterpart Merle Haggard, inventor Thomas A. Edison and the modern inventor Dan Kamen, and finally Henry Ford with the Model T and Steven Jobs with Apple Computer.

Hill concludes the section by quoting the poem "I Bargained With Life for a Penny," which reiterates the point that what you get out of life will depend a great deal on what you demand out of life.

DESIRE OUTWITS MOTHER NATURE

This is a long section in which Hill tells the story of his son Blair. The heart of the story is that although Blair was born without ears and the doctors said he would be deaf, through Hill's burning desire that his son would live a normal life, coupled with his firm belief in the power of thought, Napoleon found ways to inspire Blair and teach him to hear.

This story is a testament not only to Napoleon Hill's burning desire and his power to inspire and motivate, but also to Blair Hill's own burning desire to overcome his adversity and to find in his disability the seed of an equivalent benefit. It also speaks to the importance of a burning desire when you refuse to accept no as an answer.

EDITOR'S COMMENTARY

The chapter closes with comments by the editors and by Hill about the power of a burning desire to overcome physical illness, and the editors' confirmation that by the 1980s the concept of the body-mind connection had become a part of mainstream medical practice.

CHAPTER 3: THE WORKBOOK

THE FIVE STEPS TO SUCCESS

There are five fundamental steps that must be taken by all of those who succeed. These steps are:

1. Choice of a definite aim or purpose to be attained
2. Development of sufficient power to attain your goal
3. Perfection of a practical plan for attaining your goal
4. Accumulation of specialized knowledge to achieve your goal
5. Persistence in carrying out your plan

You cannot succeed using the Napoleon Hill method unless you begin by choosing a definite aim or purpose.

"There is no doubt in my mind that Blair would have been deaf and unable to speak all his life if his mother and I had not managed to shape his mind as we did."

A DEFINITE AIM OR PURPOSE

Napoleon Hill's research that supports the principles in *Think and Grow Rich* was first published as part of his masterwork, *Law of Success.* Because the information in *Law of Success* offers more and different examples, this workbook will often go back to that original source to clarify or expand on a point.

For example the following, which is adapted from *Law of Success: The 21st-Century Edition,* Lesson Two, presents a slightly different take on success:

SUCCESS IS POWER

Success is the development of the power with which to get whatever you want in life without interfering with the rights of others.

I lay particular stress on the word *power.* Power is *organized* energy or effort. This course explains how you may organize facts, knowledge, and the faculties of your mind into a unit of power.

For more than twenty years I have gathered, classified, organized, and analyzed information about more than 16,000 men and women. My analysis revealed that 95 percent were failures and only 5 percent were successes.

One of the most startling facts was that the 95 percent who were classed as failures were in that class *because they had no definite aim in life.* The 5 percent who were successful not only had a definite purpose, but they also had *definite plans* for the attainment of their purposes.

FOCUSING ON YOUR DEFINITE AIM

Until you select a *definite purpose* in life, you dissipate your energies and spread your thoughts over so many subjects and in so many different directions that they lead not to power but to indecision and weakness.

With the aid of a magnifying glass you can teach yourself a great lesson in the value of *organized effort.* Through the use of such a glass you can focus the sun's rays on a *definite* spot so strongly that they will burn a hole through a plank. Remove the glass (which represents the *definite purpose*) and the same rays of sun may shine on that same plank for a million years without burning it.

When you organize your thoughts, and direct them toward a *definite purpose* in life, you will be taking advantage of organized effort out of which *power* is developed.

FIRST, LET'S CLEAR UP THE TERMS

Because Napoleon Hill wrote and lectured so extensively, and because his philosophy of personal achievement developed over the years, his first principle of success has had a number of different names. It has been called *desire, a burning desire, a definite aim, a definite purpose, definiteness of purpose,* as well as other variations using the word *goal* or *objective.* Needless to say, by using words with such similar meanings, the terminology has become confusing.

In order to minimize the confusion, the editors of this workbook have created specific definitions for each of the terms, as well as a hierarchy that sets out how the terms relate to each other:

• Your **desire** is something you wish for. The term *desire* is an all-encompassing term that can refer to an aim, a purpose, a goal, or an objective.

• Your **definite purpose** (or just **purpose**) is a long-range desire. It is an overarching desire that you hold in your mind as an ideal to be achieved. We most often use the term *definite purpose* when referring to a philosophical precept that guides your whole life.

- Your **definite aim** (or just **aim**) is also a long-range desire. It is a grand plan that guides your life, but we use this term to refer to a desire that is more concrete than philosophical. It is possible that your definite aim in life is exactly the same as your definite purpose, but it is more common that your aim *contributes* to your purpose, and that you may accomplish one aim on the path to achieving your purpose, then set yourself a new aim that will take you further along that path.

- Your **goals** are medium-range desires. They are individual, targeted desires that contribute to your aim or your purpose.

- Your **objectives** are immediate desires. These are the individual steps that you desire to take to accomplish your goals.

To illustrate, following are two examples:

Example 1

Your **definite purpose** might be: "To become a major figure in the world of television, commanding a salary that will allow me to own my own home and live comfortably on the Upper East Side in New York City or above Sunset Boulevard in Beverly Hills."

Your **definite aim** at this point in your career might be: "To become the head of dramatic-series development at _____ production company, so that I have the power to greenlight projects." After you have accomplished that, you might create a new **aim** such as "To be offered the position of president of _____ network so I can put my stamp on all the programs broadcast."

One of your **goals** at this time might be: "To put together the financing for a specific pilot by April so that production can be complete by November and it can be pitched to the networks no later than February for the next fall season."

Another simultaneous **goal** might be: "To make a co-production deal for the pilot with a company that already produces programming for the network."

A third alternative **goal** might be: "To be hired as a VP of development at the network."

Your **objectives** for your **first goal** might be: "(1) Finish polishing the pitch for the investors. (2) Book meetings with two bankers and one private investor by Wednesday of next week. (3) Meet with a specific agent for lunch tomorrow to confirm the deal for the two lead actors and arrange for the actors to attend the meeting with investors. (4) Set meeting for this Saturday to rehearse investors pitch."

Example 2

Your **definite purpose** might be: "To own my own discount specialty food store that will be profitable enough annually over the next fifteen years that my wife and I can afford to keep up our mortgage payments and continue our current lifestyle while sending our children through college. Our exit strategy is to sell the store and our home at the end of fifteen years and use the proceeds to retire to Scottsdale, Arizona." In this case your **definite aim** is the same as your **definite purpose**.

Your **first goal** at this time might be: "To find an appropriate building that is at least [specify floor space], at a rate of [specify cost per square foot], that must be in an area such as [detail the factors that govern where you want to operate a small specialty food store]."

A simultaneous, noncompeting **second goal** might be: "To make exclusive agreements with regional suppliers who can provide gourmet foods at a wholesale cost that will allow me to price goods at least 25 percent less than the gourmet section of the major food chains in the region, while still maintaining a contribution to overhead of 25 percent."

NOTES & COMMENTS

Your **objectives** for your **second goal** might read something like this: "(1) Call owner of the 99 Cents Only Stores to see if he will give names of low-price specialty goods suppliers. (2) Surf Internet for names of overstock and closeout companies. (3) Call farmers co-op to arrange to meet at Saturday's Farmer's Market to discuss securing options on future berry crops."

AUTOSUGGESTION AND THE SUBCONSCIOUS

There are two basic concepts at the heart of Napoleon Hill's principles of success. First, choose to change the thoughts that dominate your actions by fixing your definite purpose in your conscious mind, and then reinforce it in your subconscious mind through autosuggestion. Both are dealt with in great detail in other chapters, but the following overview of the basic concepts pertaining to autosuggestion and the subconscious will be valuable as you proceed with the rest of this chapter.

- *The Conscious Mind:* Your conscious mind receives information through the five senses of sight, smell, taste, hearing, and touch. Your conscious mind keeps track of what you need for thinking and operating, and it filters out what you don't need. Your conscious mind (and what your memory retains) is the intelligence with which you normally think, reason, and plan.

- *The Subconscious Mind:* Your subconscious has access to all the same information your conscious receives, but it doesn't reason the way your conscious mind does. It takes everything literally. It doesn't make value judgments, it doesn't filter, and it doesn't forget. It doesn't draw a distinction between good and bad, positive and negative. The only thing it responds to is the intensity with which the idea is planted. The stronger the emotion attached to an idea when planted in your subconscious, the more prominent that idea will be.

- **Suggestion:** A suggestion is something that prompts you to take action. It comes from a source outside of yourself. It may be something that someone else says to you, or something you read, see, hear, or even smell, taste, or feel.

- **Self-Suggestion:** This is a suggestion that prompts you to action, but it is controlled by you and it comes from within yourself. It is a suggestion you give to yourself by thinking it, envisioning it in your imagination, saying it to yourself, or writing it down. If you wish to change some aspect of yourself, you can do so by creating a self-suggestion that tells your "self" that you want to make the change. By repeating your self-suggestion over and over, you will not only fix your desire to change in your conscious mind, but it will also become embedded in your subconscious mind.

- **Autosuggestion:** A prompt to action that originally came from without but now comes from within yourself. It is a suggestion that became planted in your subconscious and has now become your automatic response. It is any outside suggestion or self-suggestion that has become so deeply fixed in your subconscious that it is the response which automatically flashes into your mind. It becomes your habit, your natural reaction.

WHAT YOU CONCEIVE AND BELIEVE IS UP TO YOU

Nature has built human beings so that they can have control over the material that reaches their subconscious mind. However, this does not mean that you always exercise this control. Through the dominating thoughts that you permit to remain in your conscious mind (it doesn't matter whether these thoughts are negative or positive), the principle of autosuggestion goes to work impressing those thoughts on your subconscious mind. And, as noted above, your subconscious is not judgmental. It can be just as easily influenced by a negative idea or a bad suggestion as it can by a positive thought or a good suggestion.

When speaking of the subconscious, Hill often used the metaphor of a fertile garden in which weeds will grow if the seeds of more desirable crops are not sown. You can feed your subconscious on creative thoughts, or you can, by neglecting it, permit thoughts of a destructive nature to find their way into this rich garden of the mind.

THE POWER OF HABIT

The following comments by Napoleon Hill on the importance of using autosuggestion to create good habits are excerpted and adapted from *Law of Success*, Volume I, chapter 2, Your Definite Chief Aim:

> Having, myself, experienced all the difficulties of one who didn't completely understand how to use autosuggestion, let me tell you a little of what I learned about the principles of habit and autosuggestion.
>
> Habit grows out of doing the same thing or thinking the same thoughts or repeating the same words over and over again. Habit may be likened to the groove in a record, while the human mind may be likened to the needle that fits into that groove. When any habit has been well formed, the mind has a tendency to follow the course of that habit as closely as the needle follows the groove in a record.
>
> Habit is created by *repeatedly* directing one or more of the five senses of seeing, hearing, smelling, tasting, and touching in a given direction. After habit has been well established, it will automatically control and direct your actions and responses.
>
> When you were a child, you learned how to write by repeatedly directing the muscles of your arm and hand

over certain letter outlines, until finally you formed the habit of tracing those outlines. Now you write quickly and easily, without tracing each letter slowly. Writing has become a habit with you.

The principle of habit will take hold of the faculties of your mind just the same as it will influence the physical muscles of your body. The object in writing out and repeating a self-confidence formula is to form the habit of making belief in yourself the dominating thought of your mind until that thought has been thoroughly embedded in your subconscious mind, through the principle of *habit.*

DEFINING YOUR DEFINITE AIM AND PURPOSE

In the following section you will find these tools:

- How to identify your definite purpose
- How to identify your definite aim
- How to define your purpose and/or your aim
- How to identify your goals and objectives
- How to define your goals and objectives
- How to write the statement of your purpose and/or your aim

Settling on a definite purpose or a definite aim will take time and serious consideration, and there is no better way to explore the possibilities than by writing out your thoughts. As you work your way through this book, you will find a number of exercises and questionnaires with space set aside for you to make notes. However, as with any course of study, the editors of this workbook advise that in addition to the fill-in sections of this book, you should also keep a journal or notebook. You will find that is necessary for the longer writing exercises where it was impractical to leave enough space to adequately deal with the questions posed.

NOTES & COMMENTS

You may choose to use an actual journal or notebook in which you write by hand, or you may prefer to set up a specific folder on your computer. Choose the method you find best suited to free-flowing, stream-of-consciousness writing, and be sure to date each entry so that you can track your progress.

HOW TO IDENTIFY YOUR DEFINITE PURPOSE

Your definite purpose is a clear statement that declares your mission in life. As Hill has said earlier, the word *definite* is key. This is not just another one of the many things you wish you could have—this is a specific desire that has been arrived at after much serious thought.

Ideally, your definite purpose will be a lifelong pursuit that will be related to your occupation or career so that the work you do on a daily basis doesn't conflict with what you want to be.

The following exercise is designed to help you identify your definite purpose by posing a series of questions. This is more of a thinking exercise than a writing exercise, but you might want to make a few notes to yourself down the side of the page or in your journal so you will have a handy reference when you come to the actual writing assignment.

Your definite purpose should answer questions such as these:

- Why do I exist in this life? Do I have a purpose for being here?

- Where am I going? Is there something that I should be pursuing?

- Whom do I serve and why? Am I here just to do whatever comes my way, or do I owe it to somebody or some thing to accomplish something special?

- What do I have to offer? Is there something special about me?

- Do I need to be special to do something that will make a positive difference?

When you commit yourself to your definite purpose, it will feel like you have discovered your reason for being. Although you may decide later to change your definite purpose, it is likely that you will not change it until it is fulfilled. However, even though it may be a lifelong pursuit, the plan for achieving that purpose may change a number of times.

Very few people discover or decide upon their whole life's definite purpose on their first attempt. As you mature and gain wisdom, you may find that your purpose will take a slightly different direction. This does not mean that your first definite purpose was wrong. It may be that something has altered your priorities to the point that you need to rethink your definite purpose.

You might find that you have accomplished your definite purpose sooner than you expected, or you may simply decide that you want something more challenging. It is normal for your purpose to grow with you. However, if, after making a serious effort, it becomes apparent that your desire cannot be accomplished, you must accept that you should change your definite purpose.

HOW TO IDENTIFY YOUR DEFINITE AIM

Although not as philosophical as identifying your definite purpose, settling on your definite aim follows virtually the same procedure. The major difference is one of specificity.

Once again, this is more of a thinking exercise than a writing exercise. Make whatever notes you wish down the side of the page or in your journal. Your definite aim should answer such questions as:

- Can I specifically identify the most important thing that I want to accomplish in my life?

- If I were to continue on the same path, what will make me feel most successful?

NOTES & COMMENTS

• What accomplishment should I target to keep me on the path to success?

• What challenge can I take on that would earn me the greatest rewards?

• What challenge can I take on that I know I can accomplish and will be most successful at?

• What challenge can I take on that will benefit the most people?

• What challenge will make me feel I have done something special?

As mentioned previously, it is quite common to have a definite purpose in life and at the same time have a definite aim. In fact, if you do have both, your definite aim is almost always something that contributes to your definite purpose.

On the other hand, you can have a definite aim without having decided upon any overriding definite purpose for your life.

Although a definite aim is not stated as "the meaning of your life," it does give your life focus and a target to aim for. Those who know what they are aiming for and where they are going do not waste their time and energy trying to accomplish too many things at once. Nor do they bounce from one desire to the next, quickly abandoning anything that doesn't bring immediate satisfaction. They concentrate their efforts on a definite aim, exerting all of their powers to attain that end. When it is accomplished they reset their sights and move on to another definite aim, which becomes their new burning desire.

As with your definite purpose, your definite aim may also change either because you have accomplished it, outgrown it, or it may have become untenable. However, unlike your definite purpose, which if properly chosen will guide you for a lifetime, you very likely will accomplish more than one definite aim, and as you do, you will replace it with a new, more challenging definite aim.

WRITING OUT YOUR DEFINITE PURPOSE OR AIM

Following is a writing exercise that will go a long way toward helping you to define your definite purpose or aim. This exercise should be done in your journal.

Do not expect to create perfectly worded statements the first time you sit down to work on this exercise. It is not a test, it is a working paper. There is no time limit, and there is no limit to the number of words you have to write. The point of doing this as a writing exercise is that in the process of writing out your aim or purpose you will edit and clarify your ideas to make them specific.

- Write a description of the kind of person you would like others to think you are.

- Write an explanation of the kind of knowledge you wish to acquire in life.

- Write an explanation of the skills you would like to master.

- Write an explanation of where you would like to go and what you would like to see in your lifetime.

- Write a description of your ideal job.

- Write a statement of how much you would like to earn each year.

- Write an explanation of what you would be willing to give in return for that amount.

- Write an explanation of what success for you would mean in terms of your home and family.

- Write an explanation of what success for you would mean in terms of your place in the world at large.

- Write an explanation of why success would make you a better person.

NOTES & COMMENTS

These writing exercises are designed to open your mind about your purpose in life and what you want to achieve. When you feel that you have a clear idea of your definite purpose or definite aim, it is time to narrow your focus and define the goals and objectives that make up your aim or purpose.

DEFINING YOUR GOALS AND OBJECTIVES

Just as your definite aim or purpose must be identified, defined, and committed to, so too must your goals and objectives. Remember, to achieve your definite aim or your purpose, you set and accomplish certain goals. To achieve each goal, you set and accomplish certain objectives.

- The reason for setting your goals is to focus your effort on an overarching desire which is your definite purpose or definite aim.

- Your goal statements will then answer the question "What must I accomplish to acquire or achieve my purpose or aim?"

- You can have many goals that are nonconflicting, which help you reach your definite purpose.

- Your goals should always remain a few jumps ahead of you. Goals should be something that make you stretch to accomplish.

- Once you have accomplished a goal, it should naturally open the door to your next new goal.

- Every goal should be broken down into objectives. The more you can break it down, the more obtainable that goal will seem because you are breaking it down into units of effort that seem possible for you to handle.

- Put time limits on each goal and each objective to keep yourself focused and motivated.

When setting your goals you will find that some are almost as demanding as writing out your definite purpose or aim.

The editors recommend that even the simplest goals require some analysis and should be entered in your journal so that you can keep an accurate account of your achievements and progress.

The same is true of objectives. Even though objectives are very often nothing more than a "to-do" list for each goal, you should still write out the list in your journal.

HOW TO WRITE OUT YOUR GOALS AND OBJECTIVES

Following is a step-by-step process for determining your goals and putting them into writing:

1. Write your definite purpose or definite aim as a heading. Under the heading make a list of what you really desire or want to accomplish that will help you live out your definite purpose or aim. The list you have written is a list of your goals.

2. Next, opposite each goal write a one-sentence explanation. If you can't express it in a single sentence, it is not a goal. If it is more than a sentence, then it is an aim and you need to break it down.

3. Putting your goal statements in writing will help you to be more specific in determining what you want to accomplish.

4. Make all of your goals measurable. Each goal should allow you to easily determine if and when you have accomplished it. In order to be measurable, each goal should include specifics such as:

   • How much time will it take to do and when is the deadline up?

   • What are the quotas, threshholds, minimums or maximums that must be achieved?

   • What is the profit margin? What is the break-even point?

NOTES & COMMENTS

5. Examine your goal statements to determine if your goals are challenging and yet obtainable. Goals should be realistic but they should also stretch your knowledge, skills, and self-discipline.

6. Examine your goal statements to determine if they are stated in a positive fashion. A goal that is stated as a negative may focus your attention on what you fear rather than the result you seek.

WRITING THE STATEMENT OF YOUR AIM OR PURPOSE

The following six pages should provide everything you need to write out the statement of your aim or purpose. First there is an eight-point review of the steps you must take to clearly know your desire.

Following that is a sample statement of a definite aim written by a person whose desire is to be a sales manager.

And finally there is a blank form that you can use as a template for creating the statement of your definite aim or your definite purpose.

AN EIGHT-POINT REVIEW

1. Fix in your mind exactly what you desire as your definite purpose or your definite aim. Write it out in a clear, concise, positive statement.

2. Determine exactly what you intend to give in return for what you desire. Will it be your time, your money, your privacy, your independence? What about your sense of security? How much control will you give up in exchange for success? Remember, there is no such reality as "something for nothing."

3. Establish a definite date when you intend to possess what you desire.

4. Create a definite plan for carrying out your desire and begin at once, whether you are ready or not, to put this plan into action. Do it now—right now.

5. Start by opening a new page in your journal and writing your polished statement of your definite purpose or definite aim. Next, write out the benefits you will receive by carrying

out your purpose. Then set the time limit for its accomplishment, choosing an exact date when you want to achieve it. State what you intend to give in return for the right to fulfill your purpose, and describe clearly the plan through which you intend to accomplish it.

6. Read your written statement aloud at least twice daily. Read it just before retiring at night and read it after arising in the morning. As you read, see and feel and believe yourself already in possession of the money.

7. To guarantee success, engage in regular study, thinking, and planning time about how you can achieve your goals, aims, or purpose.

8. Set specific times for regular personal inspection to determine whether you are on the right track, so that you don't deviate from the path that leads to the achievement of your objective.

In the beginning you should evaluate your progress monthly, then quarterly, and finally semi-annually. This review process requires that in evaluating your progress toward your stated desire you must be completely honest with yourself. The main purpose of the evaluation is for you to decide if you need to change your plan, so it will be of no value to you if you are overly generous in your personal assessment.

As noted previously, revisions in your definite aim or purpose should never be made for something as minor as having failed to meet a deadline. Changes in your plan should only be made because of circumstances that are beyond your control or because you have seriously evaluated your purpose or aim and have concluded that it is wrong for you, and you have decided to commit to a different definite purpose or definite aim.

REVIEWING THE PROCESS, MAKING THE PLAN

If you are going to follow the Napoleon Hill plan that leads to success, the first thing you must do is to set your definite purpose or definite aim. You must then create within yourself a burning desire to achieve your purpose or aim. You must lay out a specific step-by-step action plan that will keep you on track to your fulfillment, and you must consciously decide that from now on you will approach life with success consciousness.

Sample Statement #1

The following sample is a completed statement written to record a specific definite aim. It is an example that is often printed in the Napoleon Hill Foundation's publications to illustrate how an individual whose desire it is to become regional sales manager might write out his definite aim, and the goals that will lead him to success.

MY DEFINITE AIM

1. My definite aim is to be regional sales manager for [insert the name of the company] by [insert date and year].

   A. I will definitely be appointed branch manager for [insert name of branch office] of [insert name of company] by [insert date and year]. This will be a step toward the position of regional sales manager because I will be the leading branch manager in efficiency and volume of business in the entire company.

   B. I will definitely lead the entire company as the most efficient field manager for the balance of this year, starting with [insert the specific work you intend to do to get people to recognize your abilities] as justification for promotion to branch manager and as a means of causing the people in power to make such a promotion.

      a) I will strictly budget my time and money. I will use time in such a way that all essentials will be taken care of each day. I will not waste time on anything nonessential.

      b) I will budget my money so as to always have sufficient funds to operate with complete freedom of mind and body.

      c) I will encourage my imagination to develop ideas by putting to work the ideas my mind produces. I will place these ideas where they will help others, and thus attract the attention of those in a position to appoint me to branch manager.

      d) I will attract to me the type of people who want to do an excellent job of selling products. These people, for the most part, are already dealers in my field manager section.

e) I will advertise in the newspapers as a means of attracting the people I want. I will constantly enlist by personal solicitation the services of others who will help me locate the type of dealers necessary to help me achieve my definite aim of being regional manager by [insert date and year].

f) In return for this help, I will give each dealer full benefit of my years of experience. I will teach each dealer all phases of the business, thus enabling him or her to qualify for an opportunity equal to what I have.

g) I will engage in study, thinking, and planning time.

h) Each week I will talk to at least one person, aside from my business associates, about the philosophy of individual achievement. By helping others, I will benefit by the law of compensation in attracting good people.

2. I am motivated in my definite aim by the love of my work, by the desire for recognition, by love for people, and by my insatiable desire to also help others attain their goals.

3. I am confident that I can discharge the responsibilities of branch manager and the responsibilities of regional manager because my methods this year have placed me fifth in efficiency and fifteenth in sales for the entire company of about 1,000 field manager sections. I know these same methods can be carried out branch- and region-wise.

4. I have faith in my ability to attract the attention of the people in power to appoint me branch manager on [insert date and year] and regional manager on [insert date and year]. Because people in power in the company, with whom I have worked, have recommended me for promotion, and as my efficiency becomes greater, I know they will work for my further promotion.

SIGNATURE: _____

DATE: _____

Sample Statement #2

This sample is a blank form that you may use to write the statement of your definite aim or purpose. As you will see, we have arbitrarily chosen to allow for six individual goals. If that is not appropriate for your aim or purpose, you may choose to use this version as a guideline for creating your own personalized statement.

MY DEFINITE AIM OR PURPOSE

My definite aim or purpose is: _____

_____

_____

_____

_____

_____

_____

I will accomplish this by _____ [month] _____ [day] _____ [year]

My first goal toward my definite aim or purpose is:

_____

_____

I will accomplish this by _____ [month] _____ [day] _____ [year]

My second goal toward my definite aim or purpose is:

_____

_____

I will accomplish this by _____ [month] _____ [day] _____ [year]

My third goal toward my definite aim or purpose is:

_____

_____

I will accomplish this by _____ [month] _____ [day] _____ [year]

My fourth goal toward my definite aim or purpose is:

_____

_____

I will accomplish this by _____ [month] _____ [day] _____ [year]

My fifth goal toward my definite aim or purpose is:

_____

_____

I will accomplish this by _____ [month] _____ [day] _____ [year]

My sixth goal toward my definite aim or purpose is:

_____

_____

I will accomplish this by _____ [month] _____ [day] _____ [year]

SIGNATURE: _____

DATE: _____

FAITH IN YOUR ABILITY

4

CHAPTER 4: OVERVIEW AND ANALYSIS

VISUALIZATION OF, AND BELIEF IN, ATTAINMENT OF DESIRE

Chapter 4, Faith, opens with Napoleon Hill's statement that when a thought is mixed with faith, that thought becomes imprinted on your subconscious mind and there it connects with Infinite Intelligence.

EDITOR'S COMMENTARY

In this Commentary the editors clarify some of the terminology as Hill defines it:

- Faith has no religious connotation. Faith means complete and total confidence in your ability to accomplish your desire.

- Infinite Intelligence refers to the part of the thinking process that produces hunches, intuition, and flashes of insight.

- The conscious mind is the intelligence with which you normally think, reason, and plan.

The following is very important in turning desire into money:

You must have complete and unwavering faith that you can do it.

Faith is a state of mind that may be created by repeating instructions to your subconscious mind through self-suggestion.

- The subconscious mind receives the same information as the conscious but it does not filter or judge the content.

HOW TO DEVELOP FAITH

Hill says that faith is a state of mind which may be created through autosuggestion by repeating positive affirmations. It is through this technique that you can emotionalize your desire. He also warns that negative thoughts which become strongly emotionalized are just as easily planted in the mind.

Because the one thing over which you have control is your thoughts, it is up to you whether your subconscious is positive or negative.

EDITOR'S COMMENTARY

To illustrate that the subconscious mind cannot distinguish between what is real and what is vividly imagined, the editors cite the experiment in which a group of basketball players who visualized making free throws each day did just as well in a test of skills as another group of players who had actually practiced.

THE MAGIC OF SELF-SUGGESTION

Hill says that thoughts which are imprinted in your subconscious will begin to influence all of your other thoughts, because thoughts that are strongly emotionalized are like magnets—they attract other similar or related thoughts.

To emphasize the point, the editors present a five-point formula for burning into your mind a set of thought impulses to help you overcome a lack of self-confidence.

Hill again warns that self-suggestion can work for you or against you. If you don't consciously counteract fear and doubt with positive thoughts, it is fear and doubt that will gradually take over and become the magnet that attracts other negative thoughts.

Hill closes the chapter with the lengthy story of how Andrew Carnegie's righthand man, Charles M. Schwab, engineered the deal that created the mining and manufacturing giant U.S. Steel Corporation.

The editors note that although the story actually illustrates six of Napoleon Hill's principles of success, the principle that is at the center of it is Schwab's faith that he could pull together such a disparate group and inspire them to put aside their differences and share the vision that would make it happen.

CHAPTER 4: THE WORKBOOK

In the previous chapter, Hill says that to make a change in your life you must first have a burning desire to change.

What is it that can make your desire burn?

According to Napoleon Hill, it is faith that makes your desire burn. But by faith Hill was not referring to a belief in a higher power. The faith that Hill means is the unquestioning belief in yourself and your abilities, and the complete, unwavering confidence that you can accomplish what you set out to do.

It should be pointed out that this does not mean that Hill was not himself a religious man. However, he made it very clear that regardless of his personal beliefs, his principles of success neither endorsed nor violated any particular religion or creed. During a series of lectures he gave in Chicago in 1962, Hill elaborated on his reasoning as follows:

> I feel exceedingly proud of this philosophy for many reasons. First of all, because it is accepted by all religions even though it does not partake of any of them. Catholics and Protestants, whites and blacks, all the races, all the colors, all the creeds accept this philosophy, and I think that's a miracle in itself.
>
> When I first started out with Andrew Carnegie, he had admonished me to never under any circumstances attach any title of an orthodox nature to this philosophy. He said the minute you do that, you will split your audience.

Plain and unemotional words will not influence the subconscious.

The repetition of emotionalized affirmations and visualizations are the only known methods of developing the emotion of faith.

NOTES & COMMENTS

And when you start the actual writing, never use a word or an illustration that will send a high school boy or girl to the dictionary or encyclopedia.

I have followed those instructions to the letter, with the result that we have a philosophy that is understandable to anybody. Anybody can apply it, and millions of people are applying it all over the world.

NOT JUST FAITH, BUT APPLIED FAITH

The faith that Napoleon Hill says you must have is the undoubting, unwavering belief that your aim can be accomplished, along with your utter and total confidence in your ability to accomplish it.

The term that Hill preferred to use in his later works was *applied faith.* When the word *applied* is added to the word *faith,* you have a term that can be used in the same way you talk about applied pressure or applied force: it is faith with power behind it.

Applied faith added to your aim or purpose is like adding the yeast when you bake bread. Yeast is what makes bread something more than a flat mixture of flour, water, and salt, and faith is what makes your aim or purpose more than a collection of words repeated over and over.

Applied faith is what you add to your desire—your aim or your purpose—in order to make it work.

IT IS CALLED APPLIED FAITH BECAUSE YOU MUST APPLY IT

Napoleon Hill also began using the term *applied faith* because it made it clearer that faith is not something you get, faith is something you have, and it is up to you to use it.

If you have faith, you don't sit around "having" it; if you have faith, you start doing. Having faith without applying it is meaningless. Only when you *apply* your faith do you *demonstrate* your faith.

If you have faith in your aim or purpose, you must start doing it and you must start now, even if you don't have a complete plan.

Someone once said, "Life is what happens to you while you are busy making other plans," which actually makes a nice, neat summation of Hill's point about applied faith. Things are almost never exactly right. And even if things aren't exactly what you want them to be, you will be much further ahead if you get started now, while you work out the rest of the details of the plan.

Hill's message is that there is always something you can do right now that will help you move forward. If you wait around for things to be exactly right, you are not only wasting time but you are delaying the arrival of your success.

IS IT JUST A WISH OR A DEFINITE AIM?

As you learned in the previous chapter, repetition of your aim or purpose is the primary method of planting it in your subconscious. However, there are no magic words that will suddenly make your desires appear. This is psychology, not hocus-pocus. The repetition is simply an effective method of planting an idea in your subconscious so that it will become your habit to think that way.

As Hill stresses often throughout the book, you may wish for something to happen, but with an aim or a purpose you must do more than wish; you must believe it will happen. If, deep down, you don't really believe it is something that is logically within your reach, you won't really have faith that you can do it.

YOU HAVE TO BELIEVE IT

If you are a forty-year-old who has spent your adult life in sales, it is not reasonable to set a definite aim of being the astronaut pilot of the space shuttle. That is a wish or dream, not a definite aim or purpose; not because the aim is too fanciful, but for purely practical reasons. At

NOTES & COMMENTS

forty your age is against you, and so are the entrance requirements. To qualify you would need to spend years learning advanced physics and aeronautics, not to mention the difficulty of qualifying to fly jets, the physical fitness requirements, and the fact that there are only a limited number of shuttle flights and many qualified astronauts ahead of you.

The point is that although you may want something to happen, and you may follow the Hill formula by repeating over and over that it *is* happening, unless there is a reasonable possibility, all the repetition in the world will not make it happen. Furthermore, by selecting an unrealistic aim and failing at it, you will have undermined your faith in yourself and created doubts in your mind about the method.

There is a fine balance between choosing a definite aim that is challenging and choosing one that is unrealistic. But that does not mean you should choose simple or easy-to-accomplish goals. In fact, Hill specifically suggests it is good to choose aims and purposes that cause you to stretch yourself.

In choosing a definite aim or purpose, you should start from the assumption that if there is nothing mental or physical preventing you from learning, there is almost nothing that can't be accomplished if you have enough time to perfect the needed skills or ability.

The only thing that should restrict your choice of a definite aim is if it requires educational degrees or minimum entrance requirements that you have not achieved, or if it requires some specialized talent or physical or mental capacity that you do not possess. In many cases even that should not stop you if what you want can be learned within a reasonable amount of time.

It is true that all the faith in the world won't get you a job that requires a Ph.D. when you only have a high school diploma, but all that means is that you've selected the wrong definite aim. Your aim shouldn't be the job, it should be getting your Ph.D. Once you've done that, your *next* aim can be getting the job.

MOTIVES AND MOTIVATION

Throughout *Think and Grow Rich,* Hill says that you must emotionalize your aim or purpose; you must mix emotion with it in order to burn it into your subconscious. To find the most effective way to emotionalize your desire, you must look inward and identify what gets you going, what stirs your emotions, what motivates you to want it.

Hill offered the following comments on the issue of motivation, excerpted and adapted from *Selling You!,* chapter 2:

> There are nine doors through which the human mind can be entered and influenced. These nine doors are the nine basic motives by which all people are influenced and to which all people respond.
>
> Every move, every act, and every thought of every human being is influenced by one or more of the nine basic motives. By understanding and applying these nine motives, you will not only learn how to influence other people but you will also learn how to motivate yourself.
>
> When sales professionals qualify prospective buyers, they look first for the most logical motive they may use to influence the buyer's thinking and decision. When an appropriate motive has been planted in the mind of the prospective buyer, it begins to work from within.
>
> If this can be done to motivate others, it can also be done to motivate yourself.

The message is to find the connection between your desire and each of the motives identified by Hill. Use the emotion that it stirs in you to help burn your aim or purpose into your subconscious mind.

On the following pages you will find Hill's nine motives listed in the approximate order of their importance and their greatest usefulness.

1. The motive of **self-preservation**: The more you believe your future depends on achieving your aim, the more powerfully emotionalized your desire will be. If you really are putting everything you have into your aim, your future well-being will truly be in jeopardy and you will be motivated to do anything you can to keep from failing.

2. The motive of **financial gain**: For many people, money is the barometer of success and, quite simply, the more money that is at stake the more powerful the motivation. The degree to which this is true for you will affect how strongly money will emotionalize your desire and motivate you to achieve your aim.

3. The motive of **love**: This is probably the easiest motive to understand. Our history is full of stories of people motivated to great achievement for the love of another person or for love of country or cause. If you have a true heartfelt love for your aim or purpose, nothing could be a stronger motivator.

4. The motive of **sexuality**: Love is psychology, but sex is biology, and there is an innate biological drive that motivates men and women to seek sexual satisfaction. You have heard it a million times: "sex sells." You will powerfully motivate yourself to achieve your aim if you can convince yourself that achieving it will enhance your stature and make you more attractive to the opposite sex.

5. The motive of desire for **power and fame**: Why people desire power or fame is a complicated sociological question, but there is no doubt that modern society tells us both are valuable, so they have become powerful motivators. As with money, love, and sex, if you convince yourself that achieving your aim will give you more power or fame, you can greatly increase your drive to succeed.

6. The motive of **fear**: Napoleon Hill says there are six basic fears: fear of poverty, fear of criticism, fear of ill health, fear of the loss of love, fear of old age, and fear of death. Here the motive is not so much to gain something as it is to overcome. If you believe the achievement of your aim or purpose will lessen any of those fears, the boost it will give your desire is obvious.

7. The motive of **revenge**: Although the desire for revenge may not be the most admirable quality, it is not hard to understand how it can be a powerful motivator if succeeding at your aim or purpose also means that you prove to your detractors you were right. If succeeding at your aim or purpose can be tied to the idea that you will get your just desserts, it can add mighty impetus to your effort.

8. The motive of **freedom** (of body and mind): Although not true everywhere in the world, in America the concepts of individual rights and freedom are integral parts of the fabric of our society. If your aim or desire is linked to your personal freedom, you will have tapped into the very principle upon which this country was founded.

9. The motive of **desire to create or build in thought or in material**: Probably the best-known theory of human motivation is Abraham Maslow's Hierarchy of Needs, a theory in psychology contending that once humans have met their "basic needs," they seek to satisfy successively "higher needs." Very near the top of the pyramid of needs, second only to spiritual transcendence, appears the desire to create or build. This is a motive that is more for the inner you. It is a desire for personal satisfaction, and if you can feel pride and satisfaction by achieving your aim or goal, you will increase your motivation manifold.

Do you want to succeed because succeeding will give you the confidence to do something? Or do you want to succeed because you are overflowing with the desire to share your good fortune? Or maybe the real reason you want to succeed is so you can show up your competitors or get even with your detractors.

Whatever your reasons, the end result is that you must want to succeed so badly you can almost taste it. Take that passion, love, anger, fear, or whatever it is and use it to emotionalize your aim or purpose.

FAITH CAN WORK IN REVERSE

When Napoleon Hill says "faith is not something you get, it is something you have," he then adds, "but if you are not careful you may be using it in reverse."

It's true that your faith is something you have and it does not come from any outside source. There is nowhere you can go and nothing you can do to get faith in yourself. Faith is similar to intelligence or talent —it is something you have within you. But your faith can be subject to outside influences, and those outside influences can be positive or they can be negative. It is the negative influences that Hill is referring to when he speaks of using your faith "in reverse."

A positive attitude needs your encouragement, but with a negative attitude it is just the opposite. You don't even have to try to be negative. Negativity comes naturally, and it easily takes over without any effort on your part.

Hill often used the example of a garden to illustrate what happens when you let your guard down. By carefully planning what you plant, and by nurturing and tending the plants, you can grow a thriving and bountiful garden. However, if you leave it untended it won't just stay fallow and do nothing. Even though you don't encourage weeds, they will soon find their way in, and before you know it they will take over the plot and destroy everything else.

There is a maxim that says if you are not part of the solution, you are part of the problem. Stated another way, if you don't actively focus your positive energy on your aim, you are not being neutral; you are in fact encouraging negativity, which erodes your faith.

FEAR IS THE OPPOSITE OF FAITH

Faith is the art of believing by doing—and fear is the opposite of faith.

First, let us clarify that there is a difference between fear as Hill uses it in this chapter, and the defense mechanism that is hardwired into your brain. The reaction to real danger, pain, or evil is called the fight or flight response, and it describes the instant reaction of your body and mind as you prepare to either attack or escape.

The fear that prompts the fight or flight response is both real and immediate: something happens, you respond. But there is another kind of imagined or anticipatory fear. These are the "what-if" fears. They are not real. Nothing has really happened to you, but you become agitated by imagining what *might* happen.

Napoleon Hill says that because such fears are only in your imagination, and because you can control the thoughts that you think, you can and must control this kind of what-if fear.

You cannot be positive that you will succeed and at the same time be fearful that you will fail. It is impossible to hold both a positive and negative in your mind at the same time.

As Hill has stressed over and over, your mind will attract anything it dwells upon. If your mind dwells on a negative such as fear, you will become full of fear and worry.

As simplistic as it may sound, the only solution to rid yourself of fear is to stop thinking about what you fear. You either believe that you will achieve your aim or purpose, or you fear that you will not achieve it. It is up to you to stop dwelling on the fear of what might happen and to stay focused on accomplishing your aim or purpose.

NOTES & COMMENTS

NOTES & COMMENTS

HOW TO INCREASE YOUR FAITH

Having *faith,* as Hill uses the term, means that you have belief in yourself and in your ability to succeed. People who don't believe in themselves generally have low expectations, and there is considerable research that supports the idea that your expectations have a lot to do with how successful you are. If you expect to win, you will win. If you expect to fail, you will fail.

There was a famous experiment done in 1968 by Jane Elliot with her third-grade class. First the school children were divided into two groups based on the color of their eyes, and Elliot told them that blue eyes were better. Within very little time it was clear that the blue-eyed children were acting superior and the children in the brown-eyed group were performing more poorly than they had before. Then she switched it around and told them that brown eyes were better. As a result, the brown-eyed children became accelerated and the blue-eyed fell behind. Nothing had changed with the children except their expectation.

Robert Rosenthal of Harvard University came up with an interesting twist on that study. He administered an IQ test to all students in an elementary school, then he picked 20 percent of the students purely at random, but he told their teacher that the test had identified those students as "intellectual bloomers." Eight months later he tested the entire student body again and found that in the first and second grades the children whose teachers had expected them to show gains actually gained between ten and fifteen IQ points.

Again, the only difference was expectation, and in this case it was the expectations the teachers had for the children.

Rosenthal did a similar experiment with rats. He gave twelve experimenters five rats each. Although the rats were identical, Rosenthal told the experimenters that half of the rats were "maze-bright" and the other half were "maze-dull."

At the end of the experiment the rats whose trainers thought they were "maze-bright" did better than the so-called "maze-dull" rats.

Although the rats were identical, somehow the expectations of the trainers were conveyed to the rats and they responded accordingly. Or it may have been that the trainers unconsciousy tried to live up to the expectations, and that could have affected the results.

In chapter 10, Persistence, in *Think and Grow Rich: The 21st-Century Edition,* the editors tell about the research program done with a group of people who considered themselves lucky and another group who thought of themselves as unlucky. When they were each asked to call a series of coin tosses, it turned out that both groups averaged the same number of right guesses.

The fact is that the lucky group wasn't really any more lucky than the unlucky group. But by interviewing each group, the researchers found that in general the so-called lucky group remembered the good things that happened to them in their lives, while the unlucky group tended to dwell on the bad things. In short, the only difference was in the lucky group's expectations.

A final example that makes the point is quoted from the September 2006 issue of *Money* magazine, in an article called Road Trip to Riches. The writer tells of an experiment developed by a British researcher, Richard Wiseman, who also worked with groups of people who considered themselves lucky or unlucky. He asked each to count the photographs in a newspaper.

The unluckies spent several minutes flipping through and counting the photos. The lucky people got it in a few seconds.

How?

On the second page of the newspaper, Wiseman had inserted a message in giant headline type: "Stop counting

—there are 43 photographs in this newspaper." The lucky people, always on the lookout for unexpected good fortune, spotted it right away. The unlucky people whose minds are closed to such signs missed it completely.

OTHERS KNOW WHEN YOU HAVE FAITH

Faith is something that other people recognize in you, and this is especially true if you are trying to present an idea or sell a product.

In professional sales, one of the most commonly heard pieces of advice is, "The first sale you must make is to yourself." If you try to sell something you don't believe in, you can say all the right words but something will be missing. And people can always spot a phony.

On the other hand, everyone has had the experience of being convinced by a speaker who is passionate about an idea, or of being persuaded to try a product because the salesperson just seemed so sincere. In such instances it isn't a slick sales pitch or overwhelming logic that does the trick; it is an attitude that emanates from the person.

If you have faith in what you are selling or explaining, it is as though you don't even have to try to sell. You simply present your story and, in doing so, your faith in it gives off a sense of confident enthusiasm that other people pick up on.

INFINITE INTELLIGENCE

Infinite Intelligence is one of Napoleon Hill's most important conceptions and it is also one of the most difficult to get a handle on. At times Hill refers to Infinite Intelligence as if it were an actual thing; at other times he seems to be discussing a location, as though it is a compartment inside the brain; and in some instances he speaks of passing an idea on to Infinite Intelligence as though it is some sort of god-like figure who sits in judgment.

Infinite Intelligence is probably best described as a process or a system, in the same way that we think of a broadcasting system or a telephone system. There are three aspects to Infinite Intelligence:

1. It is a part of your thinking process that takes bits of information and ideas which your conscious mind has filtered out or forgotten, and connects them with each other on a subconscious level to create new solutions and creative ideas

2. It is the part of your thinking process that, through the laws of nature and science, connects you to and makes you part of all other things.

3. It is the part of your thinking process through which outside information such as hunches, intuitions, and premonitions come into your subconscious mind.

WHAT DOES IT DO?

Sometimes it is easier to understand something by what it *does* rather than trying to define what it is.

What Infinite Intelligence does is give you access to ideas that wouldn't normally occur to you. It does this by taking bits of information stored in your subconscious, and mixing those bits of ideas with ideas that it is able to pull from outside of your experience or knowledge.

The result is that you find yourself coming up with new solutions, original ideas, flashes of insight, and sometimes premonitions or intuitions that can't be explained in any other way.

WHY IS IT CALLED INFINITE INTELLIGENCE?

Infinite Intelligence is a term created by Napoleon Hill to account for the fact that our world follows a set of laws of nature and science that make things happen consistently and predictably. He came up with the term in order to satisfy Andrew Carnegie's advice about avoiding any particular religious connotation, but it has still resulted in some confusion.

Some people take the words *Infinite Intelligence* to mean that there is some sort of omniscient overseer. That was not Hill's intention, and he never suggests that Infinite Intelligence is something that meddles in human affairs. Infinite Intelligence does not make things happen *to* you, but Infinite Intelligence is something you can use to make things happen *for* you.

IT IS REALLY JUST NATURAL LAW

To explain the concept of natural law, Napoleon Hill would often use his pocket watch to demonstrate. He would point out that it was made up of wheels and gears and cogs that were clearly designed to fit together and work in a very specific way to do a very specific thing.

If you were to take apart the watch and put the pieces into a hat and shake it, you could keep on shaking it for a million years and the pieces would never reassemble themselves into a pocket watch that keeps time. It is not an accident that a watch works. It works because it is designed and assembled according to a specific plan.

Hill believed that each of us exists in a time and place, in a world, in a solar system, in a universe that, like the pieces of a watch, all fit together and operate with precision. The world works according to natural laws that are part of an overall plan. Because you too are an integral part of the plan, what you do has an effect on other things that are part of the plan.

If you can understand that, you can control the thoughts you think in such a way that, working through natural law, they will produce the effect you desire.

YOU DON'T ALWAYS HAVE TO KNOW WHY

If you throw a ball up into the air you don't doubt that it will fall back down. And you believe this because of the law of gravity. But do you actually understand what gravity is or how it works?

The fact is that no one really knows how gravity works. Or exactly why electricity does what it does either. And, as Hill often liked to point out, we don't even know why a kernel of wheat knows how to extract the correct combination of things from the earth, water, and sunlight to turn itself into a stalk of wheat.

But the fact that we don't know precisely why these things work does not keep us from growing food, or making use of gravity, electricity, and all the other laws of nature. The reason we can make use of them is because we have *faith* that they will work, even though we cannot intellectually prove how they work.

All science is based on the faith that there is universal order. However, the same regularity and predictability that gives us faith also raises another issue. What *causes* the world to operate with such regularity? *Why* is it so orderly?

Although for some people this line of thinking leads straight to religion, Hill takes the position that in order to use this philosophy to become successful, it does not matter. Things work whether we know why or not.

Rather than be diverted into a rationalization of religion, Hill opted for a practical approach that does not involve any particular religious belief. Hill says that from a purely practical point of view, religion does not affect your ability to utilize the natural laws. Gravity works equally well for Protestants and Buddhists. It doesn't matter if you are Catholic, Muslim, or agnostic, the sun still rises in the east and sets in the west.

PUTTING INFINITE INTELLIGENCE TO WORK FOR YOU

It is easy to have faith that the sun will rise in the east and set in the west. You've seen it happen time after time, and all of our history tells us that is what the sun is supposed to do. It's harder to have faith that you will succeed at your aim or purpose because, almost by definition, it is something you haven't done before.

NOTES & COMMENTS

Hill's philosophy of personal achievement does not attempt to answer the question *why,* but rather focuses on *how.* For the purpose of applying the Hill method to achieving success, *why* can be set aside for philosophizing, but just the fact that there is consistency is enough for you to utilize its power.

All you have to do is look at the world around you to know that everywhere in nature there is order. Who or what created the order may be debatable, but the result is not. If you use your own experiences and reason things through, you will easily satisfy yourself that the world follows certain patterns with such regularity and predictability, it is as though the world is following an organized, definite plan.

Napoleon Hill states without equivocation that he is certain there is a set of natural laws that comprises a plan. He is certain that there is such a plan because the success of his method relies on it. Hill's method would only work if there is a plan, and since it has worked for literally millions of people, there must be a plan.

To make Hill's method work for you, you too must start from the assumption that the world works according to natural laws that are part of an overall a plan, and that you are a part of that plan. If you make the choice to assume it is a plan, and you treat it like a plan, it will work like a plan. If it works like a plan, you can make the plan work for you.

To recap the main points:

1. Hill's philosophy of success is based on the premise that there is an Infinite Intelligence that underlies the way nature operates.

2. It is this intelligent plan that makes the laws of nature predictable, consistent, and reliable.

3. Because the laws of nature follow predictable patterns, we can have faith in them even though we do not really understand why they do what they do.

4. You must have the same kind of faith in your definite aim or purpose as you have in the laws of nature.

5. You must have complete faith and confidence that the possibility for you to succeed at your aim is a natural part of the plan of things.

6. Just as you have no doubt that the sun will rise in the east, you must have no doubt that if you follow the Hill formula your aim or purpose is achievable.

7. You must have complete faith and confidence that by burning your desire into your subconscious, it will, as a part of the natural plan of things, connect you with ideas and concepts that can help you realize your desire.

You will need to practice to acquire this art of conditioning your mind to be receptive, and the first step is to relax your natural tendency to question everything. If you don't, your sense of reason will constantly get in the way by challenging you to prove it to yourself.

But you can't prove it. The only proof is when it works and you come up with a creative solution or a new and unique idea.

In practical terms, you start by assuming that if you follow principles that have worked for others, they will work for you. Then you temporarily relax your own reason and willpower, set aside your usual questioning, and open your mind to the inflow of Infinite Intelligence.

NOTES & COMMENTS

AUTOSUGGESTION

5

CHAPTER 5: OVERVIEW AND ANALYSIS

THE MEDIUM FOR INFLUENCING THE SUBCONSCIOUS MIND

This chapter opens with Napoleon Hill stating the basic principle that autosuggestion is the way your conscious mind communicates with your subconscious mind. Because you can control what you consciously dwell on, you can influence what is in your subconscious mind, and that affects every idea you have.

EDITOR'S COMMENTARY

The editors note that there is considerable research to support Hill's theory that the subconscious receives the same information as the conscious but it does not judge; it just stores it. The editors then draw the comparison between the process of intentionally planting an idea in your subconscious and the way that emotionally charged circumstances produce fixations and phobias. The more you emotionalize your burning desire, the stronger it is burned into your subconscious.

Your thoughts do remain stored in the subconscious, and they remain just as they were when they were first input.

The more highly emotionalized the thoughts are when they are input, the more influence they exert on your attitude and behavior.

Autosuggestion gives you the power to control which thoughts are burned into your subconscious.

SEE AND FEEL MONEY IN YOUR HANDS

In this section Hill recaps the six-step plan for planting your desire, and he restates the point that your desire will only fix itself in your subconscious if it is attached to a strong emotion.

HOW TO STRENGTHEN YOUR POWERS OF CONCENTRATION

Hill stresses the importance of repetition in planting an idea firmly in your subconscious. He again refers to the six-step plan as he explains the theory behind repeating positive affirmations to burn them into your subconscious, and he introduces the concept of doing the same with creative visualization.

EDITOR'S COMMENTARY

The editors provide an extensive Commentary explaining about Emile Coué's early work with affirmations and how he developed the phrase "Every day, in every way, I am getting better and better." They also note the modern resurgence and acceptance of the technique.

The editors then devote equal emphasis to visualization as a motivational tool and as a technique for treating certain medical conditions. They note that it is now used in every field from business training to Olympic athletes to NASA astronauts. The Commentary closes with notes about some of the bestsellers written by medical professionals who have researched affirmations and visualization.

STIMULATE YOUR SUBCONSCIOUS MIND

Hill explains how to use the written statement of your aim or purpose as a spoken affirmation, and how to use it as a guide to visualizing yourself achieving your aim or purpose.

The editors suggest that you can also influence your subconscious by posting written copies of your affirmations and visual illustrations symbolizing your desire.

Hill closes this chapter by acknowledging that some readers may be skeptical of these techniques, but he also reminds the reader that it is these techniques that have made millionaires.

CHAPTER 5: THE WORKBOOK

Because the four-letter prefix *auto* has the same meaning as the word *self*, technically the words *autosuggestion* and *self-suggestion* mean the same thing. However, as Napoleon Hill uses the word, *autosuggestion* doesn't just mean *self*; it is also meant to convey the idea of an automatic or repetitive action that happens as habit.

A definition of each of the words appears in the previous chapter, and the definitions make it clear that *self-suggestion* is a prompt to action that you give to yourself, while *autosuggestion* is any suggestion that has become so deeply fixed in your subconscious that it is the response that flashes into your mind without even thinking.

The following explanation from Hill's co-author, W. Clement Stone, will help to make the differences clear.

Stone developed a number of short phrases that he used to motivate himself. One such phrase was the simple statement "Try to do the right thing because it is right." In the following, Stone uses that same phrase to explain how it can be used to demonstrate all three forms of suggestion:

Suggestion comes from the outside. It is anything you see, hear, feel, taste, or smell. If I say to you, "Try to do the right thing because it is right," that is a suggestion from me to you.

Self-suggestion is purposefully controlled from within. It is a suggestion you give to yourself that you can see in your imagination, say to yourself, or write down. Each time you think or say to yourself "Try to do the right thing because it is right," that is self-suggestion.

Autosuggestion acts by itself, unconsciously, like a machine that always reacts in the same way from the same stimulus.

NOTES & COMMENTS

Each time your subconscious flashes to your conscious mind "Try to do the right thing because it is right," that is autosuggestion.

If, for the next week, every morning and every evening and frequently throughout the day you repeat this phrase—"Try to do the right thing because it is right"—when you are faced with temptation, that phrase will flash from your subconscious to your conscious mind. In this way, through repetition, you will form a habit—a good habit—that will help make your future a success.

AUTOSUGGESTION: TURNING DESIRE INTO HABIT

Napoleon Hill first published his theories on the use of autosuggestion in his 8-volume masterwork, *Law of Success,* which became a bestseller in 1928, nine years before the publication of *Think and Grow Rich.* At that time he approached it from the point of view of techniques that can be used to change your habits. The following is adapted from *Law of Success,* Volume III, Lesson Twelve:

There is a close relationship between habit and autosuggestion. Through habit, an act repeatedly performed in the same manner has a tendency to become permanent, and eventually we come to perform the act automatically or unconsciously. In playing a piano, for example, the artist can play a familiar piece while his or her conscious mind is on some other subject.

Autosuggestion is the tool with which we dig a mental path, concentration is the hand that holds that tool, and habit is the map or blueprint that the mental path follows.

The following are the rules through which you may form the habits you desire:

1. At the beginning of the formation of a new habit, put all the force and enthusiasm you can muster into expressing what you want to become. Feel what you think. Remember that you are taking the first steps toward making your new mental paths, and it is much harder at first than it will be afterward. At the beginning make each path as clear and as deep as you can, so that you can readily see it the next time you wish to follow it.

2. Keep your attention firmly concentrated on your new path-building, and forget all about the old paths. Concern yourself only with the new ones that you are building to order.

3. Travel over your newly-made paths as often as possible. The more often you go over the new paths, the sooner they will become well-worn and easily traveled.

4. Resist the temptation to travel over the older, easier paths you have been using in the past. Every time you resist a temptation, the stronger you become and the easier it will be for you to do so the next time. This is the critical time. Prove your determination, persistency, and willpower now, at the very beginning.

5. Be sure you have mapped out the right path as your goal or aim, then go ahead without fear and without allowing yourself to doubt. Select your goal and make good, deep, wide mental paths leading straight to it.

NOTES & COMMENTS

Because the subconscious mind does not distinguish between what is real and what is vividly imagined, if you convincingly plant an idea in your subconscious, it will accept the idea as though it were a fact.

If you have planted the new idea strongly enough, when your thoughts run in that direction, your new idea will be the first thought that comes to mind. It will have become your new belief, and eventually it will be your habit.

In *Law of Success,* Napoleon Hill goes on to propose a specific technique for breaking habits and making new mental pathways. Hill calls the process *concentration.*

> Concentration is defined as planting in the mind a definite aim, object, or purpose, and visualizing and repeating that objective over and over until ways and means for its realization have been created. Concentration is the principle through which you may build your habits to order.
>
> When focusing on your aim becomes a habit, your subconscious will constantly look for ways to translate your aim into its physical counterpart. And your subconscious will try to do that through the most practical and direct methods available.
>
> Nothing was ever created by a human being that was not first created in the imagination, through desire, and then transformed into reality through concentration.

This technique that Hill dubbed concentration is actually an amalgam of two separate but interrelated techniques which today are most often called positive affirmation and creative visualization.

- Positive affirmations rely upon the idea of summing up your desire in a short phrase that you repeat over and over to yourself. It is the repetition that wears away at your old thinking until it makes a new mental pathway.

- Creative visualizations rely on creating such a vivid mental image of your desire that you can experience it just as if it were reality. By making it so real in your mind you are adding emotion which, as we stressed in the previous chapter, is what is needed to burn it into your subconscious, creating a new mental pathway.

The way in which you create affirmations and visualizations is virtually identical. The only difference is that one is verbal and the other is visual, but it is completely natural and easy to do both at the same time. In fact, it is not only natural to do them simultaneously, but it may also be easier for you to create a mental image while saying a phrase that describes it. Or, to state the obverse, keeping a vivid mental image in your mind may give more passion and meaning to the words you use to state your desire.

We will examine each technique separately so that you can focus on certain aspects of each that deserve special attention. We will begin with affirmations.

POSITIVE AFFIRMATIONS

A positive affirmation is a short phrase that clearly states the change you want to make in yourself. If you emotionalize that phrase with total faith and belief that you are capable of changing yourself, and if you repeat the phrase over and over to yourself until thinking that way becomes your natural habit, then you will make the change you desire.

When French psychologist Emile Coué devised the positive affirmation "Every day, in every way, I am getting better and better," his intent was to create an affirmation that could be used by many different patients suffering from a wide range of psychosomatic disorders. This general, nonspecific phrase was designed to give the subconscious a positive instruction, but was still open enough that it did not tell the subconscious a specific problem to deal with, nor did it try to tell the subconscious how to do it.

NOTES & COMMENTS

Although Coué's affirmation may indeed make you "better and better" in general, the downside is that because it is so general and does not define what "better and better" means, it leaves the interpretation up to your subconscious, which is exactly the kind of thing that the nonjudgmental subconscious mind does not do very well. Most affirmations are directed at improving a more focused aspect of your character. Here is a list of affirmations that deals much more directly with specific issues related to self-motivation and personal achievement:

- Whatever I can conceive and believe in my mind, I can achieve in reality, as long as it does not go against the laws of nature.

- I do it now. Whenever I set a definite goal, I take immediate action to get it done. I do it now.

- I am a powerful and charismatic leader. My thoughts are creative. My decisions are fair. I lead with confidence and certainty.

- What I desire is more important than the difficulties along the way. I will overcome them to reach my goals.

- I am like a mental and financial magnet, attracting to myself all that I need to prosper.

- I maintain my enthusiasm and motivation throughout today's ups and downs.

- I am a person who thrives on challenges. Every setback gives me new opportunities for success.

- In every failure I can find the seed of an equal or greater success.

- My conscious mind is wide open to my subconscious mind, which sends me hunches, premonitions, and flashes of insight.

- When I speak to others, I look them straight in the eye and my voice sends a message of strength and confidence.

It may be that in the preceding list you found one or more affirmations that you might like to use to deal with certain issues, but the editors suggest that you will have even greater success if you use the following proven techniques to create your own affirmations that are tailor-made to deal with your life and the specific issues you want to improve.

DECIDE WHAT YOU WANT TO CHANGE

The first step in creating a personalized affirmation is to clearly identify what it is that you desire. In *Think and Grow Rich,* Napoleon Hill offers a formula for defining and writing out a statement of your aim or purpose. Hill's version is reprinted here so that you may compare it with today's style of affirmations:

> How can the original seed of an idea, plan, or objective be planted in the mind? The answer: write out a statement of your desire, purpose, goal, or objective, commit it to memory, and repeat it out loud, day after day, until these vibrations of sound have reached your subconscious mind.
>
> 1. To begin the process, write a clear, concise statement of the amount of money you intend to acquire. Fix in your mind the exact amount of money you desire. It is not sufficient merely to say "I want plenty of money." Be definite about the amount.
>
> 2. Determine exactly what you intend to give in return for the money you desire.
>
> 3. Establish a definite date when you intend to possess the money you desire.
>
> 4. Create a definite plan for carrying out your desire and begin at once, whether you are ready or not, to put this plan into action.

For example, suppose that as a general goal you intend to accumulate $50,000 by the first of January, five years from now, and that you intend to give your personal services as a salesperson in return for the money. Your written statement of your purpose should be similar to the following:

By the first day of January _____, I will have in my possession $50,000, which will come to me in various amounts from time to time during the interim.

In return for this money I will give the most efficient service of which I am capable. I will give the fullest possible quantity, and the best possible quality, of service as a salesperson of _____ (describe the service or merchandise you intend to sell).

I believe that I will have this money in my possession. My faith is so strong that I can now see it before my eyes. I can touch it with my hands. It is now awaiting transfer to me at the time and in the proportion that I deliver the service in return for it. I am awaiting a plan for getting this money, and I will follow that plan when it is received.

Signed . . . .

Place a written copy where you can see it, and read it before retiring and on arising, until it has been memorized.

Speak your written statement aloud at least twice daily. Go to a quiet spot where you will not be disturbed. Close your eyes and repeat aloud (so that you may hear your own words) the statement of the amount of money you intend to accumulate. As you speak, see and feel and believe yourself already in possession of the money.

In the reprint of Napoleon Hill's version that is provided above, the resulting written statement is quite long and uses a formal style of language that few people would feel comfortable using today. However, you should bear in mind that when Hill instructs his readers to memorize their written statement, he was giving that instruction at a time when school students were regularly called upon to stand up and declaim long heroic poems from memory, and stem-winding public lectures were considered popular entertainment. Times were very different then and it would not have been unusual for Hill's readers to follow his instructions and learn the statement by heart.

Today, the intent in creating your affirmation is not quite so all-encompassing. Now the challenge is to take just one aspect of your aim or purpose and use that one idea to create a short, easily remembered phrase that sums up what you desire. By narrowing the focus, it is quite likely you will find that it will require more than one affirmation to properly address each issue.

Because of these changes, the editors of this workbook now view the creation of an affirmation as a three-step process:

1. Identify your desire.

2. Follow Hill's template to create your formal written statement.

3. Use the information from your statement along with the techniques explained below to create a short, memorable affirmation.

You may choose to create one overarching affirmation that you feel encapsulates your major purpose or aim, or you may create a group of different affirmations that deal with the individual goals and objectives which must be accomplished in order to achieve your over-arching purpose or aim.

You might also create additional affirmations that are not directly related to your chief aim or purpose, but which deal with general improvements such as overcoming procrastination or eliminating the fear of criticism. Chances are that as you work with them you will find reason to create affirmations for all of these purposes.

When you start working with your completed affirmation(s), you will read your written statement at least twice each day and repeat your memorized affirmation(s) many times a day. Your formal written statement should be read once every night, and you should follow the reading by repeating the affirmation(s) derived from the statement at least ten times. Every morning you should again read your formal statement as the introduction to the repetition of your affirmation(s). And again, you should repeat your affirmation(s) at least ten times.

SEE IT IN YOUR MIND'S EYE

Once you are completely satisfied that you clearly know your desire, you must visualize a simple but vivid image that represents things as they are now and as they will be when the aim is accomplished or the change has taken place. It's like mental before-and-after snapshots.

WRITE DOWN THE WORDS

When you can clearly see in your mind's eye the manifestation of your desire, you then create a short, simple, easy-to-remember phrase that is like a verbal accompaniment to what you feel when you bring the before-and-after images to your mind. Following are some rules of thumb that are important when formulating affirmations:

- Affirmations should always be stated as a positive. Affirm what you do want, not what you don't want.

- Affirmations work best when they are about a single goal. Take the time to rewrite and polish your affirmation until you can express your desire in a short statement of precise and well-chosen words.

- Make the words memorable and make it feel right for you. Use powerful and inspirational words that stimulate your mind. Make up your own catch phrases or rhymes that make it easy to say. Remember, your affirmation is not just a statement; it should be an expression of your inner desire that gets you psyched-up no matter how many times you've said it.

- Keep your affirmation in the present even if saying it does not represent your reality as it is right now. You are training your subconscious mind to make your aim or purpose your new habit. By repeating an affirmation that states something is true *now,* your mind will begin to search for ways to make it happen.

- Affirmations should be specific about the desired goal but not about how to accomplish it. Infinite Intelligence working with your subconscious knows better than you what it can do and how it can do it.

- Do not make unreasonable time demands. Your subconscious can't make anything happen "suddenly" or "immediately."

SAYING IT WITH FEELING

Just saying the words will have little effect. When you affirm your desire you must do it with such faith and conviction that your subconscious becomes convinced of how important it is to you. As you affirm your desire to yourself, visualize it so that in your mind's eye it is as big as a billboard. Make it big, powerful, and memorable. More will be said about this in the section on visualization.

SAYING IT OVER AND OVER

Repetition of your emotionalized affirmation is crucial. At this time it is your habit to think one way, but by repeating your affirmation often every day, your new way of thinking will begin to be your automatic response.

Keep reinforcing it until it becomes second nature to you, and your habit will become to think the new way—the way you want to think.

If you have reservations about the value of repeating affirmations, we suggest that you consider the billions of dollars spent to run the same commercials over and over and to place the same print ads day after day. Or give some thought to the reason why astronauts and athletes train over and over, why pianists and golfers practice over and over, and actors rehearse over and over. It is why Pavlov's dog salivated when the bell rang and why Skinner's rats learned to navigate the maze.

It has been scientifically proven in the laboratory, every motivational expert acknowledges it, and you prove it to yourself every time you hum to yourself "You deserve a break today" or you remember that it's the jeans with the little red tab on the back pocket that are the real ones. Repetition makes things stick in your mind. Things that stick in your mind change the way you think. Change the way you think and you change your habits.

SAYING IT OUT LOUD

Although the most common method of using an affirmation is to silently repeat the phrase to yourself a number of times each day, Hill advises that it is most effective when you say the words out loud:

> Speaking it aloud sets into motion the vibration through which the thought behind your words reaches and embeds itself in your subconscious mind. This is why you are instructed to write it out, commit it to memory, and repeat it out loud, day after day, until these vibrations of sound have reached your subconscious mind. There it takes root and grows until it becomes a great moving force in your outward, physical activities, leading to the transformation of the thought into reality.

Speaking an affirmation out loud while looking at yourself in a mirror can be especially effective. You can either look yourself in the eye and talk directly to "you" or, as Andrew Carnegie advised Hill, you can use the mirror to observe how convincing you appear making the statement.

Carnegie told Hill to look into his mirror every morning and declare: "Andrew Carnegie, I am not only going to equal your achievements in life, but I am going to challenge you at the post and pass you at the grandstand."

This is a very well-conceived affirmation. It is a clear statement of the goal, it is short enough to easily memorize and say with feeling, and it creates a clear and colorful image that is easy to visualize.

It is worth noting that at speaking engagements Napoleon Hill often told his audiences about that affirmation and he said that it had a profound impact on him and did just what it was supposed to do. In 1962, at a lecture in Chicago, Hill said this about Carnegie's affirmation:

> The first few times I said it, I felt like a fool. But you know, eventually I commenced to believe it, and then, after I started to believe it, I knew I was going to succeed. And modestly, may I state that I have reached the place in life where, in terms of the number of people I have influenced to become millionaires, my achievements far excel those of Andrew Carnegie.

Experts on visualization techniques, Shakti Gawain, author of *Creative Visualization*, and Marilee Zdenek, author of *The Right-Brain Experience*, both use a variation on the technique that you might try from time to time. They suggest that as you repeat your affirmation, you change from saying it in the first person to saying it in the second person, and then to saying it in the third person.

NOTES & COMMENTS

The following illustrates the technique using the affirmation "In every failure I can find and use the seed of an equal or greater success."

1. First you would say: "In every failure I, [insert your name], can find and use the seed of an equal or greater success.

2. Then you would restate it as: "In every failure you, [insert your name], can find and use the seed of an equal or greater success." As you say this, think of it as being said by someone close to you who is encouraging you.

3. The third time you would say: "In every failure he/she, [insert your name], can find and use the seed of an equal or greater success." This time, as you say it, think of it as being said by someone in authority whom you admire, and they're praising you.

SAYING IT WHENEVER YOU CAN

Another technique that will help to fix your goal or desire in your subconscious is to make it a part of your daily vocabulary. Look for ways to include your affirmation in your normal everyday activities. The opportunity may not come up often, but by keeping the possibility in mind and looking for the chance to use a variation of your affirmation in conversation, you also keep it forefront in your mind.

WRITING IT WITH FEELING

You will have already written a version of your affirmation when you followed Hill's directions to create a formal written statement, and again when you refined and polished the words that you used in creating your affirmations. The suggestion here is simply that occasionally, in addition to repeating your statement and affirmations out loud, you sit down and write the words over and over.

Although this could be done at the computer, taking pen in hand and writing out your affirmation over and over makes a different kind of impression on your subconscious. In some way the act of actually writing your thoughts compels you to turn the words over in your mind. Anything that helps to distinguish the words makes them more memorable, and therefore plants them more firmly in your subconscious.

Just as saying your affirmation in the first, second, and third person can be very effective, writing these three versions over and over can make an even stronger impact. As you now know, your subconscious does not question or evaluate the information it receives. By presenting your subconscious with a written version, you have reached your subconscious through another sense. Seeing your own name written out and repeated as second- and third-person statements is a powerful way to reinforce the message.

WRITING IT TO BE SEEN

Another value in writing out your affirmations is that you can place the written versions where they will act as reminders. Write your affirmations on cards or Post-its and put them in your wallet, on your desktop, or stick them on your mirror, the refrigerator door, or anywhere else where they will catch your eye.

A variation on the idea is to surround yourself with books, pictures, mottoes, and other things that symbolize and reinforce the idea of you succeeding at your goal. Hill suggests that you constantly add to your collection of visual motivators, and move your pictures and reminders to new places where you can see them in a different light and in association with different things.

Some people clip pictures of the cities they want to visit on vacation, the dream car they want to be able to afford to buy, or clothes they want to be slim enough to wear. We know of people who compile magazine clippings illustrating an idea, put them into book form, and regularly flip through it as a visual version of an affirmation. Some use computer programs such as PhotoShop to insert their likeness into the pictures.

NOTES & COMMENTS

Bestselling motivational authors Mark Victor Hansen and Jack Canfield are perfect examples of how well visual affirmations can work. They tell the true story about the unique way they kept focused while working together to write a book. After they came up with a title they liked, they had it typed out in the same font as is used for the *New York Times* bestsellers list, then they pasted their mock-up into the number-one spot and hung copies of their version of the list in their office where they could see it as they worked on their new book.

Incidentally, the book they were writing was *Chicken Soup for the Soul,* and as the whole world must know by now, it wasn't long before they were able to replace their visual affirmation with the real thing.

Can you really make something happen just by focusing on it in your mind and repeating your affirmation over and over? Well, as we have already said, the saying it over and over doesn't make it happen, but saying it over and over does make it a part of you and your personality.

When your affirmation becomes a part of you and the way you think, your subconscious will begin to pull together bits and pieces of information that you otherwise might have missed, and you will find that you are coming up with more and better plans and ideas to accomplish your desires.

CREATIVE VISUALIZATION

The following description of the process of visualization is excerpted and adapted from the directions for writing a formal statement of your desire that appears in *Think and Grow Rich: The 21st-Century Edition.*

> To begin the visualization process, write a clear, concise statement of the amount of money you intend to acquire. Fix in your mind the exact amount of money you desire. It is not sufficient merely to say "I want plenty of money."

Be definite about the amount. As you read, see and feel and believe yourself already in possession of the money.

When you concentrate on your aim or desire, visualize yourself as you will be. Look ahead one, three, five, or even ten years. See yourself as a person of influence, due to your great ability. See yourself engaged in a life-calling in which you will not fear the loss of your position. See yourself in your own home that you have purchased with the proceeds from your efforts as the success you wish to be. See yourself in possession of a nice bank account for your retirement. See yourself, in your imagination, in possession of the money you wish to receive.

When you begin to "fix in your own mind the exact amount of money you desire," close your eyes and hold your thoughts on that amount until you can actually see the physical appearance of the money. When visualizing the money you intend to accumulate, see yourself rendering the service or delivering the merchandise you intend to give in return for this money.

Make your subconscious believe that this money is already waiting for you to claim it, so your subconscious mind must hand over to you practical plans for acquiring the money that is yours. When the plans appear, they will probably "flash" into your mind in the form of an inspiration or intuition.

CAN VISUALIZING SUCCESS REALLY MAKE IT HAPPEN?

Napoleon Hill is a convincing advocate for the theory, but is there any proof that by holding a mental image in your mind it will subconsciously change the way you think?

NOTES & COMMENTS

A dramatic illustration that most readers will be able to relate to is what would happen if you were walking along a garden path and you suddenly catch a glimpse of something coiled in the grass at your feet. Or what would happen if someone frantically points at your shoulder and shouts, "Ohmygawd, it's huge and hairy!" Fear messages race to your hypothalamus, your heart rate increases, your breathing becomes rapid, your endocrine system fills your blood with increased adrenaline, and in a split second your body is prepared for flight or fight.

It doesn't matter that what you saw was a garden hose, or that the person pointing at you was just joking. In your mind's eye you saw a snake in the grass or a spider on your shoulder, and that thought, that visualization was enough to cause your whole body to change.

The reason you react so strongly to the snake or spider is that you have attached a strong emotional charge to those images. If the vision in your mind is vivid and real, then the meaning of that image will be burned into your subconscious. The more often you visualize that image, the deeper it will penetrate, until it becomes your natural habit to respond that way. Your subconscious reacts to what is vividly imagined as if it actually happened. So if your visualization of yourself succeeding is as real to you as your mental image of the snake, then the new mental pathways will come as quickly and naturally as your flight or fight response.

CREATING THE MENTAL IMAGE

Creative visualization is like seeing in reverse. In real life, when you look at something, "seeing" it is an interaction that takes place between your eyes and your brain. If you see a real image in the real world and then close your eyes, you can still see the picture of it inside your mind as a mental image of what you saw. That is visualization.

However, what we refer to as *creative* visualization is like taking the process of seeing and reversing it.

Instead of seeing an image outside of you and re-creating it in your mind, creative visualization is seeing something inside your mind and re-creating it in reality. Obviously that does not mean you can visualize something physical, such as a book or a Rolls-Royce, and suddenly make it appear in the real world. However, what you can do is visualize something such as success, courage, or leadership and have it appear within yourself.

Can you really make something happen just by focusing on it over and over in your mind?

As we have said previously, visualizing it over and over doesn't make it happen, but it's the visualizing that makes it a part of you and your personality. Then it's up to you to take the visualization of your desire—and your faith that you can accomplish it—and turn that visualization into reality.

There are two areas in modern life where changing the way you think about yourself is crucial, and in both of those areas you will find that visualization is widely used and accepted.

In medicine it can literally mean life or death. In sports it can mean fame and wealth. Because of the long and successful history of using visualization in both sports and medicine, these two areas also have the best documentation and the most convincing statistics.

In *Think and Grow Rich: The 21st-Century Edition,* the editors note that in the time since Napoleon Hill wrote about what he called concentration, his technique of visualizing yourself succeeding has become an accepted part of athletic and sports training. In fact, if you read any book by a winning coach, sports star, or Olympic medalist written since the 1970s, you will find that they all mention the use of some form of visualization.

When you consider how much the skill levels have improved for individual competitors in every sport, and how much of that improvement is attributed to visualization, it is only logical that creative visualization applied to other nonathletic areas should have similar results.

Most athletes use this technique like a mental dress rehearsal of a skill or talent that they have already developed. But as persuasive as the athletic achievements are, even more impressive is what has been achieved in medical science. It is especially true of the work that is being done with the autoimmune system, the treatment of cancer, and the field of pain control, where the most stunning advances are not in improving performance but in *changing* performance by actually altering the way the mind thinks and the body operates.

Although Napoleon Hill and a few others were writing about the connection between the brain and the body at the beginning of the twentieth century, it wasn't until the 1960s and 1970s that the concept began to have a serious impact on the way medicine was practiced in America. Two of the medical professionals who were instrumental in introducing the technique were oncologist Dr. O. Carl Simonton, who was teaching the technique to cancer patients, and Dr. David Bresler, who was heading up the research at the UCLA Pain Control Unit.

At that time Dr. Simonton was beginning to document the success he was having teaching cancer patients to visualize their cancer and imagine an army of healthy white blood cells swarming over it like white knights riding to the rescue and carrying off the malignant cells. When used in conjunction with regular cancer treatments, Dr. Simonton's spontaneous remission rate far exceeded normal. Dr. Bresler was having similar success using visualization to help patients manage the pain of backache, migraine headaches, and arthritis.

The books and academic papers written by Dr. Carl Simonton, Dr. David Bresler, and a growing group of other pioneers in the field began to attract the interest of not only the medical establishment but also the media. This idea of self-healing was just the kind of thing that appealed to the personal-growth movement that was becoming influential in America. The media picked up on it, and terms such as *holistic medicine* and *body-mind connection* became more and more common in their reporting. The concept of the body-mind connection was soon a part of the popular vocabulary and by the 1990s various visualization techniques had found their way into mainstream medical practice.

Today there are hundreds of books citing thousands of case histories where patients learned to manage an acute medical condition, went into long remission, and in some cases were cured through the use of visualization. The method has become so accepted in the medical field that it is no longer categorized as alternative medicine; it is now a part of what is called integrative medicine.

If there are any lingering doubts in your mind that visualization works, the editors urge you to investigate the books written about the medical use of visualization. The authors are irrefutably credible and the stories will convince you beyond question that visualization can have a powerful impact on the way you think and how you succeed in life.

THE FIRST STEP IS TO RELAX

The first step in the process of visualization is to allow your body and mind to relax into a calm, open, and receptive state of mind. So the first thing to do is to select a time and a place where you can let yourself relax and you won't be disturbed.

- Choose a comfortable place to sit where you can rest your feet flat on the floor.

- Loosen any clothing that you find binding or constricting and let your arms hang loosely with your hands resting in your lap.

- Now close your eyes, place one hand lightly on your abdomen, and take a deep breath, breathing the air in through your nose and letting it out through your mouth.

- As you breathe in, do not try to fill your chest. Instead, as you take each breath, think of the air filling your whole body so that both your chest and abdomen expand.

- If you are breathing as you should, each time you breathe in, the hand you placed on your abdomen will be lifted out as your abdomen expands along with your lungs.

- Continue to breathe deeply as you let your breathing settle into a slow, relaxed rhythm and you slowly count down from ten to one, releasing all stress and tension in your body. As you count each number, envision yourself on an escalator; with each number the escalator takes you down to a deeper level of relaxed receptivity.

That simple exercise, which shouldn't take more than a few minutes, will put you in a state of relaxed but receptive attention. At the end of this chapter you will find a more detailed explanation of the ideal mental state for visualization. However, at this point, knowing the relaxation technique explained above is quite sufficient in order to move on to the next step in the process.

WHAT PICTURES DO YOU SEE?

Although there is no one right way to use the technique of creative visualization, most people find that the method works best if you can hold the images in your mind and show your subconscious what you want it to learn by moving from scene to scene.

Some people find that their visualizations are like movies, while others don't see "pictures" at all. Instead, they see in visual symbols that represent the idea behind their goal.

Napoleon Hill said that nothing has ever been created that did not start as a thought. You cannot bake a cake or build a skyscraper without first thinking about it. When you have a goal, you automatically form a picture in your mind. Research indicates that about 70 percent of people say they can easily create mental images, while the remaining 30 percent feel that although they may have some trouble, they can strengthen their ability with practice. The difference may be that what they visualized was not what they expected.

What each individual person actually "sees" when they visualize can vary greatly. Some people find that their visualizations come in full-color mental movies, while others say that what they see is more like a single scene that dissolves or morphs into something else. Others report that they can create pictures but the scenes won't stay on subject. It is also not uncommon for people who see pictures and scenes to be concerned that their visualizations are more like something they have made up or constructed rather than a picture of reality. And some people don't see "pictures" at all. Instead, their mind's eye presents them with images or visual symbols that are metaphors for the idea behind their goal. Some people report that their visualizations are more like having a thought or an idea, rather than what it is like when they see something.

If you are concerned that you won't be able to use the visualization technique because you don't think you can create clear mental pictures, you can set your mind at ease. All of these examples and practically any other variation you can think of can be worked with and intensified by practice. It is a matter of taking whatever comes to your mind's eye —whether it is a full-blown movie; a shifting, flickering snapshot; or a symbolic image—and visualizing it often enough that it will naturally start to come into clearer, cleaner, sharper focus.

What if you fall asleep, or your mind wanders, or you can't make heads or tails out of what you see, or you get so many images so fast it doesn't make sense and you can't control it? The answer to all of those questions is just give it time. Your pictures are there. You just have to find them and give yourself a chance to understand them.

NOTES & COMMENTS

Professionals who teach visualization courses say that even if your first attempts only produce vague images or flashes, in time virtually everyone can learn to visualize in mental images. Many people who see in symbols to begin with, find that as they work with their visualizations the symbols just naturally make the transformation into realistic mental pictures. The same is true for those who initially see only flashes of indistinct single images. If you practice consistently you will find that the images last longer and become clearer each time you repeat the visualization. It is a matter of practice and familiarity.

MAKING MOVIES IN YOUR MIND

One technique that many professionals suggest is to visualize your mental images as though they are literally the scenes in a film that is appearing on a movie screen. Some believe it works best when you treat it as a very personal experience in which you envision it as your own private screening and you imagine the screen as though it is just behind your eyelids. Others take exactly the opposite approach and suggest that you visualize it as though you are seated in a movie theatre, watching on a huge, towering screen that fills your entire mental field of vision.

Whether your visualizations are something that just happen inside your head, or whether you turn them into a widescreen spectacular, you will likely find that your visualization allows you to use movie techniques such as zooming in when you want to add details to your mental image, or creating a mental match-dissolve when you want to impress upon your subconscious the difference between the way things are now and how they will be when you have achieved your desire. Another especially helpful film technique is the use of slow motion to slow things down so that you can study every frame and make sure it is captured and imprinted on your subconscious.

Changing the point of view is another technique that will help burn the message of your visualization into your subconscious. Many people naturally visualize in wide shots. Even if they zoom in when they are filling out details, their master shot is to stand back and look at the complete picture of themselves having accomplished their desire.

The most effective visualizations are those that focus on vivid mental pictures that resonate with you on a personal and emotional level. Some people create visualizations that focus on the process and play like a plot that takes time to advance to the point where the aim has been realized. Others focus on the goal and create a single panoramic scene that illustrates their concept of having achieved success, and they zoom in or cut to specific areas to focus on the details.

If your visualization is like a movie that moves from scene to scene, see yourself in the scenes acting exactly as you would want to be if you were overcoming obstacles and succeeding at your goal. Project yourself and your personality so that you are acting as if you already are the person you want to become.

If your style of visualization is to create a symbolic panoramic scene, visualize your aim or desire in the present tense, as already existing the way you want it to be. Use your imagination to form the picture as if it were already a fact, and see yourself as an integral part of your vision, feeling as though you have already accomplished your desire.

As you create the visualization of your desire, fill in every detail that you can think of. If your visualization involves going somewhere or doing something, create images of your actions right down to the last detail. Where do the scenes take place? Is it outside or indoors? Is it hot or cold? Is it bright or dark? If it's inside, how are the rooms furnished? If it's outside, are there trees or pavement? Can you hear traffic or birds? Do the sounds annoy you or soothe you? Keep building up your visualization and giving meaning to every detail until it is so complete that it looks like reality and feels like a real experience.

The more real and complete the visualized experience, the more power your visualization will have to influence your subconscious.

One technique that can strengthen the impression is to talk to your mind when you visualize the images—as though you are talking to another person. Whether you do it mentally or out loud, if you use words to accompany the images, it will help impress upon your subconscious the mental picture you are visualizing and the idea behind it.

To keep your visualizations fresh and interesting, you should change your point of view from time to time—similar to the affirmation technique of saying your affirmation in the first, second, and third persons. If your natural style is to create a broad picture of your success, you might switch to seeing the entire success scenario in close-up. Or you could get a sense of what it feels like to succeed by making yourself the central figure in the scenario and looking out through those eyes to see it from that point of view. Then see it from someone else's point of view, as though you are standing beside someone you respect and that person is watching the scene and cheering you on.

Jack Canfield, co-author of the *Chicken Soup* series of books, teaches another three-step variation on the movie-theatre technique that covers all the bases. He suggests that first you view your visualization as though you are watching a movie playing on a theatre screen. Then you walk up to the screen, open a door, and step inside the movie, which plays again, but now you are in the movie and seeing it from that point of view. And as a final step, you walk out of the screen, shrink the screen down until it is like a cookie that you break into pieces and swallow, making the whole visualization literally a part of you.

WHAT VISUALIZATION CAN OR CAN'T DO

Visualizing your desire can't put actual dollars in your bank or park a Rolls-Royce in your driveway any more than it can make a cup and saucer suddenly materialize on the desk in front of you. When you visualize yourself acquiring money, a car, or any other real object, what you are really doing is confirming to yourself the belief that you are capable of making it happen. The vivid images that you create of your desire are burned into your subconscious where they connect and interact with other bits of information so that you automatically start coming up with more and better ideas of how you can earn the money to put in your bank so you can buy the Rolls-Royce.

Visualization doesn't create concrete objects; it creates attitudes and ideas. When you change your attitudes and ideas, you go from living inside your head to making things happen in the real world, and then it is *you*, not your visualization, who takes action and makes the concrete things come true.

VISUALIZATION AND NEGATIVE SELF-TALK

You are who you are because of what you keep in your mind and what you tell yourself about yourself. And we all are talking to ourselves all the time. Our minds are filled with mental chatter as we constantly flip through our memory banks of thoughts and ideas—some important, some nonsense—and a great many of which are remembrances of past failures, embarrassments, criticisms, humiliations, doubts, and fears. This negative self-talk, which some motivational experts refer to as "rerunning old tapes," has a powerful effect on your self-confidence and your faith in your abilities as you take on new challenges.

Visualization is one of the most effective ways to counteract the effect of negative self-talk and feelings of failure, and it does so by tapping into your *positive* self-talk. Just as recalling past embarrassments will cause you to cringe even now, recalling past successes and triumphs will do the same in reverse.

No one ever forgets what it felt like when they were on top of the world. It's a rush of confidence, enthusiasm, and pride that is almost as much physical as it is mental and emotional. Recapturing that winning feeling is one of the greatest motivators you can tap into, and that is what visualization can do. By mentally reexamining in detail the thoughts and emotions going through your mind when you were exhilerated with success, you can take those feelings and use them to overcome the sabotaging negative self-talk. In effect, you can remake the way you are feeling now by infusing it with the confidence and faith you felt when you were a winner.

IMPROVE YOUR PERFORMANCE

Earlier we commented on the extensive use of visualization in the medical profession, and we noted the ways it has been used by Olympic athletes and sports stars, but two of the most influential pioneers in using the technique were associated with the space program. Charles Garfield, Ph.D., who wrote the bestseller *Peak Performance,* and Dennis Waitley, author of *The Winner's Edge,* were consultants to NASA.

The intention of the program they worked on was to rehearse the astronauts in every possible way so that they would be totally familiar with everything they were to do while in space and every possible disaster that might happen. This program included using leisure time to visualize coping with emergencies. When tested, it was found that those who had visualized the tasks handled their simulated disasters most effectively. The astronauts were not just mentally convincing themselves they could do something, they were actually rehearsing the doing of it, and by rehearsing they were also improving their skills.

Because visualization allows you to zoom in for close-ups or slow down the action, it is ideally suited to doing mental practice runs or dress rehearsals to polish almost any kind of skill or talent. In addition to motivating success and inspiring personal achievement, visualization can be used to change behavior and improve performance in a wide range of areas including reducing anxiety about public speaking; getting rid of the fear of flying; improving reading speed and comprehension;

tackling weight control; eliminating bad habits such as substance abuse; improving any skill, talent, or sports ability; and improving your interpersonal skills and your relationships with others.

EDITORS' RECOMMENDATIONS

The editors recommend the following list of books which are particularly helpful in developing the technique of creating powerful mental imagery; most are also available as audiobooks: *Visualization: Directing the Movies of Your Mind* by Adelaide Bry; *Creative Visualization* by Shakti Gawain; *Psycho-Cybernetics* by Dr. Maxwell Maltz; *Peak Performance* by Charles Garfield; *The Psychology of Winning* by Dr. Dennis Waitley; *The Power of Visualization* by Lee Pulos, Ph.D.; *The Secret* by Rhonda Byrne; *The Success Principle* by Jack Canfield; *Awaken the Giant Within* by Anthony Robbins; *The Silva Method* by José Silva; and the collection of audiobooks featuring the Silva Method trainer Hans DeJong, which includes an unusual method of quieting the mind using an audio tone that is designed to put the mind in the alpha state.

PROGRESSIVE RELAXATION EXERCISE

Earlier we noted that to close this chapter we would present a description of a more advanced relaxation technique. It is called a progressive relaxation exercise, and it will take quite a bit longer the first few times you work with it, but once you have learned the method you will be able to achieve a deep state of relaxation quickly and easily.

The human brain produces certain brain-wave patterns that can be measured with an EEG machine. There are four different wave patterns: Beta waves are what you produce when you are wide awake, and theta and delta are the waves produced while deep asleep. Alpha describes the brain-wave pattern produced when you are relaxed, daydreaming, or when you are just drifting off or just waking up from restful sleep. The ideal state of mind for working with visualization is the alpha state.

NOTES & COMMENTS

You can bring yourself to this ideal state of mind for visualization by following the progressive relaxation process described below. Although we have written it in a certain sequence to convey the idea of moving from one muscle group to another, our version is not a special formula that you need to memorize and follow to the letter. This relaxation exercise is simply a sequence of breathing and releasing muscle tension that follows an obvious progression that you will quickly recognize and easily understand.

- To begin, loosen any clothing that you find binding or constricting. Sit in a comfortable place where you can rest your feet flat on the floor. Let your arms hang loosely with your hands resting in your lap.

- Now close your eyes, place one hand lightly on your abdomen, and take a deep breath, breathing the air in through your nose and letting it out through your mouth.

- As you breathe in, do not take the air in so you swell out your chest. Take it in so that you fill both your chest and your abdomen.

- As you take each breath, think of the air filling your whole body. If you are breathing as you should, each time you breathe in, the hand you placed on your abdomen should be lifted out as your abdomen expands along with your lungs.

- Breathe deeply as you settle into a relaxed rhythm. Release and relax all stress and tension in your body. As you inhale, breathe in the stillness around you. As you exhale, breathe out any tension.

- As you quiet down, take notice of how your body feels, starting with the toes on your right foot. Curl your toes, then let them uncurl and relax. When you feel you can recognize the difference between tensed and relaxed, shift your attention up to your right ankle and again stretch and flex, noting the difference. Move further up, tighten and relax the calf muscles, then bend and straighten your knee, noting the difference as your muscles contract. Move up to your thigh muscles, your hips, and finally your buttocks, tensing and releasing all the way up until your whole leg is relaxed from your toes to your hip.

- Now move to your left leg, tightening and releasing the muscles until your left leg too is completely relaxed and comfortable.

- Then work the muscles of your stomach and chest, tensing and releasing. Now move your focus to your lower back and spine.

- Next focus on your arms and upper torso. Work each arm individually, being aware of the muscles working as you curl your fingers and close your thumbs, swivel your wrists, then progress up your forearms, work your elbows, tighten and release your biceps, and continue working all the way up to your shoulder blades, your upper shoulders, and your neck muscles. With each set of muscles, tighten and release until you can feel the tension leave, allowing warmth and relaxation to flood in and spread throughout your body.

- Now pay special attention to your face and scalp. Begin by making yourself aware of how relaxed your body has become and let that feeling of relaxation rise upward until it engulfs your neck, your throat, and spreads across your cheeks, temples, forehead, and scalp. Release your frown and allow your forehead to relax. Ease the tightness in your jaw and let your mouth open a bit so the tension can flow out. Breathe deeply and release all tension. Now let go completely and enjoy the release as all tension drains away.

If you repeat this progressive relaxation exercise at the same time and in the same place every day, both your body and mind will soon learn the technique and what it is intended to accomplish.

It will not be long before you will have only to take those first few deep breaths, and your body and mind will automatically go to the alpha level of deep relaxation and receptivity.

NOTES & COMMENTS

SPECIALIZED KNOWLEDGE

6

CHAPTER 6: OVERVIEW AND ANALYSIS

PERSONAL EXPERIENCES OR OBSERVATIONS

This chapter opens with Napoleon Hill stating that general knowledge is of little use in accumulating wealth. He tells how Henry Ford took on a newspaper that had called him ignorant, and won the lawsuit by showing how he commanded access to any knowledge he desired.

YOU CAN GET ALL THE KNOWLEDGE YOU NEED

Hill introduces the concept of the Master Mind Alliance—bringing together a group of people who share your goals and who will give you access to their knowledge and advice.

EDITOR'S COMMENTARY

The editors explain that the difference between a Master Mind and team-work is that while teams share cooperation, in a Master Mind every member shares a deep commitment and a common sense of mission.

Hill had a real disagreement with the commonly held notion that to educate meant having every possible fact, figure, and bit of knowledge crammed into the minds of students.

He loved to point out that the word *educate* has its roots in the Latin word *educo,* which means to develop from within; to educe; to draw out; to grow through use.

IT PAYS TO KNOW HOW TO PURCHASE KNOWLEDGE

Hill points out that in most cases all the knowledge you need is available through our school system and public institutions. However, he reiterates the theme that the knowledge is of no value until you take it, organize it, and apply it toward achieving some end.

EDITOR'S COMMENTARY

The editors expand on Hill's point, noting that IQ has never proven to be a good indicator of whether you will be successful in life. Daniel Goleman's bestseller *Emotional Intelligence* is cited to support the idea that factors other than good grades often have much more significance.

A LESSON FROM A COLLECTION AGENCY

Hill tells the story of how a correspondence school taught him a lesson in stick-to-it-iveness by insisting he pay his tuition whether he finished the course or not.

THE ROAD TO SPECIALIZED KNOWLEDGE

Hill promotes the idea of correspondence courses as being a statement of a sincere desire to learn and a clear indication that you will pay what it costs to get ahead.

A SIMPLE IDEA THAT PAID OFF

Hill tells the story of an accountant who was fired, which prompted that accountant to get the specialized knowledge he needed to start his own mobile accounting firm.

EDITOR'S COMMENTARY

The editors draw a parallel between the accountant getting the specialized knowledge he needed for his business and the story of how Bill Gates got the specialized knowledge he needed to launch Microsoft.

Hill again picks up the story about the accountant and tells how the accountant then needed marketing advice, so he got specialized advertising knowledge from a copywriter.

The story is continued by the copywriter, who was inspired by the example of the accountant, so she went out and got the specialized knowledge she needed to start her own agency.

YOU DON'T HAVE TO START AT THE BOTTOM

In this section Hill tells the story of how Dan Halpin used his dissatisfaction with his dead-end job as the motivation for him to get the specialized knowledge that brought him to the attention of those who could promote him, and how that finally took him all the way to the top.

EDITOR'S COMMENTARY

The editors illustrate how specialized knowledge can be the key to success by telling the stories of Mary Kay Ash and Mary Kay Cosmetics, Neil Balter and California Closets, Lillian Vernon and her mail-order empire, and finally how Walter Chrysler got the specialized knowledge he needed to go into the automobile industry.

Hill closes this chapter by noting that behind all ideas is specialized knowledge. What turns specialized knowledge into great ideas is imagination, which is the subject of the next chapter.

CHAPTER 6: THE WORKBOOK

This chapter focuses on the importance of having solid facts and information on which to base your opinions and actions. In the opening section, Napoleon Hill emphasizes two key points:

1. Contrary to the often-quoted phrase "knowledge is power," knowledge is *not* power—knowledge is just *potential* power. Knowledge becomes power only when it is organized into a definite plan.

2. There is a vast difference between the kind of education program taught in schools and actually being an educated person.

These are themes that Hill first wrote about in *Law of Success* and continued to develop throughout his career.

"The individual who knows how to make use of the knowledge possessed by another is as much a person of education as is the one who possesses the knowledge but does not know what to do with it."

"I learned my first lesson in self-confidence listening in on some older men talking about capital and labor. Without invitation I joined in and said something about employers and employees settling their differences by the Golden Rule. One of the men turned to me and said: 'You are a bright boy, and if you'd get some schooling you could make your mark in the world.' . . .

It should be noted that although Hill was a great promoter of the concept of the self-made man, that does not mean he didn't value education. However, his personal experience and a life spent analyzing the rich and powerful convinced him that if your desire is to achieve wealth and success, you will succeed only through specialization. He learned his first lesson in the power of focused and specialized knowledge at an early age.

As a boy, young Nap was known as a sometime student but a full-time troublemaker until, at age nine, his new stepmother, Martha Ramey Banner, came into his life. It was she who first told Napoleon that with his keen imagination he should be a writer, and by doing so she inspired in him a lifelong love of literature. It was also Martha who convinced him to give up his six-shooter in exchange for a typewriter, and she set the schoolboy scribbler on the path that would ultimately bring him fame and fortune.

Although he was more of a truant than a student before Martha took him in hand, with her encouragement Napoleon Hill became a devoted student. So much so, that at the one-room schoolhouse in his hometown of Wise, Virginia, for years after he was remembered as the "talent of the school." He went on to graduate from the local two-year high school, then headed about a hundred miles down the road to Tazwell, Virginia, to attend the business college.

The Tazwell business school had a one-year curriculum geared to teaching young men the basic accounting and office skills needed to get hired as a male secretary, which in those days was the prime entry-level job. It was expected that from there you would learn the business and climb the corporate ladder, and that's exactly what Hill did. After completing the course, he checked out his options and decided that Rufus Ayres owned the corporate ladder he would climb.

Ayres had made a fortune in banking and the coal-mining industry, and he'd become one of the wealthiest and most powerful men in

Virginia. Following is an excerpt from the letter of application that Hill wrote to Rufus Ayres:

> I have just completed a business college course and am well qualified to serve as your secretary, a position I am anxious to have. Because I have no previous experience, I know that at the beginning working for you will be of more value to me than to you. Because of this I am willing to pay for the privilege of working for you.
>
> You may charge me any sum that you consider fair, provided at the end of three months that amount will become my salary. The sum I am to pay you can be deducted from what you pay me when I start to earn money.

Ayres was so intrigued by this self-assured young man that he offered him a job, including a salary, and over the next two years Hill met and exceeded all expectations. In fact, he proved himself so completely, and rose so quickly, that Ayres put him in charge of 350 men, and at age nineteen Hill became the youngest manager of a mine in the country.

But even though he had accomplished so much within Ayres' company, Hill realized that it was a family firm and there were two sons who were way ahead of him in line to occupy the top management positions. That, plus his admiration for Rufus Ayres' skills in legal matters, prompted Hill to quit his job and return to his studies by enrolling at Georgetown Law School in Washington, D.C.

In order to put himself through law school, Hill went to work as a writer for *Bob Taylor's Magazine.* One of his first assignments was to interview Andrew Carnegie, and it was that interview which inspired Napoleon Hill's lifelong investigation into the factors influencing success.

In addition to his years of research and studies, Hill also launched his own businesses, created and taught courses on the psychology

. . . When that old gentleman planted the suggestion in my mind that I was a bright boy, it was not so much what he said as it was the way he said it that made such a long-lasting impression in my mind. It was the way he gripped my shoulders, and the look of confidence in his eyes that drove his suggestion deeply into my subconscious."

of advertising and salesmanship, published self-help magazines, and wrote motivational bestsellers. Through it all he was developing the theories that are the basis of the philosophy of personal achievement.

THERE IS EDUCATION, AND THERE IS LEARNING

The point of recounting Napoleon Hill's background and achievements in education, research, scholarship, and literature is to make it clear that when Hill states his opinion about education, it is not meant as an observation to which you may or may not want to pay attention. When it comes to education and personal achievement, Hill knew what he was talking about, and his opinion is meant to be taken as considered advice, backed up by extensive research and experience.

How do you learn what you need to know, and where do you go to get the answers to your questions? Although Hill doesn't specifically criticize America's universities, it is quite clear that in terms of the actual education received, he thought there were many other ways you could get much more knowledge for a lot less money.

There is no doubt that a good education from a celebrated university will help you go far. Grades aside, the right class ring alone will open doors that are closed to most, and the friendships and associations made while attending the right school can be worth much more than the degrees it grants. But Hill's focus in this section is not about the value and status of a university education; it is about gaining specialized knowledge—and there is a big difference.

Although anyone can benefit from reading *Think and Grow Rich,* at the time Hill wrote it a university education was not nearly as common as it is today, so this part of the book is directed much more at the entrepreneur trying to get ahead than it is at the student pursuing the cap-and-gown route to a career. Hill's advice to those looking for the fastest way to get specific information is to give serious thought to correspondence courses, extension classes, or night schools.

Napoleon Hill would never criticize the idea of becoming a well-rounded thinker, but the goal given to him by Andrew Carnegie wasn't to add yet another voice to the elite ranks of theoretical philosophizers. Hill's goal was to create a practical philosophy, a philosophy that would help the common person to succeed. Hill called his bestseller *Think and Grow Rich,* and it offers a philosophy that is just as focused on "growing rich" as it is on "thinking."

Hill is very clear: if you want to pursue the "grow rich" part of his philosophy, you must specialize. Other people may have become rich in other ways, and other people may teach other methods, but if you are to follow Napoleon Hill's principles of success, you must specialize—and you must become single-minded in pursuit of your specialty.

STORIES AND EXAMPLES

The largest part of this chapter is devoted to stories illustrating this central theme that you must specialize if you want to succeed. The first story that Hill tells is about the accountant who got fired because his employers could no longer afford a full-time accountant. As it happened, getting fired turned out to be a kind of specialized knowledge in itself.

It was getting fired and having to look for another job that made the accountant realize that with the economy going into a recession, there would be lots of other small businesses that would be laying off their accountants too. But wouldn't they still need help with their financials, even if they couldn't afford a full-time accountant?

By getting fired he gained the specialized knowledge that made him realize the value in setting up an accounting business to fill in part-time. But to service such a wide range of different kinds of small businesses, he would need even more specialized knowledge.

The accountant then assembled all the information he could find on the accounting requirements of various kinds of small businesses, and he acquired the most recent accounting systems for each.

NOTES & COMMENTS

When the accountant realized that he didn't know how to publicize his new business, he sought more specialized knowledge by contacting the woman who specialized in writing copy and creating brochures.

The copywriter who created his marketing plan had the specialized knowledge of advertising copywriting and design to prepare the direct-response brochure, but she needed to research the specialized knowledge of accounting procedures in order to put together an effective sales piece.

When she had completed the project and reviewed what she had created, she realized that she now possessed specialized knowledge about the advertising needs of small businesses, and that gave her the insight to create her own advertising and marketing consulting firm.

The editors follow Hill's stories with more contemporary examples, citing Bill Gates and Microsoft, Mary Kay Ash starting her cosmetics business, Neil Balter franchising California Closets, Lillian Vernon learning the catalog business, and Chrysler finding out how to build an automobile.

Needless to say, in Hill's stories and in the editors' examples there are factors other than specialized knowledge that also came into play, but it is the single-minded focus on specialized knowledge that made the difference between a daydream and a viable business. If Bill Gates had not been so focused on his aim, he would not have been able to look at an article about a do-it-yourself computer kit and foresee in it the future of personal computers. Without his single-mindedness, he might have bounced around science courses and fooled around with computers on the side, just like the thousands of other guys who didn't start their own company.

Mary Kay Ash could have gone around complaining to anyone who would listen about how she wasn't appreciated by her bosses, and, like so many other salespeople who think they aren't treated the way they deserve, within a couple of years she would be just another bitter employee selling giftware for somebody else's company.

If Neil Balter did not have the desire to create his own business, he would never have seen beyond that first closet repair and he might have continued being a handyman.

Walter P. Chrysler might just as easily have stuck to railroading, which would have kept him minding steam engines in the roundhouse until he retired.

Just stop for a moment and think about all the computer geeks who didn't invent Microsoft, all the gifts salespeople who didn't revolutionize door-to-door sales, all the handymen who didn't create their own franchise businesses, and all the railroaders who didn't switch their focus from steam engines to gasoline-powered automobiles. The only difference between them and the people who became success stories is faith in their aim or purpose and a single-minded pursuit of the specialized knowledge they needed to strike out on their own.

KNOWLEDGE ATTRACTS MORE KNOWLEDGE

Specialized knowledge goes hand-in-glove with having a chief aim or purpose. If you know your aim or purpose and are committed to it, it is only logical that you will want to learn all you can about it. As you focus in on your aim, you will, as a natural matter of course, begin to seek out specialized knowledge about that aim or purpose. Whether you enroll in school or university, get a job that will give you experience in the area, or just do some reading on the subject, the more you focus on your aim, the more you will find that related material starts to show up in all aspects of your life.

It is one of those strange and inexplicable mysteries that may not make logical sense, but almost everyone has had it hapen to them. It seems that just by thinking about a particular thing, that thing begins to manifest itself in your life.

NOTES & COMMENTS

Napoleon Hill came across this theory so often as he interviewed the successful entrepreneurs, inventors, industrialists, and political leaders whom Andrew Carnegie introduced him to, that he included the concept as a part of his philosophy of personal achievement, calling it the law of attraction. This is how he wrote about it in his masterwork, *Law of Success,* published in 1928:

THE LAW OF HARMONIOUS ATTRACTION

Every seed has within it a perfect plant. This means that forces and things that are suited to the needs of one another have a natural tendency to come together, just as the acorn attracts from the soil and the air the necessary materials out of which to grow an oak. It never grows a Christmas tree.

As soon as you set an aim or purpose, things related to the aim you have set start to occur in your life. It's almost as if your mind is like a magnet that attracts the object of your desire.

In the same way, you will attract to you people who harmonize with your own philosophy. The mind feeds upon what we feed it. Therefore, give it an environment with suitable material out of which to carry on its work. Fill your mind with an aim that will attract people and circumstances that will be of help to you, not a hindrance. Associate with people who inspire you with enthusiasm, self-confidence, determination, and ambition.

Millions of people go through life in poverty and want because they have made destructive use of the law of attraction through which "like attracts like." Through the operation of this law, they are constantly attracting trouble and grief and hatred and opposition from others by their unguarded words and destructive acts. Those who remain in poverty seldom realize that they are where they are as the result of their own acts.

AS LONG AS IT WORKS, WHO CARES *WHY* IT WORKS?

Some skeptics explain away the phenomenon as nothing more than a natural response to your heightened awareness. They say that because you have increased your interest in a certain subject you are now more aware of it, and because of your heightened awareness, you recognize it in instances that in the past you would not have noticed.

Suppose the doubters are right and it *is* just a heightened sense of awareness. What does it matter *why* it works? What's important is that it *does* work. Whether your mind really does act like a magnet and draw things to you that help you achieve your aim, or if you just think it does, the bottom line is that when you expect it to happen, it happens. So who cares why it works, as long as it does work?

THE SECRET AND THE LAW OF ATTRACTION

In March of 2006 an Australian television producer, Rhonda Byrne, released a 90-minute documentary-style film based on this seeming relationship between thinking and reality that she, like Napoleon Hill, refers to as the law of attraction. The film was titled *The Secret,* and it puts forth the theory that from ancient times down through the ages the great minds of every era, including Aristotle, Plato, the Prophet Mohammed, Isaac Newton, Beethoven, Thomas A. Edison, Albert Einstein, and Winston Churchill have all known and jealously guarded the secret of transforming wishes into reality.

The Secret promises to reveal the ancient wisdom of the law of attraction. The film presents dramatizations reminiscent of the movie version of *The Da Vinci Code,* interspersed with interviews featuring twenty-four contemporary self-help experts and motivational authors who explain their personal belief in the theory that you attract into your life that which is foremost in your mind, and therefore your thoughts determine your destiny.

The Secret became a sensation. It was launched with an extremely effective Internet word-of-mouth campaign, and that was followed by appearances on *Larry King Live,* the *Oprah Winfrey Show,* and virtually all of the other daytime talk shows. As a result, the video and a companion book, also titled *The Secret,* sold many millions of copies. Eighteen months later, in September 2007, both were still the number-one sellers topping the book and video bestseller lists.

Although the editors of this workbook welcome anything that increases awareness of Napoleon Hill's philosophy—and by popularizing the law of attraction, *The Secret* has certainly done that—the version offered in *The Secret* is not quite the same as what Hill describes.

The implication in *The Secret* is that all you have to do is visualize what you desire and it will manifest itself physically without anything further required on your part.

While it is true that Napoleon Hill also wrote about the power of the mind to influence reality, in Hill's terms changing reality through visualization is a matter of using autosuggestion to create a change in your thought processes, which in turn will change your actions, and it is your resulting actions that make the changes in reality.

THE R2/A2 FORMULA

We will close this workbook chapter with a practical method for gaining knowledge that also has a relationship with the law of attraction. It was devised by Napoleon Hill and his co-author and partner, W. Clement Stone, and it is called the R2/A2 Formula.

R2 stands for Recognize and Relate, and A2 stands for Assimilate and Apply. The theory is that in order to attain any goal in life you must first learn to recognize, relate, assimilate, and apply principles from what you see, hear, think, and experience. This formula is a blueprint for gaining knowledge by treating everything in your life as a source of creative ideas.

Recognize

W. Clement Stone says that if you wish to improve your creativity, you must keep your mind open and be constantly on the lookout for interesting ideas, different angles, and new twists. This means that you are always actively on the alert for ideas, whether you are flipping through a magazine, listening in on a conversation, going to a movie, conducting a meeting, or just watching people at the mall. Don't confine your inquiry to creative thinking sessions, and don't only look where you expect to find creative answers. Opportunities pop up all the time, but unless you are looking for ideas, you will never even recognize them.

Relate

Once you do recognize something as an interesting and creative idea or a possible solution, you should ask yourself, "How does it relate to me? How can I use it to achieve my goal or solve my problems? What effect will it have on my life? How does it relate to the other ideas and concepts I have in mind?"

The key to recognizing opportunities and seeing how they relate to you is allocating a regular time every day for creative review. This is the time when you just sit alone and think. This is when you test each idea in your mind, and try them out on yourself to see what they mean to you and how they would affect your life.

NOTES & COMMENTS

Choose the time of day when you do your best thinking. If you are a morning person, get up early; if you are a night person, stay up late. Go to a quiet place that is conducive to creative thinking, and keep a notepad handy to jot down ideas. Let your mind wander if you want; try to look at things from a different perspective or in a different way than you have looked at them before. You should look for the association between old and new ideas, and find how they connect with the other solutions and concepts you have in mind.

Assimilate

When you come upon an idea or opportunity that not only grabs your attention but also feels like something you can relate to and make use of, the next step is to assimilate it. To make it a part of who you are. As you learned in the earlier chapters, in order to assimilate something you must first set your desire, put your faith into it, and then use all the tools of autosuggestion to burn it into your subconscious so that it becomes ingrained in your personality and character.

Apply

The final step in Stone's R2/A2 formula is exactly the same as the last step in Hill's formula for success: you must apply it.

Remember what was said about "applied faith"—it's not something you sit around "having"; it's something you "do." The same is true of creative ideas and solutions.

You can achieve anything in life you desire that does not violate the laws of God or the rights of your fellowmen. But first you must define your desires and then get into action to achieve them. In your quest for more and better creative ideas, you can recognize, relate, and assimilate all you want, but if you don't apply it, the most creative idea is meaningless.

IMAGINATION

7

CHAPTER 7: OVERVIEW AND ANALYSIS

THE WORKSHOP OF THE MIND

This chapter opens with Hill explaining that there are two kinds of imagination: synthesized and creative imagination. Synthesized imagination is what we use when we put together known information to create a new idea. Creative imagination is the faculty through which we receive hunches and inspirations from Infinite Intelligence.

EDITOR'S COMMENTARY

The editors expand upon Hill's explanation by citing the creation of Amazon.com and eBay.com as recent examples of synthesized imagination, but point out that to some degree they may also have tapped into creative imagination.

Hill explains that synthesized imagination is what you will use most often to transform your desire into reality. He also makes the point that the more you use it, the better it will work for you.

In the subsequent Commentary, the editors use Thomas Edison's light bulb as an example, noting that everything he used in his invention was widely known, but the way he synthesized the knowledge changed the world. The editors explain how W. Clement Stone's R2/A2 formula of recognizing and relating, assimilating and applying is a system for thinking that prompts you to use your synthesized imagination.

The editors then tell how the creation of the Barbie doll is a perfect illustration of how synthesized imagination works to create a product. In the same vein, they cite the stories behind Mary Kay Cosmetics, The Body Shop, Home Depot, and Staples.

The editors end the Commentary with a list of bestselling books on the subject of creativity and imagination.

> "First comes the thought, then organization of that thought into ideas and plans, then transformation of those plans into reality. The beginning, as you can plainly see, is in your imagination."

TAPPING INTO CREATIVE IMAGINATION

In this section Hill lays out his understanding of the way in which everything in the universe is interconnected because everything is made up of the same stuff: energy.

EDITOR'S COMMENTARY

The editors confirm that even with all the scientific advancements since Hill developed his theory, it still holds up. They use the example of the bumps and folds in a tablecloth to illustrate the idea of the interconnection of all things, and they go on to explain how this concept can also account for hunches and inspirations that come into your mind from Infinite Intelligence.

HOW TO MAKE PRACTICAL USE OF IMAGINATION

This is the beginning of a lengthy section in which both Hill and the editors tell stories illustrating how an imaginative idea was the basis of a new product or business that went on to become a huge success. These inspirational stories include the ideas that launched Coca-Cola, Colonel Sanders Kentucky Fried Chicken, Mrs. Fields Cookies, Famous Amos Cookies, McDonald's, Starbucks, and Paul Newman's Own brands.

Hill then tells how a Chicago preacher, Frank W. Gunsaulus, got the idea for a sermon that inspired the creation of a university. To follow this, the editors tell about the creation of Post-its, Velcro, the Walkman, the launch of the Piggly-Wiggly grocery stores, the invention of the shopping cart, and the stories behind Staples, Woolworth's, Wal-Mart, and the 99 Cents Only Stores.

Hill concludes the chapter by warning that if you think success depends on lucky breaks, you are in for a big surprise. You make your own luck through imaginative thinking.

CHAPTER 7: THE WORKBOOK

Napoleon Hill devotes the opening section of this chapter to explaining that human imagination is divided into two separate forms: synthesized imagination and creative imagination. But these two names that Hill has chosen to identify the forms of imagination have proven to be somewhat misleading. Generally speaking, today the word *creative* implies something better than the word *synthesized,* and most people would assume from the names that using your creative imagination is better than your synthesized imagination. That is not what Hill meant.

SYNTHESIZED IMAGINATION

To clarify, the most creative people in the world utilize synthesized imagination most of the time to come up with their best ideas. Your synthesized imagination is what you are using when you rack your brain and call upon everything you know to come up with an idea or a solution to a problem. Synthesizing, or putting the right things together in the right way, is the height of creativity. That's what scientists, cooks, inventors, mechanics, songwriters, salespeople, students, business managers, and just about everyone else does when they are using their head and working to the best of their ability.

"You will never have a definite purpose in life, you will never have complete self-confidence, you will never have initiative and leadership unless you first create these qualities in your mind and see yourself in possession of them."

NOTES & COMMENTS

Nothing makes the point about synthesized imagination more clearly than the story of how Thomas Edison synthesized various bits of knowledge to create the light bulb. Edison's invention is not only an excellent example of synthesized imagination, it is also the perfect illustration of creative thought working in conjunction with the storehouse concept of the subconscious mind.

- Edison clearly had a definite chief aim, and that was the desire to make a workable light using electricity. He certainly had faith in his ability to accomplish his desire, and he must have strongly emotionalized his desire or it never would have sustained him through ten thousand failures.

- In his conscious mind, Thomas A. Edison had a vast number of facts about electricity, scientific theory, the properties of materials, and the laws of nature. He consciously accepted or rejected the thousand of bits of information that he consciously knew, to test different combinations to see which would work.

- Because his desire was so foremost in his conscious mind, it also became deeply rooted in his subconscious mind. There it came into contact with a flood of other facts and bits of information, some of which had been forgotten and others that the conscious mind had rejected as unimportant. His subconscious mind juggled and rejuggled all of the new bits of conscious information with all of its old bits of conscious and subconscious information, looking for the right combinations.

- Out of this came the imaginative, creative thoughts that resulted not only in the electric light bulb but also in parallel circuits, the dynamo, voltage regulators, fuses, insulation, light sockets, on-off switches, and hundreds of other related products that were created, developed, and patented by Edison.

- Which of these creative ideas were developed by Edison deliberately pulling together what he knew in his conscious mind, and which were created from subconscious information he wasn't even aware that he knew? Nobody, not even Edison, could answer that. But in either case, the imaginative ideas came about because the desire was clear and firmly planted, and the creative process was encouraged.

Although the example of Thomas Edison involves working with scientific principles and materials with which the average person might not be familiar, the other stories in the book about the creation and marketing of Coca-Cola, McDonald's, Post-its, Velcro, Staples, Wal-Mart, and other icons of entrepreneurship make it clear that you can become very successful if you are just an ordinary person who is able to see ordinary things in an extraordinary way.

Using synthesized imagination, you can become hugely successful just by taking the most common everyday thing and seeing how to put it together in a new way. As Hill said about the launch of the Piggly-Wiggly stores, "Where in this story do you see the slightest indication of something that you could not duplicate?"

CREATIVE IMAGINATION

On the other hand, what Hill calls creative imagination involves tapping into something beyond the information and ideas you have in your mind. You are using creative imagination when you get a flash of insight or inspiration that comes to you completely out of the blue. At the most rarified level, it is what scientists and inventors tap into when they create new systems or discover laws of nature that previously were unknown. More commonly, it is when you get a hunch, a gut feeling, or a premonition about something that turns out to be right, but you had no way of knowing in advance that it would happen.

NOTES & COMMENTS

CAN YOU MAKE CREATIVE IMAGINATION BETTER?

Unlike synthesized imagination, your creative imagination does not depend upon getting more input. After all, what additional information would make your premonitions come earlier? Or what research could you do to make yourself have more intuitive intuitions or more inspirational inspirations?

Although you cannot intentionally make your creative imagination happen on cue, you can at least be receptive to the ideas that do come to you. You can encourage the development of your creative imagination by acknowledging to yourself that even if you don't know how it works, somehow it does actually produce ideas and plans that you can use.

How your creative imagination works and where the ideas come from is one of the most challenging of Napoleon Hill's principles of success because it relies upon the subconscious mind and what Hill termed Infinite Intelligence.

In this chapter, Hill explains just enough of the theory as to how it works to allow readers to understand the basic idea without clouding the issue with too much detail.

- Hill's original text and the Editor's Commentary spell out the basic scientific fact that there are only four things in the entire universe: time, space, energy, and matter.

- If you examine matter closely, you will see that it is made up of molecules, which are made up of atoms, which are made up of protons, neutrons, and electrons, which are not solid at all; they are bits of energy. 99 percent of each atom is empty space.

- Whether something is tangible, such as a chair, or intangible, such as a thought, it is just energy in a different form.

- All of the actual things in the entire universe are made up of one common substance: energy.

- Because everything is just a different part of energy, everything is therefore interconnected and a part of everything else.

- And finally, because everything is a part of everything else, occasionally a piece of that energy from outside yourself, in the form of a thought or an idea, will connect with you on a subconscious level and appear in your imagination as a premonition or intuition, a flash of insight or an inspiration.

CREATIVE VISION

Later in his career, when Hill wrote or spoke about imagination he devoted less attention to the division between synthesized and creative imagination, and he began using a new term, *creative vision.* Rather than dividing imagination into two separate forms, this new term embraces the idea that the two influence one another. Creative vision is a blending of the conscious mind's imagination with the subconscious mind's intuition. What this means in a practical sense is that in addition to trying to come up with an idea by consciously attempting to fit together bits and pieces of information in your imagination, you also intentionally encourage your intuitive subconscious to influence the solution.

GATHER INFORMATION

The first step in using your creative vision is to add to the information and opinions you already have in your mind by gathering all the raw material and information you can find on the subject. It is important that when you do so, you don't get so narrowly focused that you only look to the obvious sources. If you confine your research to the predictable and the tried and true, the ideas you generate will very likely be just as predictable, tried, and true. Don't lock yourself into linear, logical thinking. Cast your net wide enough that there is always the possibility you may surprise yourself and catch some off-the-wall idea that

NOTES & COMMENTS

suddenly shakes everything up. Remember, the whole point is to use your imagination, so be imaginative from the very start.

INCUBATION

As you are gathering and assembling information, you will have already begun reviewing it, integrating what you have learned with what you already know and rearranging it into new combinations. That brings us to the next aspect of the process, the germination or incubation stage, when you mull things over, try to make one concept fit with another, mentally test-drive different ideas, turn things over in your mind, try to look at it from different angles, and see it with fresh eyes.

SO WHAT'S THE DIFFERENCE?

So far, this doesn't seem any different from what Hill was describing with his earlier term, *synthesized imagination*. What makes creative vision different is the next stage, in which you use a number of techniques to open the door to your subconscious mind and allow it to influence the creative thoughts incubating in the conscious part of your imagination. This is where you make room for something to happen. This is where you intentionally put yourself in the way of the creative process in the hope that something intuitive or inspirational will come to you.

An important part of the process is learning to recognize the creative response when it happens. Very often creative vision comes to you in a kind of shorthand, appearing as images, symbols, or dreams. Because these images that emerge from your inner-self are fleeting and easily forgotten, you will need to keep close at hand a notebook or some other way to make a record of the ideas and insights before they vanish from your consciousness.

Even though the ideas dissipate quickly, you should not paraphrase or condense too much when you record your thoughts. As much as possible, you want to be sure to capture the material just the way it comes to you, because often what is good about a good idea is lost if what you recall isn't detailed enough to restimulate your senses and punch all the same buttons it did when it first hit you.

GET YOUR IMAGINATION WORKING OUTSIDE THE BOX

In the following section you will find a number of specific techniques that you can use to stimulate your creative vision. If there is one thing that is common to these techniques, it is that they offer ways to look at things differently. We often hear people talk about taking off the blinders, breaking the mold, pushing the envelope, or thinking outside the box. All of those statements suggest that the style of thinking you are now using is constricting you and, in order to think better, something has to break down the barriers that are holding you in.

The other common thread is most techniques that help you come up with better ideas are also designed to help you come up with *more* ideas. One of the biggest problems in finding new solutions and creative ideas is that people get so focused on solving the problem quickly, that as soon as they come up with a couple of good alternatives, they stop trying for more.

On the following pages you will find some of the best-known and widely used thinking techniques. They all suggest that the more ideas you have to choose from, the better the chance you'll find a superior solution, and that you should suspend your critical analysis until after you have pulled together a wide range of ideas to choose from.

LATERAL THINKING

Written by Edward de Bono, the renowned psychologist, business consultant, and bestselling author of over sixty books, *Lateral Thinking* is the classic book on creative thinking. In it de Bono explains a number of techniques to free yourself from the usual style of logical thinking, which he calls *vertical* thinking.

The difference between the two styles of thinking is that with vertical thinking all that matters is how right the answer is, whereas with lateral thinking your main concern is how diverse the answers are.

With vertical thinking your focus is to select the most promising approach to a problem. With lateral thinking you find as many approaches as you can.

With vertical thinking you move forward one step at a time, and each step has to be correct before you advance to the next one. With lateral thinking you can make leaps of logic, or jump ahead, then go back to fill in the gaps afterward.

With vertical thinking you exclude what is irrelevant. With lateral thinking it doesn't matter whether it is irrelevant; you're just interested to see what comes of it.

The whole aim of lateral thinking is to look at things in different ways, to disrupt the normal flow, to restructure patterns and to generate alternatives. In lateral thinking you are not trying to find the best approach; you are trying to come up with as many different approaches as you can. Later you will judge which are good, better, and best.

LATERAL THINKING AND OUTSIDE STIMULI

One way to shake things up and force yourself to look at things from a different point of view is to intentionally interrupt your thinking by interjecting a non sequitur that sends your thoughts off on a tangent. This is the complete opposite of a rigid, vertical style of thinking in which you only focus on what is relevant. With this approach, you intentionally look for the irrelevant.

In some ways it is similar to the practice of looking for spiritual guidance by randomly opening the bible and seeking the answer in the first passage your eye falls on. The same principle is at work in the ancient Chinese practice of throwing three coins and then looking up the interpretation in the I-Ching.

In the case of lateral thinking, the source of stimulating words could be anything from a dictionary to a romance novel to an item in your desk drawer or what you see on a walk down the street. The idea is that you set up a system to produce random words or chance events. It could be that you select a book then throw dice to come up with a page number, paragraph, and word. Or if you wanted to use a location or a visual as the stimulant, you could decide that the thing to throw into the mix will be the first blue object you see, or whatever is in the window of the fifth store with a neon sign.

One of the most interesting ways of coming up with random words is to use a random-word generator. A random-word generator is exactly what the name implies, and if you log on to any search engine and type in "random-word generator," it will offer you page after page of listings for free Web sites. Click on any of these sites, and there on the home page you will see a word to set your mental wheels spinning. Most of the sites also offer other possibilities, such as random names or random phrases, and some give you the opportunity to set certain parameters to your word search. Some sites also offer a picture option that gives you a visual image as your cue.

LATERAL THINKING: RANDOM-WORDS STIMULATION

You can do this on your own or you can do it as part of group, but there must be certain ground rules that you set about the amount of time you will devote to following the ideas stimulated by a word, how many words you use in any one session, and who will act as the referee to keep everyone on track or to prompt a new direction.

Once you have decided on your method for selecting a random word or object, you state the problem you have been wrestling with, choose your random word, and then start throwing out whatever new thoughts and ideas are stimulated by thinking of the random word in association with your problem. Some ideas will be one-offs, while

NOTES & COMMENTS

others will generate a whole chain of related ideas. Sometimes a chain of linked thoughts will continue on for the whole session, while at other times the chains will lead nowhere and you'll have go back to the word and start a new train of thought.

You do not want to devote more than about three to five minutes to exploring the possibilities opened by the random word you have selected. Also, once you have reached the predetermined time-limit you should not immediately look for another stimulus word. If you do, you will find yourself going through word after word as if you are searching for the best word. That is not the point. There are no best words, because you are not trying for anything in particular; you are just looking for ideas to stimulate your mind, so you should be satisfied with whatever you get from the exercise.

AN EXAMPLE USING THE DICTIONARY

To illustrate what you might expect when you use the random-word method, the following is adapted from an example that appears in the classic *Lateral Thinking* by Edward de Bono.

A group studying the problem of the housing shortage decided to see if they could open up the discussion by introducing a random word. They decided they would get their word from the *Penguin English Dictionary*. They used a table of random numbers to come up with the numbers 473 and 13, then they went to the dictionary and found that the thirteenth word on page 473 was *noose*.

The group then set a three-minute time period and restated their problem: What to do about the housing shortage?

Next they started free-associating ideas relating *noose* to the shortage of houses.

In just those three minutes, the following are the new ideas that were generated:

noose; tightening noose; execution . . . What are the difficulties in executing a housing program? What is the bottleneck? Is it capital, labor, or land?

noose tightens . . . Things are going to get worse with the present rate of population increase.

noose; rope; suspension construction system . . . Tent-like houses but made of permanent materials; easily packed and erected, or on a large scale with several houses suspended from one framework; much lighter materials possible if walls did not have to support themselves and the roof.

noose; loop; adjustable loop . . . What about adjustable, round houses that could be expanded as required, just uncoil the walls? No point in having houses too large to begin with, because of heating problems. Extra attention to walls and ceilings, furniture, etc., but facility for slow, stepwise expansion as need arises.

noose; snare; capture . . . Capture a share of the labor market; people captured by home ownership due to difficulty in selling and the complications; lack of mobility; houses as exchangeable units, classified into types; direct exchange of one type for a similar type, or put one type into the pool and take out a similar type elsewhere.

By using a random word, the group stimulated a large number of different ideas in a short period of time, and in this case all of the word-chains grew out of the base word. However, as an alternative, at some point a pun or a play on words might have become the stimulus (such as "no noose is good news"), or they might have switched to using an opposite of the random word (perhaps *lifeline*). The random word that is selected is used only to get things going, not to prove anything. There is no one correct way to use the word.

LATERAL THINKING: REVERSAL

The object of lateral thinking is to create a different arrangement of information that will provoke a different way of looking at the situation. Reversal is another mental exercise that you can do as a way of jogging your thinking into a different arrangement. You take some actual feature of the problem you are working on and begin to modify it by envisioning its opposite. You take things as they are, then turn them around, inside out, upside down, back to front.

Here is an example of one kind of reversal thinking that de Bono uses in his book:

A man who is late for an important meeting is driving his car down a narrow European road when he comes upon a shepherd and a large flock of sheep that block the road. There is no way the sheep can move forward any faster, and the shepherd is afraid that he can't keep his sheep from being run over if the car forces its way through the herd.

How does the car get past the sheep?

It doesn't. The shepherd reverses the situation. He tells the man to stop the car, the shepherd turns his flock around, and he herds the sheep back past the now stationary car. The sheep are then behind the car and the road in front of the car is wide open. The car speeds off.

LATERAL THINKING: THE OTHER POINT OF VIEW

A variation on reversal thinking is looking at your problem from another person's point of view. The most common version of this is when manufacturers are designing products and they say that they try to look at it from the customer's point of view.

If you were trying to come up with a revolutionary design for an office chair, it would certainly be helpful to consider the person who will buy it and sit in it. But what might produce even more creative insights would be to look at it from the point of view of the desk it will sit in front of, or see it from the point of view of the carpet its wheels will sit on, or what about the way the office cleaning crew would see it? Or consider looking at it from the point of view of the environmentalists who are trying to shut down the junkyard where it will get dumped when it is old and broken.

With either the reversal or the other point of view, your goal is to generate as many variations as possible, so remember to avoid the obvious and the tried and true. You should make sure that your other points of view are not all as directly related to the subject as indicated previously in the office-chair example. For instance, you might get even better ideas if you looked at it from a kid's point of view, from an entertainment point of view, from the point of view of a clothing manufacturer, from a historical point of view, or consider what your mother-in-law would think of it.

Once you have run through a reasonable number of viewpoints, you can magnify your results even more by challenging your team to come up with what is good about each of the ways you have looked at it. Then turn it around and come up with what's bad about what you see from each point of view.

BRAINSTORMING

Brainstorming is a term that is often misused because it is assumed that it is just a synonym for kicking around ideas. However, brainstorming is actually a very specific technique that was first defined and formalized in 1939 by advertising executive Alex F. Osborne. According to Osborne, the distinguishing features of a brainstorming session are:

- It is a group method of generating ideas about a specific problem.

- There is an appointed moderator.

- There is an appointed note-taker.

NOTES & COMMENTS

- The group should be no larger than a dozen people.

- All ideas, no matter how far-fetched, are equally welcomed and considered.

- Don't allow logic to deter an idea.

- No criticism of any idea is allowed during the process.

- Bosses cannot shoot down ideas or have any more control than anyone else.

- No judgment is made about any idea until after the session has been completed.

A brainstorming session starts with a specific problem, and by the end of the session you will have a list of good ideas, bad ideas, top-of-the-head concepts, and wild and crazy solutions. After the session is over, the list is analyzed and the suggestions are evaluated. It is only then that critical analysis is brought to bear and the ideas are reviewed to see which ones might yield practical solutions.

THE BRAINSTORMING MODERATOR OR LEADER

Brainstorming is a perfect way for you to work with your Master Mind alliance. As moderator, it is your job to set the problem and guide the session without trying to control it. The moderator keeps people from talking over one another, stops them from criticizing or killing ideas, and offers new ideas to stimulate other ways of looking at the problem. Probably the most important job is to make sure the participants keep moving on so that the session doesn't fall into critical analysis.

THE NOTE-TAKER OR SCRIBE

The note-taker writes on a chalkboard, large flip-chart sheets, or uses some kind of projector or large video screen, so that everyone in the group can keep track of the ideas as they are written down. The note-taker must record every idea and must refrain from judging or filtering out "crazy ideas." Between the note-taker and the leader, they make sure that every idea is recorded in enough detail that if anyone wants to review the notes later they will be able to easily recall the point.

THE BRAINSTORMING SESSION

In commenting on his technique, Alex Osborne said: "Brainstorm means using the brain to storm a creative problem in commando fashion." He also advised that you should get every idea out of your head, no matter how crazy you think it is, because "it is easier to tone down a wild idea than to think up a new one."

The moderator begins the session by going around the room giving everyone a chance to throw in ideas and suggestions. After a few such rounds, the floor is opened up to the free exchange of ideas.

From the beginning every idea is welcome and no one is expected to defend an idea or even to discuss any one idea for very long. Every effort should be made to encourage even the most reticent members of the group to say whatever comes into their minds. The challenge is to keep the ideas coming and to keep them building on each other, and it doesn't matter if your idea is totally original or if it is based on someone else's idea. Your idea can then get picked up by another person and another person until it becomes a chain of ideas that keep piggybacking on the ideas that came before them.

The session terminates at the end of a predetermined period, or when the moderator senses that creativity or enthusiasm is beginning to flag. Most creative-thinking brainstorming sessions last only an hour at most.

Most groups usually take at least a coffee break, and sometimes as much as a few hours, before they tackle the evaluation. In some

NOTES & COMMENTS

cases the evaluation is done by the whole group; at other times it may just be the leader and two or three others who are closest to the problem. Their task is to combine and modify the raw ideas to come up with a list of the best practical ideas, to discard those that are totally impractical, and to create another list that identifies the kernel of a good idea that is at the heart of some of the wilder, off-the-wall suggestions.

MIND-MAPPING AND CLUSTERING

Mind-mapping is an idea-generating method that is mostly associated with author, educator, psychologist, and brain specialist Tony Buzan. *Clustering* is the term that was created to describe the right-brain thinking method advocated by author and creative-writing instructor Gabriel Rico. Both are similar creative-thinking techniques that are designed to organize your thinking and generate creative ideas. The easiest way to differentiate between the two is to see the examples below and on the following page.

IF NAPOLEON HILL HAD MADE A MIND MAP TO PLOT *THINK AND GROW RICH* . . .

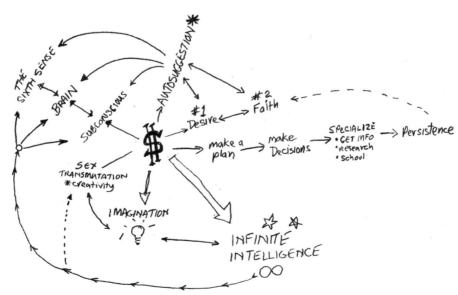

A mind map is used to generate and classify ideas, and as an aid in problem-solving and decision-making. It is a diagram that shows how new ideas are spun off a central keyword or idea, and it visually illustrates the connections between bits of information. By drawing what amounts to a picture of the way ideas are generated, it encourages a brainstorming approach to any organizational task.

Unlike a list that is made from top to bottom, the mind map starts from the center or main idea and branches out in different directions. The relative importance of the ideas is readily apparent from how and where they appear in the map. Although there are exceptions, usually the most important ideas cluster near the center and grow less important as they spread out. The way you write or draw an idea, and how it looks on the page, can play a large part in recalling not just the facts about the idea you wanted to capture but also the feeling you had about the information when you put it on the mind map.

Tony Buzan suggests the following for mind-mapping:

- Start in the center with a word or an image of the topic.

- Use multiple colors to emphasize special words or ideas.

- Use images, symbols, and codes to make certain ideas stand out.

- Don't overthink where things should go; it will restrict creativity.

- Select keywords and print using upper- or lowercase letters.

- Each word or image must be alone and sitting on its own line.

- The lines must be connected, starting from the central image.

- Use emphasis and show associations in your mind map.

- Feel free to start a new branch whenever an idea hits, or to go back and add new details to branches you started earlier.

- Do not worry about order or organization; it will take care of itself.

A mind-mapping session ends when you feel that you have set down all the information you wish to record at a particular time, or when you feel that your creativity is losing its freshness. You can always come back at a later time and add more ideas to a mind map.

CLUSTERING

Clustering is a technique devised by Gabriel Rico to break writer's block, to pull together your creative ideas and get yourself ready to start writing about your idea(s). It is a technique that jump-starts creativity and generates ideas by forcing you to break out of the linear thinking that views things in an organized, prioritized way. Clustering is more random, less restricting. It is a form of brainstorming that generates ideas, images, and feelings around a topic or stimulus word.

Clustering ideas is usually done by yourself with a pad and pencil, although you can also adapt it to a group. It normally does not take more than a few minutes, but the session is left open-ended to allow for the "felt shift," which we will explain at the end of the following description:

THE EDITOR'S CLUSTER PRIOR TO WRITING ABOUT HILL'S CHILDHOOD

Begin with a blank page. In the center of the page write the word or phrase that describes your problem and draw a circle around it. This is the seed or nucleus from which you will start. Now, as quickly as possible, without censoring any ideas that may come to mind, draw a line out from the circled word at the center and write the first idea that pops into your head. Draw a circle around it, then draw a connecting line; write down the next idea, circle it, draw a line; write the next idea, circle it, draw a line, and so on and so on, until you run out of ideas to add to that chain of thoughts.

Whenever your mind shifts to a new direction, go back to the center circle, draw a new line extending out in a different direction, and start a new chain of thoughts. Keep on creating clusters of circled words or ideas and starting new chains of thoughts, until you feel what Gabriel Rico calls a "felt shift." This is an odd but very descriptive term that captures something quite unique that happens when you use this technique.

When you start working outward from a central circled word, the new ideas will come quite quickly and easily. However, as you continue clustering, you will come to a point where you feel as though something about the process has changed or shifted, and that this is the time to stop because now you know what you want to do or write. This "felt shift" is the clustering equivalent of the aha or eureka moment. It's your subconscious telling you that you've hit on something good and it's time to stop clustering and start writing it down.

One last note on clustering: Gabriel Rico is quite specific about drawing a circle or an oval around each new word or idea, as opposed to a square, rectangle, or any other shape. She does not know why, but from her many years of experience with the technique, she has found that there is something in the clusters and connections of rounded shapes that produces better results.

NOTES & COMMENTS

MASTER MINDS

In later chapters of *Think and Grow Rich,* Napoleon Hill writes about certain concepts that should also be mentioned in this chapter about imagination and creative vision. The first of these is what Hill calls the Master Mind alliance. The Master Mind is defined as two or more people coming together and blending their minds in perfect harmony as they work to achieve a common goal. Following is how Hill describes his experience with it:

> When you tap into the power of your Master Mind group, you will find that the more you work together the more each member will learn to anticipate the ideas of others and to connect immediately with their intense enthusiasm and inspiration. The strange thing about this method of mind stimulation is that it places each participant in communication with unknown sources of knowledge definitely outside their own experience. By adopting and following a similar plan, you will be making use of the famous Carnegie formula. You cannot completely control this process, but the more you use it the more it will come into play.

Having a Master Mind group is an excellent thing to do if you want to increase your creativity and your productivity. Surround yourself with a group of smart people and you not only get to tap the smarts of each individual, but you also get the sparks that start to fly when you rub smart against smart. In simple terms, mentally and creatively the whole is greater than the sum of its parts.

There is much more in the later chapters about how to organize a Master Mind, who you should ask to join, how often to meet, and so on, but its primary purpose is the subject of this chapter: how to create more and better creative ideas.

HILL'S INVISIBLE COUNSELORS

In chapter fifteen, The Sixth Sense, Napoleon Hill goes into detail about a mental exercise that he originally developed as a character-building device to overcome what he called the handicap of being born and raised in an environment of ignorance and superstition. He called the technique his invisible or imaginary counselors.

Each night Hill would imagine that he was conducting a meeting of the nine men in history he admired most. He would pose a question, and then each of his imaginary guests would give their answer. To prepare for this mental exercise, Hill intently studied the lives of these historical personages so that the answers they gave were completely in keeping with their character.

The answers, of course, were Hill's own thoughts and words that he was mentally putting into the mouths of his invisible counselors. But because he was coming up with the answers "in character," so to speak, those answers exhibited an intelligence and wit that Hill did not normally exhibit when he was being himself.

Once Hill became aware of how insightful these answers could be, he switched focus from asking personal questions designed to improve his character, to posing questions about a wide range of problems that required creative solutions. It proved to be such an effective method for creating more and better ideas that he used it not only for personal purposes but also to create solutions for certain clients he advised.

Napoleon Hill's counselors are a variation on the use of visualization as a means of accessing knowledge stored in the subconscious and tapping into Infinite Intelligence. However, even though the editors have confirmed the principle underlying Hill's method of posing questions to his invisible counselors, many readers may find it hard to imagine themselves going to the lengths of choosing counselors and doing the extensive research into their personal histories as Hill did with his

NOTES & COMMENTS

counselors. The following explanation of creative visualization will offer you a version that is less demanding but that can be just as effective.

CREATIVE VISUALIZATION

In previous chapters, creative visualization was examined as a way to burn your major aim or purpose into your subconscious. Visualization can also be used to stimulate your imagination and heighten your creativity. You can do this by approaching it almost as though your subconscious mind is an actual place where you can take your concept or problem, and by taking it there it will become transformed into something better and more creative.

If you have doubts that creative visualization can really work, if you feel self-conscious or uncomfortable trying, or if you feel that this kind of pretending is more silly than it is serious, just remind yourself about Thomas Edison, Alexander Graham Bell, Albert Einstein, the NASA astronauts who perform without a hitch, all the sports stars who have improved their game, and all the doctors who have saved lives by using this very technique.

It is a fact that you have in your mind almost endless facts and experiences that could help you make more creative and better decisions. Some of these hidden ideas and bits of knowledge have been forgotten because you learned them long ago or they were superseded by more immediate concerns. Other bits of information didn't seem to fit anywhere when you learned them so they were just set aside, waiting for the time you'll have need of them.

If you choose to, you can open yourself to these thoughts, ideas, and solutions by creating a mental scenario in which your subconscious believes it is right and natural for it to open the way and allow you free access to the information in the deepest regions of your mind.

Following is a method for using creative visualization to provide you with creative ideas, answers to questions, and solutions to problems.

THE FIRST THING TO DO IS RELAX . . .

Choose a time and place where you can relax and won't be disturbed. Loosen any clothing that you find binding or constricting. Choose a comfortable place to sit where you can rest your feet flat on the floor, and let your arms hang loosely with your hands resting in your lap.

- Now close your eyes, place one hand lightly on your abdomen, and take a deep breath, breathing the air in through your nose and letting it out through your mouth.

- As you breathe in, do not try to fill your chest. Instead, as you take each breath, think of the air filling your whole body so that both your chest and abdomen expand.

- If you are breathing as you should, each time you breathe in, the hand you placed on your abdomen will be lifted out as your abdomen expands along with your lungs.

- Continue to breathe deeply as you let your breathing settle into a slow, relaxed rhythm and you slowly count down from ten to one, releasing all stress and tension in your body. As you count each number, envision yourself on an escalator; with each number the escalator takes you down to a deeper level of relaxed receptivity.

- That simple exercise, which shouldn't take more than a minute or two, will put you in a state of relaxed but receptive attention—the perfect condition for creative visualization; the ideal state of mind in which to create clear, convincing, fully realized mental images.

- When you are relaxed you will imagine yourself in a place that feels very calming and peaceful to you. It can be any place you want. It could be in a forest glade or in front of a cozy fireplace; it could be a vast library or an ocean cove, a castle on a hill, or any other place that gives you peace of mind. It is any place that you want

NOTES & COMMENTS

it to be, and it looks and feels just exactly the way you want it to look and feel.

- Take a moment or two to look around and explore this new place of yours. Notice all the details. Imagine the textures. Listen for the sounds. Feel, see, examine, and experience your chosen place.

- When you have explored enough and you are satisfied that it is everything you want it to be, you will become aware of a path or passageway. Somehow you know that if you follow that path it will lead you to a place where you will find the answer you are seeking.

- You lower your eyes for a moment, and when you raise them you find yourself transported and standing before a door that leads to the ideas and answers you seek. You are now entering a room, and there, almost filling one entire wall, is a large video screen. Displayed on the screen is a representation of the idea you are looking for or the problem you wish to solve.

- It might be as complete as a three-dimensional scene, as simple as a symbol rotating in space, or maybe it is just the pure essence of the idea or problem and it doesn't really have a solid shape. As you watch it on the screen you are aware that there are forces at work, adjusting and molding and shaping it to complete it in the best possible way.

- In your mind you know that whatever is causing the image to appear on the screen also has access to the subconscious memories of everything you have ever learned or experienced and every thought or feeling you have ever had. You also know that whatever it is that is controlling the images can draw upon that vast resource of your subconscious and it can use all of that information to transform the illustration of your problem into the solution to your problem.

- In your mind you settle on what you think is a reasonable number of ideas that you can deal with in one sitting, and you then instruct your subconscious that, one after another, the screen will begin showing you a series of creative ideas that will help you solve your problem. You will be able to help develop the solutions that appear on the screen so that each finished idea is the best combination of what you know, combined with what your subconscious knows.

VISUALIZATION: TAKE TWO

A variation on this visualization follows exactly the same procedure up to the point where you encounter the path or passageway. But this time, as you follow the path or passageway, you will encounter a person who will become your mentor or adviser.

How you picture this person is entirely up to you. You may think of your mentor as an ancient sage, a mythical oracle, or, alternatively, you might choose a hugely successful CEO, or some other kind of well-known leader. In fact, if you choose an actual living person whom you admire, it opens it up to some very interesting results, because you already know a good deal about the person and you have a feel for the kind of advice he or she would give.

Whomever you choose as your mentor, this person is everything you could ever ask for in an adviser. He or she has access to everything you have ever experienced and every thought you ever had, and is the personification of wisdom and creativity. You can ask this person to help you develop your idea or provide the answer to your problem.

WHAT TO EXPECT

Will your subconscious provide you with a set number of clear and distinct solutions to your problem, or will you get a couple of fuzzy ideas that may or may not be good? Will you see images on the screen, or will the answers come to you like ideas in your mind? Will your mentor sit you down and explain the answer, or will you just pick up a feeling for what to do? And what do you do if you don't get anything?

There is no right answer to any of these questions. What comes of working with creative visualization is completely dependent on you and how prepared you are to make it work and let it work. It is well documented that creative visualization has been the source of scientific breakthroughs and multimillion-dollar inventions. It has also been the source of a lot of fanciful ideas, numerous impractical solutions, plenty of daydreaming, and more than a few unplanned midday snoozes.

Creative visualization is a tool. It is a fact that it does work. It works better for some people than it does for others, but the more it is used the better the quality and quantity of results.

Approach your visualization sessions with faith and confidence, and have a pen and paper handy so you can quickly make notes of the thoughts and ideas that come to you. As with the other techniques, you should never try to evaluate or analyze during the process. Write down as clear a description as you can of each idea. Review what you have written later, when you can take the time to give your ideas and your solution serious consideration.

ACTING AS IF, AND RECAPTURING THAT WINNING FEELING

This acting-as-if technique is actually quite closely related to Napoleon Hill's counselors and to creative visualization, but for many this is a much more straightforward and easy-to-understand version of the concept. This technique is simply to act as if you are just as smart and intelligent and creative as you would like to be.

To restate that in a way that should make it a little clearer, you may not think you are very creative, but if you *act* as if you are creative, you will be surprised how creative you become.

The editors of this workbook assure you that it works to some degree for everyone, and if you give it a fair chance it will work for you.

The next time you have to come up with a creative idea or solution, think of someone whom you believe to be as smart and creative as you would like to be. In your mind, put yourself into that person's shoes and come up with the kind of idea you imagine that person would think of. In effect, if you pretend that you think like a creative person, you really will come up with creative ideas.

A variation on this technique would be to go back in your mind to a time when you were really on roll, when you were at the top of your game, when everything was clicking, and you felt like a winner. In your mind, recall that feeling of success, vividly picture yourself full of self-confidence, clear-headed, in command, bold and decisive. Now, in your mind, project yourself into that winning frame of mind, and use that mind-set to solve your problem.

NOTES & COMMENTS

ORGANIZED PLANNING

8

CHAPTER 8: OVERVIEW AND ANALYSIS

THE CRYSTALLIZATION OF DESIRE INTO ACTION

This chapter opens with Napoleon Hill recapping his basic theory that everything you create starts with desire, to which you must apply your imagination to turn that desire into a practical plan.

One of the best ways to develop your plan is to put together a Master Mind group who will share their knowledge and abilities with you to help you achieve your goal. Hill then lays out a brief overview of the six rules for assembling your Master Mind group.

IF YOUR FIRST PLAN FAILS, TRY ANOTHER

No reader should expect to succeed without experiencing some setbacks along the way. All the great fortunes were built on plans that failed, but those setbacks only served to convince the entrepreneurs that what they needed was new and better plans. Hill cites James J. Hill and Henry Ford as examples, and comments on their leadership abilities.

You must plan your work and work your plan.

Your achievement can only be as good as the plans you make.

If you fail to plan, you had better plan to fail.

Failure is not defeat. Everyone fails, but you are not defeated until you quit in your own mind.

A winner never quits, and a quitter never wins.

LEADERS AND FOLLOWERS

Hill introduces this section by saying that while there is nothing wrong with following a leader, becoming the leader yourself will bring you much greater rewards. He also makes the point that most great leaders begin as intelligent followers who grow into the position.

Hill presents a list of the eleven major attributes of leadership, followed by a list of the ten major causes of failure in leadership.

WHEN AND HOW TO APPLY FOR A POSITION

Following the section on leadership, Napoleon Hill turns his attention to a completely different aspect of organizing and planning. He devotes ten pages to the ins and outs of finding and applying for a job. The editors provide new commentary and material that update and reflect the modern business climate.

HOW TO GET THE EXACT POSITION YOU DESIRE

Hill says that first you must identify what you really want, and he sets out a seven-point plan for presenting your abilities in the best light.

THE NEW WAY OF MARKETING SERVICES

Hill says that customer service will become the future watchword of American business.

WHAT IS YOUR QQS RATING?

Hill says that to succeed in selling yourself, you should measure the Quality, Quantity, and Spirit with which you deliver your service.

THE CAPITAL VALUE OF YOUR SERVICES

Hill explains a formula that says the price for your services should be at least equal to the annual interest rate on borrowed money.

THE THIRTY-ONE MAJOR CAUSES OF FAILURE

With this list of the major causes of failure, Hill instructs you to go through the list point by point in order to find how many of the causes stand between you and success.

DO YOU KNOW YOUR OWN WORTH?

Hill returns to the subject of your personal worth in order to introduce a list of twenty-eight questions designed to help you analyze how you are progressing on your road to success.

WHERE AND HOW TO FIND OPPORTUNITIES TO ACCUMULATE RICHES

Napoleon Hill closes this chapter with an overview of the freedoms that are guaranteed to Americans by the Constitution, followed by a brief description of what that means in real terms, using the most basic needs of food, shelter, and clothing to illustrate.

Hill goes on to explain how organized capital in the form of investors and their investments create the industries and the institutions and the jobs and the products that provide the goods and services that meet our demands that support and encourage our way of life. The point is rarely better made than Hill's explanation of what it would take to make breakfast if there was no such thing as capital.

CHAPTER 8: THE WORKBOOK

In this chapter, Organized Planning, Napoleon Hill places great emphasis on the importance of leadership in creating the plans needed to achieve your definite aim or purpose. In fact, the most important segments in this chapter are the lists and questionnaires designed to assess your leadership abilities:

- the 11 major attributes of leadership

- the 10 major causes of failure in leadership

- a breakdown of the 31 causes of failure in general

- a 28-question self-inventory questionnaire

We will deal with each of these four lists in detail, but before we do we would like to comment briefly on one or two other subjects.

"Perhaps you have wondered why a few will advance to highly paid positions while others, who have as much training and who work just as hard, do not get ahead.

The ones who advance believe in themselves, and they back their belief with such dynamic and aggressive action that others recognize it in them."

NOTES & COMMENTS

THE MASTER MIND ALLIANCE

In this chapter, Hill writes a very brief overview of how a Master Mind group can be helpful in organizing a plan. The explanation is so brief because the Master Mind is covered in more detail in Chapter 11. This workbook follows the same approach and deals with the Master Mind in a corresponding later chapter.

WHEN AND HOW TO APPLY FOR A JOB

The purpose of this workbook is to supplement the information in *Think and Grow Rich: The 21st-Century Edition.* When this updated edition of the book was being assembled, the editors included new commentary and material that expanded the coverage of how to apply for a job to ten full pages.

After reviewing the revised and updated text, the editors of this workbook concluded that the new edition of *Think and Grow Rich: The 21st-Century Edition* had been so thoroughly annotated and updated that we do not believe there is anything more needed to augment what is now a very complete treatment of the subject.

MR. HILL MAKES A PLAN

There was nothing Napoleon Hill liked better than telling a true story that illustrated how his principles of success worked. So naturally he had worked up a great personal story that he almost always told when he was lecturing on the importance of turning your aim or purpose into a practical plan of action. But, for some reason, when he was writing *Think and Grow Rich,* the story never made it into the final edition of this chapter.

For your enjoyment, and because it illustrates the point so well, we are including the following version of Napoleon Hill's Lumberport story, excerpted and adapted from *Law of Success,* Volume II, Lesson Five:

Some eighteen years ago I made my first trip to the little town of Lumberport, West Virginia. At that time the only means of transportation leading from Clarksburg, the largest nearby center, to Lumberport was either the Baltimore & Ohio Railroad, or an interurban electric line which ran within three miles of the town. If you chose the trolley it meant you had to arrange for someone to pick you up or you'd have to walk the three miles to town.

Upon my arrival at Clarksburg I found that the only train going to Lumberport before noon had already gone, and not wishing to wait for the later afternoon train, I made the trip by trolley, with the intention of walking the three miles. On the way down, the rain began to pour, and those three miles had to be navigated on foot, through deep yellow mud. When I arrived at Lumberport my shoes and pants were muddy, and my disposition was none the better for the experience.

The first person I met was V. L. Hornor, who was then cashier of the Lumberport Bank. In a rather loud tone of voice I asked of him, "Why do you not get that trolley line extended from the junction over to Lumberport so your friends can get in and out of town without drowning in mud?"

"Did you see a river with high banks, at the edge of town, as you came in?" he asked. I replied that I had. "Well," he continued, "that's the reason we have no street-cars running into town. The cost of a bridge would be about $100,000 and that is more than the company own-ing the trolley line is willing to invest. We have been trying for ten years to get them to build a line into town."

"Power grows out of organized knowledge, but only through application and use.

A person may be a walking encyclopedia of knowledge without possessing any power of value."

"Trying!" I exploded. "How hard have you tried?"

"We have offered them every inducement we could afford, such as free right of way from the junction into the town, and free use of the streets, but that bridge is the stumbling block. They simply will not pay the expense. Claim they cannot afford such an expense for the small amount of revenue they would receive from the three-mile extension."

Right then the principles of success began to come to my rescue. I asked Mr. Hornor if he would take a walk over to the river with me, that we might look at the spot that was causing so much inconvenience. He said he would be glad to do so.

When we got to the river I began to take inventory of everything in sight. I observed that the Baltimore & Ohio Railroad tracks ran up and down the river banks, on both sides of the river, and that the county road crossed the river on a rickety wooden bridge, both approaches to which had to cross over several railroad tracks because the railroad company had its switching yards at that point.

While we were standing there, a freight train blocked the road to the bridge, and several teams of horses stopped on both sides of the train, waiting for an opportunity to get through. The train kept the road blocked for about twenty-five minutes.

With this combination of circumstances in mind, it required little imagination to see that three different parties could be interested in the building of the bridge such as would be needed to carry the weight of a streetcar.

It was obvious that the Baltimore & Ohio Railroad Company would be interested in such a bridge, because that would remove the county road from their switching tracks. It would also save them a possible accident on the crossing, to say nothing of much loss of time and expense in cutting trains to allow the wagon teams to pass.

It was also obvious that the County Commissioners would be interested in the bridge, because it would raise the county road to a better level and make it more serviceable to the public. And of course the street railway company was interested in the bridge, but it did not wish to pay the entire cost.

All of this passed through my mind as I stood there watching the freight train being cut for the traffic to pass through.

A definite chief aim took place in my mind. Also a definite plan for its attainment. The next day I got together a committee of townspeople, consisting of the mayor, councilmen, and some of the leading citizens, and called on the Division Superintendent of the Baltimore & Ohio Railroad Company at Grafton. We convinced him that it was worth one-third of the cost of the bridge to get the county road off his company's tracks.

Next we went to see the County Commissioners and found them to be quite enthusiastic over the possibility of getting a new bridge by paying for only one-third of it. They promised to pay their one-third, providing we could make arrangements for the other two-thirds.

We then went to the president of the Traction Company that owned the trolley line at Fairmont, and made him an offer to donate all the rights of way and pay for two-thirds of the cost of the bridge, providing he would

"The successful lawyer is not the one who memorizes the greatest number of the principles of law.

The successful lawyer is the one who knows where to find a particular principle of law, plus a variety of opinions supporting that principle, which fit the immediate needs of a given case."

"Any modern railroad bridge is an excellent example of the value of organized effort, because it demonstrates quite simply and clearly how thousands of tons of weight may be borne by a comparatively small group of steel bars and beams which are arranged so that the weight is spread over the entire group."

begin building the line into town promptly. We found him receptive also.

Three weeks later a contract had been signed between the Baltimore & Ohio Railroad Company, the Monongahela Valley Traction Company, and the County Commissioners of Harrison County, providing for the construction of the bridge—one-third of its cost to be paid by each.

Just two months later, the right of way was being graded and the bridge was under way. And three months after that, the streetcars were running into Lumberport on regular schedule.

This incident meant much to the town of Lumberport, because it provided transportation that enabled people to get in and out of the town without undue effort.

It also meant a great deal to me, because it served to introduce me as one who "got things done."

Two very definite advantages resulted from this transaction. The chief counsel for the Traction Company gave me a position as his assistant, and later on it was the means of an introduction that led to my appointment as advertising manager of the LaSalle Extension University.

Lumberport, West Virginia, was then and still is a small town, and Chicago was a large city located a considerable distance away, but news of initiative and leadership has a way of taking on wings and traveling.

Although initiative and leadership were the key elements of my success, there were five of the principles of success that combined in the transaction I have described here: a definite chief aim, self-confidence, imagination, initiative, and leadership.

It would be helpful here to take note of the part that imagination played in this transaction. For ten years the townspeople of Lumberport had been trying to get a streetcar line built into town. It must not be concluded that the town was without any citizens of ability, because that would be inaccurate. In fact there were many able people in the town, but they had been making the mistake of trying to solve their problem through one single source, whereas there were actually three sources of solution available to them.

One hundred thousand dollars was too much for one company to assume for the construction of a bridge, but when the cost was divided among three interested parties, the amount to be borne by each was more reasonable.

The question might be asked, why did some of the local townspeople not think of this three-way solution?

In the first place, they were so close to their problem that they failed to see it from a perspective which would have suggested the solution. This is a common mistake, and one that is always avoided by great leaders.

In the second place, these people had never before co-ordinated their efforts or worked as an organized group with the sole purpose in mind of finding a way to get a streetcar line built into town. This is another common error made by people in all walks of life—that of failure to work in unison, in a thorough spirit of cooperation.

I, being an outsider, had less difficulty in getting cooperative action than one of their own group might have had. Too often there is a spirit of selfishness in small communities that prompts each individual to think that

"Real power is organized energy or effort.

This book will teach you how to organize facts, and knowledge, and the faculties of your mind into a unit of power."

their ideas should prevail. It is an important part of the leader's responsibility to induce people to subordinate their own ideas and interests for the good of the project or goal.

Success is nearly always a question of your ability to get others to subordinate their own individual interests and follow a leader. The person who has the initiative, the personality, and the imagination to induce followers to accept his or her plans and carry them out faithfully is always an able leader.

Leadership, initiative, and imagination are so closely allied and so essential for success that one cannot be gainfully applied without the other. Initiative is the moving force that pushes the leader ahead, but imagination is the guiding spirit that tells him or her which way to go.

Imagination is what enabled me to analyze the Lumberport bridge problem, break it up into its three component parts, and assemble those parts into a practical working plan. Nearly every problem may be broken up into parts that are more easily managed as parts than they are when assembled as a whole. Perhaps one of the most important advantages of imagination is that it enables you to separate all problems into their component parts and to reassemble them in more favorable combinations.

It has been said that all battles are won or lost not on the firing line but through the sound strategy, or the lack of it, used by the generals who plan the battles.

Organized effort is effort that is directed according to a plan conceived with the aid of imagination, guided by a definite aim, and given momentum with self-confidence and initiative. These principles of success blend into one and become a power in the hands of a leader. Without the blending of these principles, and the initiative to pull them together and make use of them, effective leadership is impossible.

LEADERSHIP

Everything Napoleon Hill says in the final paragraphs of his story makes a perfect lead-in to the following section on leadership: you have to turn your aim or purpose into a burning desire, create a plan to accomplish it, and use your initiative, personality, and imagination to induce others to accept your plan and help you make it happen. Success is nearly always a question of your ability to motivate others and get them to follow your lead.

Later in the chapter, Hill says:

Broadly speaking, there are two types of people in the world —leaders and followers. It is no disgrace to be a follower. On the other hand, it is no credit to remain a follower. Most great leaders began as followers. They became great leaders because they were intelligent followers. The person who can follow a leader most efficiently is usually the person who develops into leadership most rapidly. An intelligent follower has many advantages, including the opportunity to acquire knowledge from the leader.

Our assumption is that the reason you are reading this workbook is because you have no intention of remaining a follower any longer than is necessary.

How good a leader are you? That is what the following section will help you determine.

LEADERS, FOLLOWERS, FAILURES

Following are four self-tests designed to help you learn what kind of leader you are:

- the 11 major attributes of leadership

- the 10 major causes of failure in leadership

- a breakdown of the 31 causes of failure in general

- a 28-question self-inventory questionnaire

If you give serious consideration to each of the questions and answer them truthfully, by the time you have completed all four questionnaires you will have learned a great deal about yourself, and you will have a very good idea of how good a leader you are.

THE 11 MAJOR ATTRIBUTES OF LEADERSHIP

After describing each of the attributes of a successful leader, we have provided a self-analysis scale. Consider how well you have mastered each of the qualities, then circle the appropriate number.

In the space provided following the numbers, record the date and write a brief note to yourself explaining what each quality means to you and how it fits into your life on this date.

In three months, come back to this exercise and record how much you think you have improved. Return again after another three months, and note your further improvement.

1. Unwavering courage based upon knowledge of yourself and your occupation. No follower wishes to be dominated by a leader who lacks self-confidence and courage. Certainly no intelligent follower will be dominated by such a leader for very long.

1 2 3 4 5 6 7 8 9 10 _____

_____

_____

_____

2. Self-control. The person who cannot control themself can never control others. Self-control sets a strong example for your followers, which the more intelligent followers will emulate.

1 2 3 4 5 6 7 8 9 10_____

_____

_____

_____

3. A keen sense of justice. Without a sense of fairness and justice, no leader can command and retain the respect of their followers.

1 2 3 4 5 6 7 8 9 10_____

_____

_____

_____

4. Definiteness of decision. Those who waver in decisions show that they are not sure of themselves, and therefore cannot lead others successfully.

1 2 3 4 5 6 7 8 9 10_____

_____

_____

_____

5. Definiteness of plans. Successful leaders must plan their work, and work their plans. Leaders who move by guesswork, without practical, definite plans, are like a ship without a rudder. Sooner or later they will land on the rocks.

1 2 3 4 5 6 7 8 9 10_____

_____

_____

_____

6. The habit of doing more than paid for. One of the penalties of leadership is the necessity of the leaders to willingly do more than they require of their followers.

1 2 3 4 5 6 7 8 9 10_____

_____

_____

_____

7. A pleasing personality. Leadership calls for respect. Followers will not respect a leader who does not grade high on all of the factors of a pleasing personality.

1 2 3 4 5 6 7 8 9 10_____

_____

_____

_____

8. Sympathy and understanding. Successful leaders must be in sympathy with their followers. Moreover, they must understand them and their problems.

1 2 3 4 5 6 7 8 9 10_____

_____

_____

_____

9. Mastery of detail. Successful leadership calls for mastery of the details of the leader's position.

1 2 3 4 5 6 7 8 9 10_____

_____

_____

_____

10. Willingness to assume full responsibility. Successful leaders must be willing to assume responsibility for the mistakes and the shortcomings of their followers. If a leader tries to shift this responsibility, that leader will not remain the leader. If one of your followers makes a mistake, or is incompetent, you must consider that it is you who failed.

1 2 3 4 5 6 7 8 9 10_____

_____

_____

_____

11. Cooperation. The successful leader must understand and apply the principle of cooperative effort and be able to induce followers to do the same. Leadership calls for power, and power calls for cooperation.

1 2 3 4 5 6 7 8 9 10_____

_____

_____

_____

THE 10 MAJOR CAUSES OF FAILURE IN LEADERSHIP

Starting on the following page are the ten most common faults of leaders who fail. It is just as important for you to know what not to do as it is to know what you should do.

After the explanation of each fault, we have again provided a self-analysis scale. As you read each item, measure yourself against the kind of person you think you should be, and circle the number on the scale that you believe truthfully reflects where you stand. Make a note of the date.

In three months come back to this exercise and record how much you think you have improved.

Return again after another three months, and note your further improvement.

1. Inability to organize details. Efficient leadership calls for the ability to organize and master details. No genuine leader is ever "too busy" to do anything that may be required of them as leader. Whether a leader or follower, when you admit that you are "too busy" to change your plans or to give attention to any emergency, you are admitting your inefficiency. The successful leader must be the master of all details connected with the position. That means, of course, that you must acquire the habit of relegating details to capable lieutenants.

1 2 3 4 5 6 7 8 9 10_____

_____

_____

_____

2. Unwillingness to render humble service. Truly great leaders are willing, when occasion demands, to perform any sort of labor that they would ask another to perform. "The greatest among ye shall be the servant of all" is a truth that all able leaders observe and respect.

1 2 3 4 5 6 7 8 9 10_____

_____

_____

_____

3. Emphasis of the "authority" of leadership. The efficient leader leads by encouraging, and not by trying to instill fear in the hearts of those who follow. If you are a real leader, you will have no need to advertise that fact. It is apparent in your conduct—by your sympathy, understanding, fairness, and a demonstration that you know your job.

1 2 3 4 5 6 7 8 9 10_____

_____

_____

_____

4. Fear of competition from followers. Leaders who fear that one of their followers may take their position are practically sure to realize that fear sooner or later. Able leaders train understudies. Only in this way can leaders multiply themselves and be at many places, and give attention to many things, at one time. It is a fact that leaders receive more pay for their ability to get others to perform than they could possibly earn by their own efforts. A good leader may, through knowledge of the job and a magnetic personality, get followers to render more and better service than they could render without the leader's guidance.

1 2 3 4 5 6 7 8 9 10_____

_____

_____

_____

5. Lack of imagination. Without imagination, the leader is incapable of meeting emergencies or of creating plans by which to guide followers efficiently.

1 2 3 4 5 6 7 8 9 10_____

_____

_____

_____

6. Selfishness. Leaders who claim all the honor for the work of their followers are sure to be met by resentment. The really great leader claims none of the honors. Great leaders are content to see the honors go to their followers, because the great leaders know that most people will work harder for commendation and recognition than they will for money alone.

1 2 3 4 5 6 7 8 9 10_____

_____

_____

_____

7. Intemperance. Followers do not respect an intemperate leader. You may be "one of the guys," but you won't be looked up to or admired.

1 2 3 4 5 6 7 8 9 10_____

_____

_____

_____

8. Disloyalty. Leaders who are not loyal to their duty, or to those both above and below them, cannot maintain their leadership for long. Disloyalty will bring contempt. Lack of loyalty is one of the major causes of failure in every walk of life.

1 2 3 4 5 6 7 8 9 10_____

_____

_____

_____

9. Expectation of pay for what you "know." The world does not pay you for what you know; it pays you for what you do with what you know, or what you can get others to do.

1 2 3 4 5 6 7 8 9 10_____

_____

_____

_____

10. Emphasis of title. Competent leaders require no "title" to give them the respect of their followers. The doors to the office of a real leader are open to all and are free from formality.

1 2 3 4 5 6 7 8 9 10_____

_____

_____

_____

THE 31 MAJOR CAUSES OF FAILURE

As Napoleon Hill assembled and analyzed his research of more than 25,000 individuals, he identified thirty-one major reasons for failure. Following, we have listed the causes of failure in the form of a questionnaire to help you to discover how many of these thirty-one reasons may stand between you and success.

As you go through the list, measure yourself point by point, record how you measure up on the self-test scale, record the date, and, as with the two previous questionnaires, make a few brief notes to remind yourself how you felt when you first went through this review.

Hill suggests that because people often cannot see themselves as clearly as others see them, it might also be helpful if you get someone who knows you well to go over this list with you and help you to analyze yourself by each of these causes of failure.

1. Unfavorable hereditary background. There is little, if anything, that can be done for people who are born with a mental deficiency. This is the only one of the thirty-one causes of failure that may not be easily corrected by any individual. Hill's philosophy can offer only one method of bridging this weakness—through the aid of the Master Mind.

1 2 3 4 5 6 7 8 9 10 _____

_____

_____

_____

2. Lack of a well-defined purpose in life. There is no hope of success for the person who does not have a definite aim or purpose. Ninety-eight out of every hundred people Hill analyzed had no such aim. Perhaps this was the major cause of their failure.

1 2 3 4 5 6 7 8 9 10 _____

_____

_____

_____

3. Lack of ambition to aim above mediocrity. Napoleon Hill can offer no hope for those who are so indifferent that they do not want to get ahead in life, and are also not willing to pay the price.

1 2 3 4 5 6 7 8 9 10_____

_____

_____

_____

4. Insufficient education. This is a handicap that may be overcome. Experience has proven that the best-educated people are often those who are self-made or self-educated. It takes more than a college degree to make you a person of education. Education consists not so much of knowledge, but of knowledge effectively and persistently applied. As noted above, you are paid not merely for what you know, but for what you do with what you know.

1 2 3 4 5 6 7 8 9 10_____

_____

_____

_____

5. Lack of self-discipline. Discipline comes through self-control. Before you can control conditions, you must first control yourself. If you do not conquer yourself, you will be conquered by yourself. By stepping in front of a mirror, you may see both your best friend and your greatest enemy.

1 2 3 4 5 6 7 8 9 10_____

_____

_____

_____

6. Ill health. No person may enjoy outstanding success without good health. Many of the causes of ill health, such as poor diet and lack of exercise, are up to you to control. If you can't control yourself, you can't control your destiny.

1 2 3 4 5 6 7 8 9 10_____

_____

_____

_____

7. Unfavorable environmental influences during childhood. "As the twig is bent, so shall the tree grow." If you are growing up in a bad environment, it most likely won't change until *you* change it. As hard as that may sound, most people who have criminal tendencies acquire them as the result of a bad environment and improper associates during their childhood or youth.

1 2 3 4 5 6 7 8 9 10_____

_____

_____

_____

8. Procrastination. This is one of the most common causes of failure. Most of us go through life as failures because we are waiting for "the time to be right" to start doing something worthwhile. Do not wait. The time will never be just right. Start where you stand, work with whatever tools you have at your command, and you will acquire better tools as you go along.

1 2 3 4 5 6 7 8 9 10_____

_____

_____

_____

9. Lack of persistence. Most of us are good "starters" but poor "finishers" of everything we begin. People are prone to give up at the first signs of defeat. There is no substitute for persistence. The person who makes persistence his or her watchword discovers that "failure" finally becomes tired and makes its departure. Failure cannot cope with persistence.

1 2 3 4 5 6 7 8 9 10_____

_____

_____

_____

10. Negative personality. There is no hope of success for the person who repels people through a negative personality. Success comes through the application of power, and power is attained through the cooperative efforts of other people. A negative personality will not induce cooperation.

1 2 3 4 5 6 7 8 9 10_____

_____

_____

_____

11. Lack of control of sexual urges. Sexual energy is the most powerful of all the stimuli that move people into action. Because it is the most powerful of the emotions, if it is controlled it can be converted into other creative channels.

1 2 3 4 5 6 7 8 9 10_____

_____

_____

_____

12. Uncontrolled desire for "something for nothing." The gambling instinct drives millions of people to failure. Evidence of this may be found in the Wall Street stock market crash of 1929, during which millions of people tried to make money by gambling on stock margins.

1 2 3 4 5 6 7 8 9 10_____

_____

_____

_____

13. Lack of a well-defined power of decision. Those who succeed reach decisions promptly and change them very slowly. Those who fail reach decisions very slowly and change them frequently, and quickly. Indecision and procrastination are twins. Kill off this pair before they completely tie you to the treadmill of failure.

1 2 3 4 5 6 7 8 9 10_____

_____

_____

_____

14. One or more of the six basic fears (fear of poverty, criticism, ill health, loss of love, old age, and death). You will find an in-depth analysis of these six basic fears in the final chapter. They must be mastered before you can market your services effectively.

1 2 3 4 5 6 7 8 9 10_____

_____

_____

_____

15. Wrong selection of a mate in marriage. This is a most common cause of personal failure. The relationship of marriage brings people intimately into contact. Unless this relationship is harmonious, failure is likely to follow. Moreover, it will be a form of failure that destroys ambition.

1 2 3 4 5 6 7 8 9 10_____

_____

_____

_____

16. Overcaution. The person who takes no chances generally has to take whatever is left when others are through choosing. Overcaution is as bad as undercaution. Both are extremes to be guarded against. Life itself is filled with the element of chance.

1 2 3 4 5 6 7 8 9 10_____

_____

_____

_____

17. Wrong selection of associates in business. This is one of the most common causes of failure in business. In marketing your services, use great care to select an employer who will be an inspiration and who is intelligent and successful. Pick your employer and your associates who are worth emulating.

1 2 3 4 5 6 7 8 9 10_____

_____

_____

_____

18. Superstition and prejudice. Superstition is a form of fear. It is also a sign of ignorance. Successful people keep open minds and are afraid of nothing.

1 2 3 4 5 6 7 8 9 10_____

_____

_____

_____

19. Wrong selection of a vocation. You cannot have outstanding success in work that you do not like. The most essential step in the marketing of personal services is that of selecting an occupation into which you can throw yourself wholeheartedly. Although money or circumstances may require you to do something you don't like for a time, no one can stop you from developing plans to make your goal in life a reality.

1 2 3 4 5 6 7 8 9 10_____

_____

_____

_____

20. The habit of indiscriminate spending. You cannot succeed if you are eternally in fear of poverty. Form the habit of systematic saving by putting aside a definite percentage of your income. Money in the bank gives you a very safe foundation of courage when bargaining for the sale of your personal services. Without money, you must take what you are offered and be glad to get it.

1 2 3 4 5 6 7 8 9 10_____

_____

_____

_____

21. Lack of concentration of effort. The jack-of-all-trades seldom is good at any. Concentrate all of your efforts on one definite aim.

1 2 3 4 5 6 7 8 9 10 _____

_____

_____

_____

22. Lack of enthusiasm. Without enthusiasm you cannot be convincing. Enthusiasm is contagious, and the person who has it (under control) is welcome in any group of people.

1 2 3 4 5 6 7 8 9 10 _____

_____

_____

_____

23. Egotism and vanity. These qualities serve as red lights that warn others to keep away. They are fatal to success.

1 2 3 4 5 6 7 8 9 10 _____

_____

_____

_____

24. Intemperance. The most damaging forms of intemperance are connected with overeating, alcohol, drugs, and sexual activities. Overindulgence in any of these can be fatal to success.

1 2 3 4 5 6 7 8 9 10 _____

_____

_____

_____

25. Inability to cooperate with others. More people lose their positions, and their big opportunities in life, because of this fault than for all other reasons combined. It is a fault that no well-informed businessperson or leader will tolerate.

1 2 3 4 5 6 7 8 9 10_____

_____

_____

_____

26. Possession of power that was not acquired through self-effort (sons and daughters of wealthy parents, and others who inherit money that they did not earn). Power in the hands of one who did not earn it over time is often fatal to success. Quick riches are more dangerous than poverty.

1 2 3 4 5 6 7 8 9 10_____

_____

_____

_____

27. Intentional dishonesty. There is no substitute for honesty. You may be temporarily dishonest because of circumstances over which you have no control, but there is no hope for you if you are dishonest by choice. Sooner or later your deeds will catch up with you, and you will pay by loss of reputation and perhaps even loss of liberty.

1 2 3 4 5 6 7 8 9 10_____

_____

_____

_____

28. Intolerance. The person with a closed mind on any subject seldom gets ahead. Any intolerance connected with religious, racial, or political differences is unacceptable.

1 2 3 4 5 6 7 8 9 10_____

_____

_____

_____

29. Guessing instead of thinking. Most people are too indifferent or lazy to acquire facts to think accurately. They prefer to act on "opinions" created by guesswork or snap-judgments.

1 2 3 4 5 6 7 8 9 10_____

_____

_____

_____

30. Lack of capital. This is the most common cause of failure in first-time businesses. You must have sufficient capital to absorb the shock of your mistakes and to carry you over.

1 2 3 4 5 6 7 8 9 10_____

_____

_____

_____

31. Here, name any particular cause of failure from which you have suffered that has not been included in the foregoing list.

1 2 3 4 5 6 7 8 9 10_____

_____

_____

_____

TAKE INVENTORY OF YOURSELF

Napoleon Hill says that in life you go ahead, stand still, or go backward. Naturally, you want to move forward, but unless you have some reliable method of measurement, how will you know if you are on the right track? Hill recommends that you undertake a yearly self-analysis, and by using the following self-inventory questionnaire you will be able to assess for yourself whether you are getting ahead the way you want or if you are slipping behind.

We have provided a scale to record how well you are doing with each question, and space to make a few brief notes. Hill suggests that this is another instance where you might want to check your answers with the aid of someone who will not permit you to deceive yourself.

PLEASE NOTE: Because this is an annual analysis, we have provided two copies of this questionnaire. The one that follows is for you to fill in now, as you read this book. At the back of this workbook you will find another copy to remove and make copies for future years.

SELF-INVENTORY QUESTIONNAIRE

1. Have I attained the goal that I established as my objective for this year? (You should work with a definite yearly objective to be attained as a part of your major life objective.)

1 2 3 4 5 6 7 8 9 10 _____

_____

_____

_____

2. Have I delivered service of the best possible quality of which I was capable, or could I have improved any part of this service?

1 2 3 4 5 6 7 8 9 10 _____

_____

_____

_____

3. Have I delivered service in the greatest possible quantity of which I was capable?

1 2 3 4 5 6 7 8 9 10_____

_____

_____

_____

4. Has the spirit of my conduct been harmonious and cooperative at all times?

1 2 3 4 5 6 7 8 9 10_____

_____

_____

_____

5. Have I permitted procrastination to decrease my efficiency and, if so, to what extent?

1 2 3 4 5 6 7 8 9 10_____

_____

_____

_____

6. Have I improved my personality and, if so, in what ways?

1 2 3 4 5 6 7 8 9 10_____

_____

_____

_____

7. Have I been persistent in following my plans through to completion?

1 2 3 4 5 6 7 8 9 10_____

_____

_____

_____

8. Have I reached decisions promptly and definitely on all occasions?

1 2 3 4 5 6 7 8 9 10_____

_____

_____

_____

9. Have I permitted any of the six basic fears to decrease my efficiency?

1 2 3 4 5 6 7 8 9 10_____

_____

_____

_____

10. Have I been either overcautious or undercautious?

1 2 3 4 5 6 7 8 9 10_____

_____

_____

_____

11. Has my relationship with my associates at work been pleasant or unpleasant? If it has been unpleasant, has the fault been partly or wholly mine?

1 2 3 4 5 6 7 8 9 10_____

_____

_____

12. Have I dissipated any of my energy through lack of concentration of effort?

1 2 3 4 5 6 7 8 9 10_____

_____

_____

13. Have I been open-minded and tolerant in connection with all subjects?

1 2 3 4 5 6 7 8 9 10_____

_____

_____

14. In what ways have I improved my ability to render service?

1 2 3 4 5 6 7 8 9 10_____

_____

_____

15. Have I been intemperate in any of my personal habits?

1 2 3 4 5 6 7 8 9 10_____

_____

_____

16. Have I expressed, either openly or secretly, any form of egotism?

1 2 3 4 5 6 7 8 9 10_____

_____

_____

17. Has my conduct toward my associates been such that they respect me?

1 2 3 4 5 6 7 8 9 10_____

_____

_____

18. Have my opinions and decisions been based on guesswork, or on accuracy of analysis and thought?

1 2 3 4 5 6 7 8 9 10_____

_____

_____

19. Have I followed the habit of budgeting my time, my expenses, and my income, and have I been conservative in these budgets?

1 2 3 4 5 6 7 8 9 10_____

_____

_____

_____

20. How much time have I devoted to unprofitable effort, which I might have used to better advantage?

1 2 3 4 5 6 7 8 9 10_____

_____

_____

_____

21. How may I rebudget my time and change my habits so that I will be more efficient during the coming year?

1 2 3 4 5 6 7 8 9 10_____

_____

_____

_____

22. Have I been guilty of any conduct that was not approved by my own conscience?

1 2 3 4 5 6 7 8 9 10_____

_____

_____

_____

23. In what ways have I rendered more service and better service than I was paid to render?

1 2 3 4 5 6 7 8 9 10 _____

_____

_____

_____

24. Have I been unfair to anyone and, if so, in what way?

1 2 3 4 5 6 7 8 9 10 _____

_____

_____

_____

25. If I had been the purchaser of my own services for the year, would I be satisfied with my purchase?

1 2 3 4 5 6 7 8 9 10 _____

_____

_____

_____

26. Am I in the right vocation and, if not, why not?

1 2 3 4 5 6 7 8 9 10 _____

_____

_____

_____

27. Has the purchaser of my services been satisfied with the service I have rendered and, if not, why not?

1 2 3 4 5 6 7 8 9 10_____

_____

_____

_____

28. What is my present rating on the fundamental principles of success? (Make this rating fairly and frankly, and have it checked by someone who is courageous enough to do that for you accurately.)

1 2 3 4 5 6 7 8 9 10_____

_____

_____

_____

In this chapter you should have found adequate descriptions of every principle necessary to present yourself successfully. These include the major attributes of leadership, the most common causes of failure in leadership, the main causes of failure in all walks of life, and the important questions that should be used in self-analysis.

This extensive and detailed presentation has been included because it will help you to become more analytical and capable of judging people, and it will prove invaluable to you if you are going to earn your riches through the power of your personality.

DECISION

9

CHAPTER 9: OVERVIEW AND ANALYSIS

THE MASTERY OF PROCRASTINATION

This chapter opens with Napoleon Hill's statement that his research revealed people who are successful reach decisions promptly and change decisions slowly. The opposite is true of those who are failures.

EDITOR'S COMMENTARY

Further to Hill's reference to Henry Ford's reluctance to change the design of the Model T, the editors say the same about the color.

MAKING YOUR OWN DECISIONS

Those people who fail to achieve what they want out of life are generally too easily influenced by the opinions of others.

Hill warns against revealing your plans to friends or family because of the tendency for those people who are closest to you to belittle your dreams and undermine your self-confidence.

"In your search for the secret method, do not look for a miracle, because you will not find it. You will find only the eternal laws of nature. These laws are available to every person who has the faith and the courage to use them. They may be used to bring freedom to a nation, or to accumulate riches."

He advises that the only people you should take into your confidence are the members of your Master Mind. Hill's epigram is: "Tell the world what you intend to do, but first show it."

Hill says you should never give in to the temptation to show off your knowledge. You should remember that every time you open your mouth to talk you either give away too much or you show how little you actually know. Either way, you will not have done yourself any good in achieving your aim or purpose.

FIFTY-SIX WHO RISKED THE GALLOWS

Hill opens this rather long section by pointing out to the reader that although we are familiar with the names of the men who fought and the dates of the battles that led to the Declaration of Independence, little attention is paid to the force that was behind those events: the power of decision. Hill reminds readers that it began with the life-or-death decision first taken by John Hancock and Sam Adams, and subsequently taken by the other fifty-four founding fathers who joined in the world's greatest Master Mind alliance.

Throughout this book is the concept that a thought backed by burning desire will find a way to transmute itself into physical reality. The story of the founding of America is a perfect example of how, once a decision has been made, a thought can become reality.

This is not magic, and it is not a secret. It is simply recognizing and making use of natural law to realize your decision.

KNOW WHAT YOU WANT AND YOU WILL GENERALLY GET IT

If you make a decision promptly and definitely, the chances are you will get what you want out of life. The world makes room for those who know where they want to go.

If you are indecisive, slow to act, but quick to change your mind, you are the one who should get out of the way, because the world is going to walk right over you. If you don't make up your mind right now to stop and change your habit of procrastinating, it is quite likely you will fail to achieve much in your life.

CHAPTER 9: THE WORKBOOK

Napoleon Hill advises that you should never let others have undue influence on how you make your decisions. It should make no difference to you what other people might decide for themselves. Hill is especially critical of the way in which family and friends can put pressure on you to do what they think is right, while insisting that they are only doing it for your own good.

Hill's advice is based not only on his extensive research into the people who achieved outstanding success, but also on his own personal experience. Hill began his quest to assemble the philosophy of personal achievement in 1908. *Law of Success,* the first version of his philosophy, was published twenty years later in 1928, and he finally published *Think and Grow Rich* nine years after that, in 1937. For almost thirty years, Hill personally paid for the research needed to write the philosophy, and practically every day of that time he had to decide to keep doing so despite constant opposition.

During those years he was severely criticized by his family and his friends. They criticized him for putting his family at risk by not taking a stable job, they made fun of him for being so naïve as to work for one of the richest men in the world at no salary, they scoffed at his business schemes, and they ridiculed him for being so full of himself as to think he could write a philosophy. The fact is, if Napoleon Hill had listened to his family and friends, the world would not have the philosophy of personal achievement of which *Think and Grow Rich* is a direct result.

Following is a series of questions that will help you to understand your own susceptibility to the influence of friends and family. This is not a questionnaire that can be graded, because there are no absolute right or wrong answers. But by taking the time to answer the questions, noting how you have dealt with friends and relatives in the past, you will gain some valuable insights into yourself and your decisions.

1. Do you give undue attention to what your friends or family say about you?

_____

_____

_____

2. Have you ever not done something because you feared what your family would say?

_____

_____

_____

3. Have you ever not done something because you feared what your friends would say?

_____

_____

_____

4. Whose opinion do you value most?

_____

_____

5. Whose opinion do you fear most?

_____

_____

6. Is there something you would like to be doing right now that you are not doing because of your concern for what your family or friends might think or say?

_____

_____

_____

7. Do you feel you have an obligation to live up to someone's expectations? Who is that person or persons?

_____

_____

_____

8. Is someone making demands upon you that you do not deserve? What do they expect?

_____

_____

_____

9. Do you have an idea or a plan or a concept that you would be pursuing right now if it wasn't for the opinions of others?

_____

_____

_____

10. Are your family or friends more afraid to take a chance than you are?

_____

_____

_____

11. Are you confident in your own ability to assess risk and act in your own best interests?

_____

_____

_____

12. Do you believe that your family or friends are sincerely concerned about you when they give advice, or are they looking out for their own interests?

_____

_____

_____

13. Is there someone in your family or among your friends whom you suspect may secretly want you to fail because they would be jealous if you succeeded?

_____

_____

_____

TELL THE WORLD OR SHOW IT?

There are some motivation and self-help experts who suggest that the best way to make sure you stick to your decisions is to declare yourself and let the world know what you plan to do. Their theory is that if you let everyone know what you plan to do, you will be so afraid to embarrass yourself or to let people down that you will stick to your announced plan and see it through to completion.

Napoleon Hill's advice is exactly the opposite. He cautions against being too outspoken about your aims and plans for the simple reason that there are too many unscrupulous people who, given the chance, will steal your ideas. Once again, Hill's advice is not only based on his research and interviews with those who achieved success, but also on his own personal experience.

In the years when Hill was starting his own businesses to support his family and fund his research, he lost at least three businesses because he trusted dishonest people who he had thought were his friends. He mistook the intentions of bankers who extended him credit; his reputation was tarnished by associates who embezzled funds; and on more than one occasion, companies that he founded and built were literally stolen away from him by unscrupulous partners.

Hill's conclusion became to take no one into your confidence except members of your Master Mind alliance. Never tell people what you plan to do, and don't call attention to your plans by bragging or showing off your knowledge. In short, do not "tell" the world what you can do —show it!

The following six questions are designed to bring to mind those occasions when you allowed your ego to get the best of you. If you answer these questions honestly, you will very likely be surprised at how easily you can lose sight of what is really important.

1. Have you ever tried to impress someone in business by exaggerating your position or bragging about who you know?

_____

_____

_____

2. Did it benefit you in the long run?

_____

_____

_____

3. Have you ever resisted the opportunity to make yourself look important, and just listened instead of talking about yourself or your ideas?

_____

_____

_____

4. What was the result?

_____

_____

_____

5. Have you ever regretted having given away too much because you couldn't resist the urge to show how smart or important you are?

_____

_____

_____

6. Has the fear of embarrassment ever motivated you to do what you said you would do?

_____

_____

_____

THIS IS NOT A HISTORY TEST

This chapter is among the shortest and most straightforward in the entire book. The largest part of the chapter is Napoleon Hill's version of the motivating power behind the American Revolution, which illustrates the importance of being firm in your decisions.

Hill devotes six pages to his retelling of the events that led up to the signing of the Declaration of Independence by the Founding Fathers. As Hill tells it, this is the story of a Master Mind alliance of men who knowingly made a decision that required great courage, and then risked their lives to stand behind that decision until their purpose was realized.

This workbook is not meant to be a history text, so there would be little point in testing your recall of Hill's story. However, his conclusion about what the story of the Founding Fathers tells us is the very heart of Hill's philosophy: a burning desire followed by a firm decision will set into motion laws of nature that, when supported by appropriate action, will transmute that desire into physical reality.

Hill's advice that you should make decisions firmly and quickly is repeated often in his writing, but he also makes it very clear that he is not advising that you jump to conclusions or act impulsively. Hill's advice is to collect all the facts, study what you have learned, then be decisive and take action. Good leaders don't procrastinate.

STRONG LEADERS MAKE PROMPT DECISIONS

The habit of prompt and firm decision is the first essential step in the development of initiative and leadership. The leader who hesitates between vague notions of what he or she wants to do or should do generally ends by doing nothing.

If you are a leader who changes your mind often, you will lose the confidence of those you are leading. One of the natural tendencies of human nature is willingness to follow the person with great self-confidence. If you are not sure of yourself, how can you expect others to be sure of you? No one will want to follow you if you are not sure of yourself.

There are circumstances, of course, that call for slow deliberation and the examination of facts before an intelligent decision can be reached. However, after all the available facts have been gathered and organized, there is no excuse for delaying decision. The person who procrastinates cannot become an effective leader.

MAKE BOLD DECISIONS FIRMLY AND QUICKLY

The following is excerpted and adapted from *Law of Success: The 21st-Century Edition,* Volume II, Lesson Five, Initiative and Leadership:

> One of the major requisites for leadership is the power of quick and firm decision! One of the peculiarities of leadership is that it is never found in those who have not acquired the habit of taking the initiative. Leadership is something that you must invite yourself into; it will never thrust itself upon you.
>
> If you will carefully analyze all leaders whom you know, you will see that they have not only exercised initiative and decisive action, but they also have a definite purpose backed by faith in their ability, or self-confidence. The chief reason followers don't reach decisions firmly and quickly is that they lack the faith in their ability to do so.
>
> To know that the majority of people cannot and will not reach decisions quickly, if at all, is of great help to the leader who knows what he or she wants and has a plan for getting it.

NOTES & COMMENTS

DECISION-MAKING QUALITIES OF A LEADER

In applying initiative and leadership, there are certain steps that are essential:

- Know definitely what you want.

- Build a practical plan for the achievement of what you want, making use of the counsel and advice of your Master Mind group.

- Surround yourself with an organization made up of people who have the knowledge and experience essential for carrying out your definite aim.

- Have sufficient faith in yourself and in your plans to envision your goal as a reality even before you begin to carry out your plans.

- Do not become discouraged, no matter what obstacles you may meet. If one plan fails to work, substitute other plans until you have found the one that *will* work.

- Do no guessing. Get the facts as the basis for all of your plans.

- Do not be influenced by others to abandon your plans or your aim.

- Have no set hours of work. The leader must devote whatever hours are necessary for success.

- Concentrate on one thing at a time. You cannot dissipate thought and energy and still be efficient.

- Whenever possible, delegate to others the responsibility of details, but have a system for checking to see that these details are being dealt with.

- Hold yourself accountable at all times for carrying out all of your plans, bearing in mind that if subordinates fail, it is you yourself who has failed.

HOW YOU MAKE DECISIONS

Whether you are making a major decision with ramifications that could affect your entire life, or a snap-decision between chocolate and vanilla, the important factors in determining how long you take to make the decision are how much data you think is necessary, and how much you are prepared to rely on instinct.

When faced with the need to make a decision, almost everyone reacts the same way: first, review everything you know, and second, get as much additional information as you can, keeping in mind that it is impossible to ever have all of the facts.

As you are mentally running through the facts and information, you also take into account your own personal feelings and biases. Many decisions do not involve absolutes, so hunches and gut-feelings can often be the deciding factor.

After juggling all of the possibilities, and going back and forth between facts and feelings, something will shift in the way you "feel" about the decision. That's when it feels right and you take action.

IN MAKING DECISIONS, LESS CAN BE MORE

Most decision-making is not like scientific experimentation in which theory after theory is tested until some consensus is reached. It would be impractical to apply such rigorous demands on most things. In fact there is research indicating that most decisions are actually made early in the process, and that the rest of the time is taken up searching for reasons to support your original gut-feeling.

In real life there is no guarantee that a decision based on more facts and information will be more correct than one based on fewer facts. Although it seems logical that the more facts you have the better your decision will be, it is entirely possible that while you may have more facts, your interpretation of those many facts may still be incorrect. Or

NOTES & COMMENTS

it could take too much time to process because having all the facts presents you with far more information, possibilities, and choices than can be reasonably dealt with, or because you've got so much to choose from you just select the points that support your preconceived desire. Or you could just get worn down by too much to deal with.

All of these possibilities add up to delayed decisions or bad decisions because you tried to assimilate too much input.

GOOD DECISIONS AND BAD DECISIONS

Before we go any further we should point out that the chances are you are probably using the term *bad decision* incorrectly. It is likely that what you are really referring to is the bad result of the decision, not the decision itself. As you will see below, bad decisions are ones that are rushed and poorly conceived. Therefore, by definition, bad decisions have no place in the Napoleon Hill method.

- A good decision is one that has a clear objective, is based on appropriate research, is well thought-out, and is rational.

- A bad decision is one that may have a clear objective but it involves little research, or inappropriate facts, and it is arrived at on a whim or out of impatience.

This should make it clear why we say that bad decisions are not even worth considering in the Napoleon Hill method. If you practice the Hill method you would never make a rushed or ill-conceived decision. However, that does not mean that you may not get a bad result.

The problem is that good decisions don't always produce good results, and bad decisions don't always yield bad results. You may make a good decision that is well considered, rational, and takes into account all the available information and preferences, and you can still end up with an outcome you don't want.

On the other hand, a bad decision that isn't well thought-out, or is made on a whim, could be the one that hits the jackpot.

The lesson that you should take away from this is that you can't beat yourself up about a good decision that ends up with a bad result any more than you can take credit for a bad decision that turns out to be a winner.

BAD RESULTS DO NOT MEAN DEFEAT

This is the same point that Hill made in earlier chapters when he was discussing how you should view failure. A good decision that produces a bad result is a failure, but failure is not defeat. Failures are what show you how to do it better next time. Similarly, bad results show you how to make better decisions next time.

Every problem presents you with a chance to make a decision. It's up to you whether you see a failed decision as a problem or an opportunity. You can treat it as just another annoyance that you don't want to deal with, or you can use it as an opportunity to find out what is wrong with your decision-making practices.

It is a mind-set, a state of mind, and Hill always says there is only one thing over which you have absolute control, and that is your mind. If it is a state of mind, you can change it, because you can control what you think. If you choose, you can welcome failure as a way to learn what to do and what not to do. Failure is only temporary. Failure is a lesson you needed to learn in order to succeed. Success is built on decisions that failed. Great successes are created by those people who see the problems and turn them into opportunities.

HOW TO ELIMINATE PROCRASTINATION

If you procrastinate you are not just wasting your time, but you are wasting the time of everyone else who is waiting for you to decide. The age-old advice is that procrastination is the thief of time.

NOTES & COMMENTS

The method through which you may eliminate procrastination is based on self-suggestion and autosuggestion. Copy the following formula and put it in a conspicuous place where you will see it often. This formula is designed to prompt you to take the initiative and make firm decisions. As you know from the chapter on autosuggestion, every time you read the written version of the formula, it will deepen the imprint on your subconscious mind and it will help you stick with your decision. This is adapted from *Law of Success: The 21st-Century Edition,* Volume II, Lesson Eight:

PROCRASTINATION

Having chosen a definite aim or purpose as my life's work, I now understand it to be my duty to transform this aim into reality. Therefore I will form the habit of taking some definite action each day that will carry me one step nearer the attainment of my definite aim or purpose.

I know that procrastination is a deadly enemy of all who would become leaders in any undertaking, and I will eliminate this habit from my makeup by:

- Doing some one definite thing each day, something that ought to be done, without anyone telling me to do it.

- Looking around until I find at least one thing that I can do each day that I have not been in the habit of doing, and that will be of value to others, without expectation of pay.

- Telling at least one other person each day of the value of practicing this habit of deciding to do something that ought to be done without being told to do it.

I can see that the muscles of the body become strong in proportion to the extent to which they are used. Therefore I understand that the *habit* of initiative and decision also becomes fixed in proportion to the extent that it is practiced.

I realize the place to begin developing the *habit* of initiative and decision is in the small, commonplace things connected with my daily work. Therefore I will go at my work each day as if I were doing it solely for the purpose of developing this necessary *habit* of initiative and decision.

I understand that by practicing this *habit* of taking decisive action in connection with my daily work I will be not only developing that *habit* but I will also be attracting the attention of those who will place greater value on my services as a result of this practice.

Signed . . . .

Every day brings you a chance to render some service, outside of the course of your regular duties, that will be of value to others. You render this service not only because it is of help to others, but also because it provides you with ways of taking the initiative and making firm decisions, qualities that you must possess before you can ever become an outstanding figure in your chosen field.

HOW DO YOU KNOW WHEN TO CHANGE YOUR MIND?

In the chapter on your definite aim or purpose, Hill says that you should be prepared to change your aim or purpose if, after making a reasonable effort, you conclude that it is not right for you.

NOTES & COMMENTS

In the chapter on the Master Mind, Hill advises that you will almost surely make changes in your Master Mind group because you will find that some of your choices were wrong.

The question is, how will you ever know for sure when you should stick with something or when you should give up on a goal and move on to another?

The answer is, there are no magic answers. You are the person who must decide for you. It is up to you to decide what your aim or purpose will be, and for each goal you set it is up to you to make the decision at which point you should stop pursuing that goal and choose a new one.

As we have pointed out, even well-reasoned, good decisions can produce bad results. You must simply accept the fact that you may not know until after you have made a decision whether you were right or wrong. The smart move is to make contingency plans a part of your decision-making process so that you have a fall-back position in case something goes seriously wrong. That way you can stay the course with your decision, but if it becomes clear that it is producing a bad result, you are prepared to switch gears to another course of action without panicking.

PERSISTENCE

10

CHAPTER 10: OVERVIEW AND ANALYSIS

THE SUSTAINED EFFORT NECESSARY TO INDUCE FAITH

This chapter begins with Napoleon Hill's statement that lack of persistence is one of the major causes of failure. Two of the best techniques for developing your persistence are autosuggestion and the formation of a Master Mind group.

ARE YOU MONEY-CONSCIOUS OR POVERTY-CONSCIOUS?

You must work at it if you want to make money-consciousness your natural habit. On the other hand, you don't have to work at poverty-consciousness—it just sneaks in if you don't guard against it.

SNAP OUT OF MENTAL INERTIA

Life puts roadblocks in the way of success to test you. If you have persistence, you will continue no matter how often you are deterred. Every failure brings with it the seed of an equivalent advantage.

"Weak desires bring weak results, just as a small amount of fire makes a small amount of heat."

"There may not be a heroic connotation to the word *persistence*, but persistence does for your character what carbon does to iron—it hardens it to steel."

"Every failure brings with it the seed of an equal or greater benefit."

PERSIST PAST YOUR FAILURES

If you have learned the importance of persistence, you know that failure is not defeat. Failure is only temporary. It is a lesson you needed to learn in order to succeed.

EDITOR'S COMMENTARY

This section is devoted to the seven turning points in Napoleon Hill's life, which offers a perfect example of how persistence in the face of rejection can pay off. It also demonstrates why this book has become the standard against which all self-help books are measured.

TAKE YOUR OWN PERSISTENCE INVENTORY

Hill says that persistence is a state of mind. He suggests that readers take an inventory of themselves to see if they are lacking any of the qualities of persistence. Hill provides a list of the eight causes on which persistence is based.

He then sets up a second list of sixteen weaknesses that must be mastered by anyone who wants to accumulate riches. The last item on the list is the fear of criticism.

IF YOU FEAR CRITICISM

Hill says that many people never succeed because they fear criticism from friends and family. They stay in bad marriages, don't take chances, and let duty to family keep them from succeeding.

EDITOR'S COMMENTARY

Napoleon Hill says that the only lucky break is the one you make for yourself. The editors elaborate on the point by citing the book *How to Make Your Own Luck*, as well as studies which prove that although certain people appear to be lucky, it is really a result of specific actions that they may not even be aware they are taking.

He closes the section with the statement that riches do not respond to wishes. Riches respond to a definite desire emotionalized with faith, which is turned into a specific plan, action, and persistence.

HOW TO DEVELOP PERSISTENCE

Hill offers a four-step plan to develop persistence: (1) a definite purpose, (2) a definite plan, (3) a mind closed to negativity, (4) an alliance with a Master Mind group. He concludes with a list of benefits that result from persistence.

HOW TO MASTER DIFFICULTIES

Hill says that in closely studying both Henry Ford and Thomas Edison, the only thing he could determine they had that set them apart from others was persistence. When they started out, they weren't smarter or richer or luckier; they were persistent, and that's what it took to change the world.

He says that if you study the great prophets and philosophers, you will see that definiteness of purpose, concentration of effort, and persistence is the source of their achievements.

Hill suggests the biography of Mohammed as an example of a prophet-philosopher whose success was based solely on persistence.

CHAPTER 10: THE WORKBOOK

As Napoleon Hill states often throughout *Think and Grow Rich,* each of his principles of success builds upon the other principles. This chapter, Persistence, begins by referring back to the concept of a chief aim or purpose. The degree to which you have persistence is a direct result of how clear you are about your desire and how committed you are to accomplishing your aim or purpose.

Hill also says in an earlier chapter that there is a vast difference between wishing and desiring. All your wishing and hoping for success accomplishes nothing. The only thing that counts is what you do to condition your mind for success and what you do to make it happen. That brings us to what some consider to be the most controversial aspect of this book: money-consciousness.

"I had the opportunity to analyze both Mr. Edison and Mr. Ford, year after year, over a long period of time. So I can speak from actual knowledge when I say that I found no quality except persistence, in either of them, that even remotely suggested the major source of their stupendous achievements."

NOTES & COMMENTS

MONEY-CONSCIOUSNESS

Money-consciousness, or prosperity-consciousness, is the term Hill uses to describe the state of mind that attracts riches.

You can grow rich spiritually, emotionally, or intellectually, and to some degree all of those things are true for students of Napoleon Hill's philosophy, but the truth is that most people who read this book do so to learn how to grow richer financially.

In these days of political correctness, you might have reservations about admitting that you want to make a lot of money, but Napoleon Hill wrote *Think and Grow Rich* during the time that America was just beginning to recover from the worst depression in history, and the whole point of the book was to help people make money.

Today, even though the Great Depression is long behind us, *Think and Grow Rich* continues to be a bestseller year after year, right up to this very day. No matter if it's depression, recession, boom, bubble, or bust, people want to know how to succeed and make more money. This book tells you how to do it.

NOBODY SAID IT WAS EASY

If you are going to adopt Hill's money-consciousness methods, then you must be prepared to accept some ways of thinking and doing things that are much more demanding than most other motivational or self-help programs.

To succeed by using the Hill method, you must first commit yourself to an aim that offers the possibility to yield the riches you desire. Next, through autosuggestion, you fire up your faith in your ability until you are convinced that you can achieve your aim. Now, in order to turn that aim into money-consciousness, you must begin to see everything in your life from the point of view of how it relates to your aim or purpose. To be money-conscious, you must begin to evaluate the things that interest you in terms of whether they will help you to achieve your aim. Keep in mind the R2/A2 formula:

- **Recognize:** When something catches your attention, you should try to recognize whether it involves a principle or technique that can be learned or adopted.

- **Relate:** Ask yourself, "What will the success principle, idea, or technique do for me?" You must be able to relate it to yourself and your own actions and thoughts.

- **Assimilate:** Ask yourself, "How can I use this principle, idea, or technique to achieve my goals or solve my problems?"

- **Apply:** "What action will I take? When am I going to start?" Then follow through with action.

If you follow Hill's method, you will become a very focused and goal-directed person, and most people would agree that's a very good thing. However, there are some negatives that you must guard against.

On one hand you may become so preoccupied with your goal that it becomes all you can talk about and other people begin to lose interest in you. On the other hand, there is the danger that by becoming so obsessed with your goal, it's you who loses interest in other people.

The editors of this workbook would expect that anyone who is smart enough to succeed with Napoleon Hill's philosophy is also smart enough to know the difference between being a person with a passionate interest and being a self-obsessed bore. However, even if you don't become a bore or a recluse, if you embrace prosperity-consciousness with the commitment Hill says it requires, there are going to be some changes in you.

So the question is whether you should choose a definite aim and go into it with everything you've got, or whether you should play it safe as you give it a shot while not letting yourself go too overboard.

You may be able to make an argument for either point of view, but if you decide to put less than 100 percent into it, you must accept that what you get back will be less than 100 percent of what you could have achieved.

SUCCESS-CONSCIOUSNESS IS NOT FOR EVERYONE

What Napoleon Hill offers is a philosophy of personal achievement and a specific method that, if followed, will produce success and make you rich. But it will change who you are, and some of the changes may not be entirely to your liking.

It's true that you might become successful without following Hill's principles. There are people who make huge fortunes just by being in the right place at the right time or by taking a gamble and winning or by exploiting their natural talent or ability. That may be the kind of success that you wish for, but it is not the kind of success that you can plan on. Hill's methods cannot help you have that kind of success.

It is up to you to decide if you are prepared to commit yourself to a method that is this focused on being a success and making money. Your challenge is to decide what your monetary aim or purpose is, and then to decide how persistent you will be in pursuing your desire to have that money. You will become rich in direct proportion to the degree to which you apply these principles.

POVERTY-CONSCIOUSNESS

Just as money is attracted to those who deliberately set their minds on it, poverty is attracted to those whose minds are open to it.

Money-consciousness is something you have to work hard at to achieve. Poverty-consciousness requires no work at all. It is always there, waiting for you to let down your guard. Money-consciousness is demanding, but poverty-consciousness is easy. It's easier than working hard. It's easier than taking responsibility. It's easier to blame your failure and poverty on others who don't understand you, or who don't appreciate you, or don't give you the breaks, or don't like you, or any of the other excuses that let you off the hook for your own lack of ambition and persistence.

Poverty-consciousness and poverty are not the same thing. There are people right now who are living in poverty who don't have poverty-consciousness. For them, poverty is only a temporary circumstance. They have every intention of getting themselves out of poverty and they see the possibility of success in every opportunity.

On the other hand, there are people who are living in much better circumstances with much better opportunities, but they will never see an opportunity as the possibility of success. All they see is the possibility of failing, the possibility of embarrassing themselves, the possibility of being turned down, the possibility that someone else will do better than they will, the possibility they might be wrong, the possibility of losing what they have. And because they are locked into such a poverty-conscious mind-set, they will never see the upside of the possibilities and they will never rise to the top.

Money-consciousness and poverty-consciousness are not what you *are*—they're what you *think*. Both are states of mind, and you *can* change your mind and change your habits.

TAKE YOUR OWN PERSISTENCE INVENTORY

Napoleon Hill suggests that you review the following Persistence Inventory point by point to see how many of the eight factors of persistence you lack.

While there are no right or wrong answers, by noting your thoughts —as they are now—about each of these items, it will give you a point of reference by which to judge how your understanding changes as you continue the study of Hill's philosophy of personal achievement.

PERSISTENCE INVENTORY

1. Definiteness of purpose. Knowing what you want is the first and most important step toward the development of persistence. A strong motive will force you to surmount difficulties.

_____

_____

_____

_____

2. Desire. It is comparatively easy to acquire and maintain persistence in pursuing the object of intense desire.

_____

_____

_____

_____

3. Self-reliance. Belief in your ability to carry out a plan encourages you to follow the plan through with persistence. (Self-reliance can also be developed through autosuggestion.)

_____

_____

_____

_____

4. Definiteness of plans. Organized plans, even ones that may be weak or impractical, encourage persistence.

_____

_____

_____

_____

5. Accurate knowledge. Knowing that your plans are sound, based upon experience or observation, encourages persistence; "guessing" instead of "knowing" destroys persistence.

_____

_____

_____

_____

6. Cooperation. Sympathy, understanding, and cooperation with others tend to develop persistence.

_____

_____

_____

_____

7. Willpower. The habit of concentrating your thoughts on making plans to attain your definite purpose leads to persistence.

_____

_____

_____

_____

8. Habit. Persistence is the direct result of habit. The mind absorbs and becomes a part of the daily experiences upon which it feeds. Fear, the worst of all enemies, can be overcome by forcing yourself to perform and repeat acts of courage.

_____

_____

_____

_____

IDENTIFY THE WEAKNESSES YOU MUST MASTER

Following is a list of the real enemies that stand between you and achievement. These are not only the "symptoms" indicating weakness of persistence, but also the deeply seated subconscious causes of this weakness. Study the list carefully and face yourself squarely, if you really wish to know who you are and what you are capable of doing.

As you go through the list, analyze yourself point by point, record how you measure up on the self-test scale, record the date, and, as with the previous questionnaires, make a few notes to remind yourself how you felt when you first went through this review. These are the weaknesses that must be mastered by anyone who really wants to accumulate riches:

1. Failure to recognize and to clearly define exactly what you want.

1 2 3 4 5 6 7 8 9 10 _____

_____

_____

2. Procrastination, with or without cause (usually backed up with a long list of excuses).

1 2 3 4 5 6 7 8 9 10 _____

_____

_____

3. Lack of interest in acquiring specialized knowledge.

1 2 3 4 5 6 7 8 9 10 _____

_____

_____

4. Indecision, and the habit of "passing the buck" instead of facing issues squarely.

1 2 3 4 5 6 7 8 9 10 _____

_____

_____

5. The habit of relying on excuses instead of making definite plans by which to solve your problems.

1 2 3 4 5 6 7 8 9 10_____

_____

_____

6. There is little remedy for the weakness of self-satisfaction, and little or no hope for those who suffer from it.

1 2 3 4 5 6 7 8 9 10_____

_____

_____

7. Indifference, usually reflected in your readiness to compromise rather than meet opposition and fight it.

1 2 3 4 5 6 7 8 9 10_____

_____

_____

8. The habit of blaming others for your mistakes, and accepting circumstances as being unavoidable.

1 2 3 4 5 6 7 8 9 10_____

_____

_____

9. Weakness of desire because you neglected to choose motives that will push you to take action.

1 2 3 4 5 6 7 8 9 10_____

_____

_____

10. Willingness to quit at the first sign of defeat (based upon one or more of the six basic fears).

1 2 3 4 5 6 7 8 9 10_____

_____

_____

11. Lack of organized plans that you have written out so they can be analyzed.

1 2 3 4 5 6 7 8 9 10_____

_____

_____

12. The habit of neglecting to act on ideas, or to grasp opportunity when it presents itself.

1 2 3 4 5 6 7 8 9 10_____

_____

_____

13. The habit of wishing instead of willing.

1 2 3 4 5 6 7 8 9 10_____

_____

_____

14. The habit of compromising with poverty instead of aiming at riches. A general lack of ambition to be, to do, or to own.

1 2 3 4 5 6 7 8 9 10_____

_____

_____

15. Searching for all the shortcuts to riches. Trying to get without giving a fair equivalent, usually reflected in the habit of gambling or trying to drive unfair bargains.

1 2 3 4 5 6 7 8 9 10_____

_____

16. Fear of criticism, resulting in failure to create plans and put them into action, because of what other people might think, do, or say. This is one of your most dangerous enemies, because it often exists in your subconscious mind and you may not even know it is there.

1 2 3 4 5 6 7 8 9 10_____

_____

IF YOU FEAR CRITICISM

As is clear from the number of times it is mentioned in *Think and Grow Rich,* Napoleon Hill considers the fear of criticism to be one of the greatest enemies of success. In fact, the reason people have a fear of failing has more to do with their concern about what other people will think or say about them than it does with their concern for not being able to accomplish the task at hand. No one likes to try something and fail, but, more important, no one wants to be blamed for failing. Failure may make you mad at yourself, but blame and criticism diminishes you in front of others, which erodes your self-confidence.

Many people make mistakes in marriage but stay married, then go through life miserable and unhappy, because they fear criticism.

Millions of people will not go back to get an education after having left school, because they fear criticism.

Countless numbers of men and women permit relatives to wreck their lives in the name of family duty, because they fear criticism.

NOTES & COMMENTS

People refuse to take chances in business because they fear the criticism that may follow if they fail.

Too many people refuse to set high goals for themselves because they fear the criticism of relatives and friends who may say, "Don't aim so high, people will think you are crazy."

Although for some people the fear of being criticized can act as a motivator to succeed, for others the anxiety it causes has just the opposite effect. Like stage fright or first-time jitters, the fear of criticism can cause panic attacks, shortness of breath, rapid breathing, irregular heartbeat, sweating, nausea, and other physical symptoms.

The problem with even moderate fear of criticism is that it can keep you from being your best because it keeps you from taking chances. It's easier to go the safe route and not attract attention to yourself. But the safe idea that is not likely to be criticized is also not likely to be a big breakthrough.

The most creative ideas and the most audacious statements are the ones that are most likely to be laughed at. It's those risky ideas, the ones that someone might hate or laugh at, that usually have the best up-side, but you don't put them out there because you don't want to get shot down.

For many people, the criticism doesn't even have to be directed at you. Just seeing someone else get taken down a peg is enough to keep you from wanting to suffer the same fate yourself.

The way to deal with the fear of being criticized is the same as dealing with any other fear or phobia. Psychologists may use various confrontation therapies to desensitize you, and there are drugs that might ease your anxiety, but basically the answer is, as Susan Jeffers says in the title of her bestseller: "feel the fear and do it anyway."

What have you got to lose? What happens if you take the chance that you will be criticized?

If the downside is that you could lose your job or someone could get hurt, then the risk is probably not worth the reward.

On the other hand, if the downside is that you feel foolish for a while, but the up-side is that you will achieve your burning desire, then the answer is obvious.

What would be really foolish is if you didn't give it a shot.

POWER OF THE MASTER MIND

11

CHAPTER 11: OVERVIEW AND ANALYSIS

THE DRIVING FORCE

Power is essential for success, and power is organized and directed knowledge. You get knowledge from experience, research, or Infinite Intelligence, but to make it useful it must be organized.

GAINING POWER THROUGH THE MASTER MIND

A Master Mind is the coordination of knowledge and effort in a spirit of harmony between two or more people for the attainment of a definite purpose. No individual can have great power without forming a Master Mind.

A Master Mind creates two kinds of power: economic and psychic. Hill says when you pull together bright people to help you, it naturally results in economic power. The psychic aspect is that by pulling bright people together, the combined intellect is greater than the sum of the parts. Great fortune can be gained in no other way.

"When two or more people harmonize their minds and produce the effect known as a Master Mind, each person in the group becomes vested with the power to contact and gather knowledge through the subconscious minds of all the other members of the group."

HOW TO MULTIPLY YOUR BRAIN POWER

Hill compares a Master Mind to joining batteries together to increase the power. Similarly, when brains are connected, the total of all brains are available to each individual brain. People take on the nature and habits of the people with whom they associate. Hill mentions Ford's Master Mind comprised of Edison, Firestone, and Luther Burbank.

EDITOR'S COMMENTARY

The optimum size of a Master Mind group is no more than twelve members. Be prepared that it will be difficult to find people who will commit and give of themselves so freely.

FINDING YOUR MASTER MIND MEMBERS

Choose people with whom you share common values, and choose the best candidate, not your best friends. They must all work in harmony and subjugate their own ambitions for the good of the project.

COMPENSATING YOUR MASTER MIND MEMBERS

You must not take advantage of your members. You must make a fair financial offer, and you must also offer recognition and the opportunity for self-expression.

MEETINGS

These must be regular and organized, without killing spontaneity.

MAINTENANCE

You must create a nonthreatening environment in which everyone feels confident that they are valued.

MARRIAGE

You must involve your family in your Master Mind and your aims.

MASTER MIND AND INFINITE INTELLIGENCE

By joining a Master Mind group you not only get access to the knowledge of others, but by coming together, the minds interact and create a source of ideas that is more than the sum of the individual minds.

EDITOR'S COMMENTARY

The editors tell the story of how Napoleon Hill came to meet W. Clement Stone, and how their meeting resulted in the creation of the greatest Master Mind of either man's career.

THE POWER OF POSITIVE EMOTIONS

Hill closes this chapter with his theory that in life there is a great stream of power, like a river that flows in two directions. One side is positive and it flows to success and wealth; the other side is negative and flows to failure and poverty. If you are headed toward poverty, *Think and Grow Rich* can be the oar to steer you out.

CHAPTER 11: THE WORKBOOK

In many ways, the importance of the Master Mind principle is so obvious that it is easy to ignore or miss altogether. In fact when Napoleon Hill wrote his first bestseller, *Law of Success,* his philosophy of personal achievement was still evolving, and the Master Mind had not yet been identified as one of his principles of success. Hill's manuscript was constructed around fifteen concepts, and it wasn't until after the first edition had been published that he realized this idea he had included in the introduction was a separate principle unto itself. He dubbed this principle the Master Mind Alliance, and in future editions it was given its own chapter and identified as a unique and important principle.

It may be that it was overlooked because, when you first hear it described, it doesn't seem all that different from teamwork, and the need for teamwork seems so obvious that it hardly needs to be pointed out. The following excerpt, from a Commentary in the chapter Specialized Knowledge from *Think and Grow Rich: The 21st-Century Edition,* is included here to recap and clarify the difference between teamwork and a Master Mind, which takes the concept and steps it up to another level:

"If the group is meeting to discuss a given subject, ideas will come pouring into the minds of all present, as if an outside influence were dictating them. The minds of those in the Master Mind are like magnets, attracting ideas and thoughts from no one knows where."

NOTES & COMMENTS

Teamwork can be achieved by any group, even if the members of the team don't like each other or have anything in common. That's because all that teamwork requires is that the members cooperate and work together. In teamwork you might work together not because you have the same goals, but simply because you like the leader, or because the team is paying you enough to buy your services. Sometimes there is good teamwork *because* different members have different agendas. For instance, a board of directors may be very unfriendly and still run a business successfully. Musical groups are made up of notoriously self-centered people who work as a team if it will help them get ahead.

Master Minds, on the other hand, are formed of individuals who work together because they have the same agenda, a deep sense of mission, and commitment to the same goal. However, don't mistake enthusiasm and commitment for altruism. The members of your Master Mind must have a true passion for your vision, but regardless of their motivation, if they are as good as Hill says they must be, their expertise won't come cheap. If you want to bring together the brightest and the best to help you, you must be prepared to share the rewards that come from success.

The Master Mind is defined as "coordination of knowledge and effort, in a spirit of harmony, between two or more people for the attainment of a definite purpose. No individual may have great power without utilizing the Master Mind."

That level of commitment and cooperation sounds wonderful, and who wouldn't love to work in that kind of environment, but does Hill really mean that you cannot achieve success without it?

The answer is yes.

As Hill defines success and power, he really does mean it. Although you may achieve some measure of success without a Master Mind alliance, you will never have *great* success or the great power that comes with it. Power must be applied before it is effective. Individuals are limited as to the amount of power they can apply.

No matter how intelligent or well-informed you may be, no single individual, functioning independently, can ever possess great power. You have to get others to cooperate with you if you are going to organize your knowledge so that you can turn your plans into power. If you try to do everything yourself, it will take you longer to do things that others could have done faster and better; in the end you will waste time, money, and energy.

THE MASTER MIND AND INFINITE INTELLIGENCE

In *Law of Success,* Napoleon Hill used the following example to convey the value of bringing minds together in a Master Mind group:

> It is a fact that a group of batteries will provide more energy than a single battery. It is also a fact that the amount of energy provided by each individual battery depends upon the number and capacity of the cells it contains.
>
> The mind functions in a similar fashion. Some minds are more efficient than others. A group of minds coordinated (or connected) in a spirit of harmony will provide more thought-energy than a single mind, just as a group of electric batteries will provide more energy than a single battery. The strongest battery in a group will boost the power of the weaker ones.
>
> When a group of individual minds is coordinated and function in harmony, the increased energy created through that alliance becomes available to every mind in the group.

NOTES & COMMENTS

You will recall that in previous chapters the subconscious is described as the part of the human mind that can, under some circumstances, have access to Infinite Intelligence. Infinite Intelligence is described as the part of our subconscious where bits and pieces of information come together to create flashes of insight, hunches, leaps of logic, and original ideas.

You will also recall the explanation that every "thing" in the universe is one form or another of energy. A human is made up of energy, the human mind is energy, and the thoughts and ideas that come into the mind are also energy. When the minds of two people are working together in a spirit of harmony, the energy of each mind seems to pick up on the energy of the other mind(s).

Two heads are not only better than one, they are better than two—because the combination is greater than the sum of its parts. No two minds ever come together without creating this third invisible, intangible force, which, in the case of a Master Mind, will produce insights and ideas that neither of the individual minds would have come up with independently.

ANDREW CARNEGIE CREATED THE FIRST MASTER MIND

Napoleon Hill explained that at his first meeting with Andrew Carnegie, one of the questions he asked Carnegie was to what did he attribute his success. Carnegie's answer is excerpted from *Law of Success: The 21st-Century Edition,* Volume I, Lesson Two:

> With a twinkle in his eyes, he said: "Young man, before I answer your question, will you please define your term 'success'?"
>
> After waiting until he saw that I was somewhat embarrassed by this request, he continued: "By success you make reference to my money, do you not?"

I assured him that money was the term by which most people measured success, and he then said: "Oh, well, if you wish to know how I got my money—if that is what you call success—I will answer your question by saying that we have a Master Mind here in our business, and that mind is made up of more than a score of men who constitute my personal staff of superintendents and managers and accountants and chemists. No one person in this group is the Master Mind of which I speak, but the sum total of all the minds in the group, coordinated, organized, and directed to a definite end in a spirit of harmonious cooperation, is the power that got my money for me. No two minds in the group are exactly alike, but each man in the group does the thing that he is supposed to do and he does it better than any other person in the world could do it."

For years afterward, I wondered just what Carnegie meant by "Master Mind." In the light of more mature years, it began to dawn on me that he had stated a whole life's philosophy in a few words. Carnegie knew the value of organized effort. He knew that no one man could accomplish very much without the coordinated effort of other minds. He knew the value of cooperation. He had on his staff men who did not always agree with him. He had men whom he did not always admire in every respect and who, perhaps, did not always admire him, but each knew that he needed the others; therefore, they harmonized their efforts toward a common end with the result that all profited.

Andrew Carnegie was one of the wealthiest and most powerful men the world has ever known. He made his enormous fortune by dominating the iron and steel industry, but the fact is that he knew very little about the inner workings of that business. What he did know was people. He knew how to find the best person for each job, and he knew how to motivate them to be even better.

It was readily conceded even by Carnegie's rivals that he was a brilliant judge of character and an inspirational manager of men. And it was equally agreed that although he made his fortune in steel, he could just as easily have done the same thing in coal mining, banking, the grocery business or anything else he set his mind to. The secret was not that he would have learned how to dig a mine, make a loan, or harvest tomatoes. The secret was that he would have assembled a Master Mind alliance of people who were brilliant at doing those things and he would have done so by inspiring in each of them the desire to share with him the benefit of their knowledge, talent, and ability.

Let us again stress that finding such people does not come easy or cheap. Hill often made that point in his lectures by telling about Charles Schwab, who was an integral part of Carnegie's Master Mind alliance and the president of Carnegie's steel operations. Schwab earned a salary of $75,000 a year, which at that time would have made him one of the highest-paid employees in America. What's more, Mr. Carnegie not only paid Mr. Schwab's salary, but he gave him an annual bonus of as much as one million dollars.

When asked, Mr. Carnegie said, "I gave him his salary for the work he actually performed, and the bonus for his willingness to go the extra mile, thus setting a fine example for his fellow workers."

MASTER MIND GROUPS ARE ALL OVER THE INTERNET

At this point it would be well to note that the basic idea behind the concept of the Master Mind has been adopted and popularized by a number of motivational gurus and self-improvement organizations who promote the idea that you should become a member of their Master Mind group. This is largely an extension of the personal-growth phenomena that got started in the 1970s, gained momentum with the infomercial boom in the 1990s, and took off with the coming of Internet marketing.

As this is being written, when you Google the words *Master Mind group*, it tells you that there are more than 2,290,000 Web sites that use the term. Many of these groups are run by motivational gurus or life coaches who charge for the leadership and guidance they provide. There are also companies that offer membership in their Master Mind group as a free service, usually provided by an author or organization that promotes self-help books or other products and services.

While such groups can be beneficial, strictly speaking, they do not meet the criteria Napoleon Hill set forth in this chapter on the power of the Master Mind. It is very unlikely that you can join a phone-in or online group and find that all the members will, as Hill suggests, ". . . not only share your vision but will also share their ideas, information, and contacts with you. They will let you use the full strength of their experience, training, and knowledge as if it were your own. And they will do it in a spirit of perfect harmony."

Phone-in or online groups can help you generate new ideas simply because joining one puts you in a situation with other people where the sole purpose is to come up with ideas. However, for most of these groups, the main benefit you will receive would be in encouragement and enthusiasm.

The reality is that you would be joining a group of people, all of whom want to get ahead at different things in different ways, and all of whom are hoping that by linking up with others they will pick up some ideas or contacts that will help them. And although all of these people, including you, are willing to give off-the-top-of-their-head advice to the others, if, during the give-and-take, one of the members is hit with what

NOTES & COMMENTS

he or she really believes is a million-dollar idea, what are the chances that person is going to blurt it out and give it to you for free?

Would you?

If you have been following this workbook, you know the answer to that question is no. Remember Hill's advice that every time you open your mouth you either give away too much or you show how little you actually know. This does not mean these groups don't provide some value; they can be stimulating and they can be encouraging, but you should go into them with your eyes wide open. They can offer you another way to network and some cheerleading, but they do not really provide what Hill had in mind for a Master Mind.

WHAT ALL CAN A MASTER MIND BE?

Napoleon Hill got his first exposure to a Master Mind when Andrew Carnegie described it to him. Hill also saw a Master Mind in action when he observed the group Henry Ford assembled, which included inventor Thomas Edison, famed botanist Luther Burbank, naturalist and essayist John Burroughs, and industrialist and founder of the rubber and tire company, Harvey Firestone.

In describing his own personal experience with the concept, Hill tells about the meetings he conducts with his staff for the purpose of blending their minds to develop creative solutions. He also mentions that his visualization technique of tapping into advice from his invisible counselors is in its own way a variation on the Master Mind.

From the above examples it is clear that Master Minds come in a variety of shapes and sizes. The most obvious is the business model, but there are other kinds that can be of great benefit to you. For instance, in the example of Henry Ford's Master Mind, his intention wasn't to have these famous men help him achieve his business goal. He was already fabulously wealthy, and he did not need their money or their advice about building cars. What Ford wanted was to learn their sensibilities.

Although Henry Ford was brilliant in vision, he was from a very poor and humble background and had little education. It was his hope that he would improve his character and his intellect by being in association with such brilliant minds as Burbank, Burroughs, Edison, and Firestone. Apparently these educated and successful men felt it was worth it to spend time with Henry Ford, because he had just as much to offer them in the form of what today we would call his street smarts.

You can create a Master Mind in your marriage, in your family, in a partnership, in a division of a company, in a team, in a corporate board, a service club, a faith-based group, a charity, or in a thousand other ways in which two or more people get together with the idea that by being together they will come up with more and better ideas.

If you assemble a Master Mind to help you achieve your definite aim in business, there is no question about how you will keep the members motivated and loyal: you involve them in the process and you pay them from the financial rewards that come with success.

That is also how you should reward your spouse or other family members, whether they are directly involved in your business or not. Those in your immediate family are a part of everything you do, whether or not they actually go to work with you.

To be blunt, if you need the help you get from those at home so that you have what you need to succeed at your work, then you should reward them just as you would anyone else who helps you make it. If you rely on them, they are just as deserving of recognition and financial compensation as any of your business associates.

Assembling nonbusiness or nonfamily Master Minds can be more complicated. When your Master Mind is based on a shared interest, such as Ford's group, or with the members of amateur teams, civic associations, clubs, nonprofits, or volunteer organizations, pulling together a Master Mind can make a huge contribution to the success of the organization. The question is, if the members are not being financially

NOTES & COMMENTS

rewarded for the success of the organization, how do you ensure their commitment and motivation?

If you are the one in charge of the nonbusiness Master Mind, it is your job to inspire the members to share your vision, and it is your obligation to find out what each wants to get out of it so that he or she feels properly compensated. Instead of dollars and cents, you will be giving praise, recognition, and honors, while making sure they have a sense of self-satisfaction, accomplishment, and self-expression.

WHAT'S IN IT FOR ME?

There are at least three distinctly different advantages that you gain by working with a Master Mind alliance.

1. A Master Mind increases the amount you can do. As mentioned previously, no matter how intelligent or well-informed you may be, no one person, functioning independently, can ever possess great power. If you try to do it on your own, it will take you longer to do things that others can do faster and better, and in the end you will waste time, money, and energy.

2. A Master Mind improves the quality of what you can do because, in addition to more manpower, it also gives you more knowledge than any single person can have. Through your Master Mind alliance you combine your advice and knowledge with the advice and knowledge of others who join with you, and the others give you the use of their counsel and contacts just as if they were your own.

3. A Master Mind improves your creativity. When the minds of two or more people are coordinated in a spirit of harmony, when you are working with other people and everyone is on the same wavelength, the energy of each mind seems to pick up on the energy of the other minds. This results in more and better ideas than any one person could ever come up with working alone.

HOW TO ASSEMBLE YOUR MASTER MIND ALLIANCE

Following are sixteen guidelines that will help you to set the agenda and select the right kind of people for your Master Mind group. Although this is not a questionnaire, many people find it helpful to write a note or a reminder to themselves about their initial thoughts when reading the concepts, so we have provided a few lines for that purpose.

1. Clearly know your chief aim or purpose. Your desire will tell you what kind of people you need for your Master Mind.

_____

_____

_____

2. Your Master Mind should be no more than a dozen people, and generally the smaller the group the better.

_____

_____

_____

3. Decide what financial reward or advantages and benefits you will offer the individual members of your group in return for their cooperation. If you have trouble talking about money, you will just have to get over it. You *must* talk about money, and you must be absolutely honest about how you arrived at what you are offering. There is no reason to be embarrassed by any offer if it is truly the best you can make.

_____

_____

_____

4. Each member must agree at the outset on the contribution each will make, and on the division of benefits and profits.

_____

_____

_____

5. Do everything you can to attract the best people. Do not select people merely because you know them or because you like them.

_____

_____

_____

6. Choose people who not only share your vision but who will also share their ideas, their information, their contacts, and who will let you use their knowledge as if it were your own.

_____

_____

_____

7. Personal ambition must be subordinated to the achievement of the purpose of the alliance, otherwise you will have wasted everyone's time, you will ruin friendships, and your venture will be destroyed.

_____

_____

_____

8. Arrange to meet with the members of your Master Mind group at least twice a week, and more often if possible.

_____

_____

_____

9. Don't let the meetings become so regular and formalized that they inhibit phone calls, emails, and other less formal contact.

_____

_____

_____

10. The members must know with certainty that you are reliable, trustworthy, and loyal. You must maintain perfect harmony between yourself and every member of your Master Mind group.

_____

_____

_____

11. Everyone must deal with everyone else on a completely ethical basis. No member should seek unfair advantage at the expense of others.

_____

_____

_____

12. Create a nonthreatening environment. Explore all ideas with equal interest and concern for the originator's feelings.

_____

_____

_____

13. Attune yourself to every member of the group. Try to imagine how you would react in a given situation if you were in his or her shoes.

_____

_____

_____

14. Don't try to force the group along too quickly. Allow for those who want to test ideas by playing devil's advocate.

_____

_____

_____

15. Insist on confidentiality. Some people can give away an idea simply because they love to talk. You don't need them in your group.

_____

_____

_____

16. You cannot succeed when surrounded by disloyal and unfriendly associates, no matter what the object of your definite chief aim may be. Success is built on loyalty, faith, sincerity, and cooperation.

_____

_____

_____

NOTES & COMMENTS

_____

_____

_____

_____

_____

_____

_____

_____

_____

_____

_____

THE MASTER MIND AND CHANGE

In preparing the earlier workbook chapter about selecting your desire, the editors made it clear that over time you should expect your aim or purpose to change. Just as you may not get your chief aim or purpose absolutely right the first time out, you probably won't assemble the absolutely right Master Mind the first time either. Andrew Carnegie said that practically every member of his alliance was removed and replaced with some other person who could adapt himself more loyally and enthusiastically to the spirit and objective of the alliance.

More common than making the wrong choice is selecting someone who was right in the beginning but whose contributions have become less relevant as your business succeeds and grows. All businesses that succeed hit a point where they have to either scale up or fail. This is when you suddenly realize that demand is too great for your manufacturing capacity. This is when you realize your business is too big to be small, but still too small to be big. This is when you have to step up and buy the new machinery, or borrow the money, or find new investors, or get a new distributor, or buy out the competitor, or take some other drastic action that could catapult you to the next level. Regardless of the particulars, there are times when you have to scale up or you will stop succeeding.

The same thing will almost surely happen to your Master Mind. There will come a point when you have to scale up your Master Mind to keep pace with your business. What you needed as a startup is not what you need as an expanding business. What helped grow a partnership may not be the same thing you need when you incorporate and take on debt. What was perfectly fine as an S-Corp is nowhere near the financial sophistication you need to launch an IPO when you decide to go public. And so it goes.

It is up to you to find the right people for your Master Mind. It is up to you to make sure they feel they are generously rewarded for their contribution. It is up to you to recognize when it is time to change the mix of the Master Mind to keep pace with your success. And it is up to you to find the way to make sure that those who leave do so feeling they succeeded at what they set out to do.

By now it should be crystal clear why it is mandatory that your members are satisfied with the compensation arrangements when they sign on. No one should ever feel they were used up and tossed aside, or that they were undercompensated. And you should never have to feel obligated to pay to keep a member whose contribution is not living up to expectations.

The advice of the editors is that the only way to avoid anyone ever feeling that they were used or undercompensated is to be certain that everyone is completely happy with their compensation when they sign on, and that they know changes will be made in the Master Mind as the aim evolves. They must also be told at the beginning that it will be you who decides when changes must be made.

Be honest, and be prepared to be turned down by some of the people you would love to have in your group. Any other course will only create problems down the road. Don't fool yourself into thinking it is worth the risk to convince them to join now and you'll deal with the money problems later. It's not worth the risk, and all you will do later is lose friendships and create bad feeling.

We also advise that on a very regular basis you review the progress of the project toward its stated objective, and at the same time you review the issue of compensation with all Master Mind members. That is the only way to make sure your people know if they are living up to your expectations, and it is the only way to make sure disagreements and resentments are dealt with before they become problems.

MARRIAGE AND THE MASTER MIND

Napoleon Hill says that if you are married you must involve your wife or husband in your Master Mind. (Today that advice would apply to so many other kinds of domestic relationships, that we will also use the terms *spouse* or *partner.*)

Hill's point is that if you are serious about using his techniques to create success-consciousness within yourself, it will change who you are and how you live your life. So if you are going to make yourself over, it is imperative that you involve your spouse or partner in the process.

We have all been told over and over that we shouldn't bring our work home with us, and it may be true in most cases, but that advice does not work with Hill's method. The change in you is going to be too great to ignore, and it is going to affect others close to you. Therefore, to make it work, you should plan on setting aside time each day to involve your partner in deciding what you want to achieve and how you can work together to accomplish it. This may not be the way the average couple does things, but Hill wasn't writing for the people who wanted to be average.

On the other hand, you should know that trying to integrate input from your spouse or partner into your work is bound to be difficult, because of the natural resistance of the people you work with toward ideas from outside. Unless it is handled with tact and diplomacy, you will create jealousies and resentments that will negate the value of the additional creative input. However, like it or not, you still have to do it.

Regardless of the difficulty, Napoleon Hill's advice is that you must build your Master Mind into your domestic relationship from the start. It may not be easy, but if you are going to adopt Hill's philosophy and follow his methods, you will have to find the right way to make your spouse or partner a part of your work, and your work a part of your home life.

SEXUALITY: CHARISMA AND CREATIVITY

12

CHAPTER 12: OVERVIEW AND ANALYSIS

CHARISMA AND CREATIVITY

This chapter opens with an Editor's Commentary that cites Maslow's Hierarchy of Human Needs and explains that Napoleon Hill's research focused on the correlation between sexuality and high achievement.

CHARISMA

Hill says people are influenced more by emotion than by logic. He lists the top ten desires and notes that when motivated by sexual desire, a person may exhibit extraordinary courage, persistence, or imagination. A person's sexuality can also project itself as a feeling of confidence and a sense of control that can be used to influence others.

EDITOR'S COMMENTARY

Numerous contemporary studies have corroborated Hill's conclusions. Sexuality is not always good looks and youth. It can also be charisma.

"The world is ruled by human emotion. People are influenced more by feelings than by reason.

The desire for sexual expression is at the top of the list of stimuli that step up the mind and start the wheels of physical action.

When harnessed, it has been used as a creative force in the arts and other pursuits, including the accumulation of riches."

CHARISMA (continued)

Hill says that focusing your charisma is "transmuting sexual energy." You can project charisma in your handshake, your tone of voice, the way you act, and your general style.

EDITOR'S COMMENTARY

Having established a link between sexuality and success, the editors comment on the connection between sexuality and creativity.

CREATIVITY

Hill draws on his own research, plus what he is able to derive from historical biographies, to support his theory that the greatest and most successful men in history possessed a highly sexual nature.

EDITOR'S COMMENTARY

Hill did not include women in his analysis, but today there are numerous biographies of successful women that reveal to what degree sexuality plays a role in their success.

GENIUS AND CREATIVE IMAGINATION

Hill defines a genius as someone who can tap into sources of knowledge that many people refer to as the sixth sense. He calls it the "creative imagination," and says it is the area of the thinking process that links your mind to Infinite Intelligence.

Hill says that ideas come to you from: (1) someone who tells you something, (2) something stored in your subconscious, (3) tapping into someone else's subconscious, and (4) Infinite Intelligence. When your mind is working at its best, it can sometimes connect with Infinite Intelligence and come up with flashes of genius that appear in your creative imagination.

DEVELOPING YOUR CREATIVE IMAGINATION

Hill explains about Elmer R. Gates, one of America's most successful scientist-inventors, who became famous for using an isolation chamber in which he would "sit for ideas." Although Gates' method of tapping into what Hill called Infinite Intelligence was unconventional, it often resulted in amazing insights that were turned into practical inventions.

METHODS USED BY GENIUSES ARE AVAILABLE TO YOU

Hill explains the creative method used by Gates and other inventors: (1) draw upon one of the ten stimulants to get your mind working, (2) review in your mind the known facts about the project, (3) picture in your mind the unknowns about the project, and (4) let your subconscious take it over and see what flashes into your mind.

EDITOR'S COMMENTARY

In addition to Hill, many of the greatest scientific minds have studied intuition, insight, hunches, and precognition. Some have dreamed solutions, or had hunches that turned out to be scientific breakthroughs, and a number of artists and authors have had important premonitions and inspirations.

METHODS USED BY GENIUSES (continued)

Certain artists have used alcohol or narcotics to stimulate their mind, but there are no artificial mind stimulants that are as powerful as the natural mental stimulants.

EDITOR'S COMMENTARY

The editors cite the VH1 series *Behind the Music* to reinforce Hill's point on the dangers of turning to artificial stimulants for creative inspiration.

METHODS USED BY GENIUSES (continued)

Hill advises that sex can be just as addictive as alcohol or drugs. From this he concludes that many people do not succeed until late in life because they never learned any way except through physical expression to channel their sexuality and sexual energy.

THE IMPORTANCE OF LOVE

This last section is focused on the importance of balancing the biological aspect of sexuality with the emotional and spiritual aspect of love. It is Hill's contention that love can be the moderating force that channels sexuality into creativity, motivation, and success.

"When there was evidence available in connection with the lives of men of achievement, it indicated that each one possessed a highly developed sexual nature."

"When driven by these emotions, people become gifted with a superpower for action. Understand this, and you will also understand why it is that transmutation contains the secret of creativity."

CHAPTER 12: THE WORKBOOK

The basic principles of success identified and explained by Hill have not changed in the years since the first edition of *Think and Grow Rich* was published. However, the social climate and what are often called traditional values have gone through a cultural revolution during that time. Because this chapter deals with the ways human sexuality can affect motivation, success, and achievement, and because society's attitudes toward sexuality have changed so dramatically, modern readers often find this to be the most challenging chapter in the book.

When the editors prepared the revised and updated *Think and Grow Rich: The 21st-Century Edition,* this chapter was the only one that was substantially altered from the original text. In all other chapters, the updating was accomplished by adding additional material but no deletions of content were made. However, this chapter, which was originally titled The Mystery of Sex Transmutation, was based on the moral standards of the day as opposed to verifiable research or facts. The conventional wisdom that it presented was based on the opinion about sex and the moral standards common in the 1930s.

Although Napoleon Hill was a very forward thinker, people's lives in the America of 1937 were vastly different from the way people live in the America of the twenty-first century. As Hill was writing *Think and Grow Rich,* America was still deep in the Great Depression, jobs were scarce, the stock market had not recovered, the middle of the country was a dustbowl, soup kitchens were still feeding the hungry, and many men were riding the rails looking for any kind of work or a handout.

As for sex, the average home was a married husband and wife with children, most mothers didn't work outside the home, people could still leave their front doors unlocked at night, children had the run of their neighborhoods, divorce was uncommon, very few people were unconventional enough to openly "live in sin," cursing or using "dirty words" in mixed company just wasn't done, sex education was usually an embarrassing conversation between mothers and daughters or fathers and sons, books that had "good parts" were banned in Boston because they offended the public's morals, love scenes in movies dissolved to skyrockets bursting in the air, and, to quote an old joke, that was back in the days when the air was clean, and sex was dirty.

Because this chapter was influenced by the moral climate of the day, it contains a number of statements that are now considered sexist and which are contradicted by the reality of modern life. It also meant that Napoleon Hill could not be as frank in writing about sexuality as would now be the case. This created passages in the original edition where Hill seemed to be writing all around the issue instead of tackling it head-on. In the light of what is now blasted at us on radio, television, in movies, the Internet, magazines, books, and in advertising, it is hard to imagine there could be anything in Hill's message that would offend the sensibilities of today's readers.

THE KEY POINTS IN THIS CHAPTER

The following is an overview of what Hill wrote in the original edition:

- Sexuality is a natural and normal part of everyone's life.

- The desire for sex tops the list of the ten most powerful stimulants that prompt a person to take action.

- People who are good at influencing others do so by knowing how to transmute their sexuality into charm or charisma.

- You can learn to transmute your sexuality into charisma which can be used to influence others.

- Most creative people have a highly sexual nature.

- You can develop your creativity by learning techniques that will increase the possibility of accessing your creative imagination and Infinite Intelligence.

- Artificial stimulants are not as good as your internal emotional stimulants.

- Many people don't hit their stride until after the age of forty or fifty because they haven't learned they can channel their sexual drive into success.

- Love is the safety valve that can help you control your sexuality.

Most of these concepts are made clear in *Think and Grow Rich: The 21st-Century Edition.* However, there are a couple of issues that should be expanded in this workbook, and the first of these is the concept of sexual transmutation.

Although Hill stated his belief in the theory of sexual transmutation in a number of his books and programs, the version that he included in *Think and Grow Rich* does not explain the process in much detail. When the editors assembled the revised and updated *21st-Century Edition* of the book, they used Hill's statements about his belief in the theory, but they offered no further interpretation or commentary. They approached the subject from the point of view that it was one of those notions from the 1930s that would appeal to only a small portion of the readers, so rather than belabor the point, they decided to just reprint what Hill had written and let the reader choose how to apply it.

Because the purpose of this workbook is to present an examination of the entire Napoleon Hill philosophy, here we will offer further interpretation and explanation. To do so, we have drawn upon some of Hill's later writings on the subject where he was more explicit as to how you might make sexual transmutation a part of your success program.

DOES HILL REALLY MEAN WHAT I THINK HE MEANS?

Today, in an age when large segments of the population accept laissez faire sexuality and live by an as-long-as-they-are-consenting-adults moral standard, when people hear the words *sexual transmutation,* it definitely has an old-fashioned ring to it. Morality has changed so much that many people are taken aback by the notion of doing anything that would inhibit sexual expression. To them, the idea that you would do anything with your urges other than enjoy them is so far out of the modern mainstream, they find it difficult to relate to.

Does Hill really mean that you should repress your sexual urges so you can get ahead and make money?

It may not mesh very well with contemporary theories about sexuality, but the answer to the question is yes.

And can you really take something as visceral as the desire to have sex and turn it into a desire to do something else?

Once again, Hill's answer may not be in line with modern thinking, but his answer is not only "yes you can" but "yes you should."

Hill had a very idealistic and romantic view of sexual relations between a man and woman. To him, sex was more than an act of passion or procreation; it was the manifestation of nature's great creative force.

Sex transmutation is the ability to switch a desire for physical contact into a desire for another kind of expression. It was Napoleon Hill's belief that if you chose to, you could refocus the desire to create in one way, and turn it into a desire to create in another way.

It should be noted that the basis of this concept is by no means limited only to Hill's philosophy. Sigmund Freud also wrote about the same response, calling it sublimation, which he considered a defense mechanism that gives humans a way to let out emotions that otherwise would not be socially acceptable. Certain Hindus and Buddhists practice a technique called Tantra, which is a way to control raw, sexual energy and transform it into a higher, spiritual form of energy.

Although most explanations refer to transforming sexual desire into some more rarified form of expression, in Napoleon Hill's view the point of sexual sublimation doesn't have to be as exalted as a path to spiritual enlightenment. To Hill, turning your sexuality into success and money are also worthwhile goals. To emphasize the point, in one of Hill's books he says channeling sexual energy applies just as much to bricklayers as it does to great painters. Hill says even bricklayers will lay more bricks faster and in straighter rows if they apply sexual energy to the process. In his own case, he was certain that there was a difference between books he had written when he was channeling sexual energy and those written without that extra intensity.

The purpose of transmuting sexual energy is to channel the energy into a dynamic drive that brings success. What is success? It could be creative success, it could be successful self-expression, it could be laying bricks successfully, or it could be transmuting your sexual energy into personal magnetism or charisma.

OKAY, BUT HOW DO YOU ACTUALLY DO IT?

Perhaps the clearest explanation of how you actually transmute sexual energy can be conveyed by the following examples:

- Anyone can sing the words to a blues song. But if the next time you sing that song you are feeling heartsick because the person you love has just left you for someone else, the words will be charged with meaning they didn't have before.

- Your attitude during a sales call you made just before the person you love agreed to meet you at your favorite restaurant is entirely different than what your attitude will be on the sales call you'll make five minutes later.

- If you are frustrated from a lack of love and physical contact, you can channel those inner yearnings into a fierce determination to overcome the roadblocks that have held you back, and you will then succeed where you failed before.

In effect, you can take the sexual emotion—whether it is frustration, loneliness, joy, satisfaction, or any other sexually charged emotion—and use the strength of your feelings to push yourself beyond what you thought was a limitation.

The preceding examples should give you a good feel for the concept of sex transmutation, but it still leaves some unanswered questions about how to use it as a practical technique:

- Do you decide one day that you will take every sexual feeling you have and transmute them all until you accomplish your aim or purpose?

- Do you start with one urge and see if transmuting that one works before you try another?

- Do you do it for a month? Or do you do it for a year?

- Do you do it just when you want something in particular? Or is it something you keep in the back of your mind all the time and you use it whenever it occurs to you?

Napoleon Hill says he came to believe in this theory of sexual transmutation because of what he learned from his research into the lives of the successful men to whom he was introduced by Andrew Carnegie and by studying the great achievers throughout history. He also says he personally used sexual transmutation in his own work.

Unfortunately, he does not explain the specifics of what he learned through his research, and nor does he tell us how often or under what circumstances he used the technique himself.

NOTES & COMMENTS

PUTTING THE THEORY INTO PRACTICE

Although there is not much specific detail about putting the method to use in *Think and Grow Rich,* by going through Hill's books, lectures, and other writings, the editors of this workbook have assembled a visualization exercise targeted at transmuting sexual energy to enhance your sex appeal or charisma.

This exercise is a variation on creative visualization, and like all autosuggestion techniques, the more often you practice it the better the results will be. However, it is unlikely that you will be in a position to go into a deep visualization every time you want to turn on your charisma, so we have included a cue that you can use to give you instant recall of what it feels like to be full of confidence. As part of your visualization, you will tell yourself that by pressing your thumb and middle finger together, it will act as a triggering device that instructs your subconscious to instantly recall what it feels like to be at your best. As simple as that sounds, it is a technique that is widely used by psychiatrists and motivational experts.

In order to educate your subconscious mind about how you want to feel, you should practice the transmutation visualization as often as you can find adequate time to be by yourself and completely relax. Once you have taught yourself the visualization, including the instant recall cue, when the occasion arises that you need an extra boost, you can use the cue to call up your confidence and charisma.

Begin by looking inward and going back in your mind to recall a specific time when you were at your most confident, sexually. Find in your memory one specific time when you were completely satisfied, confident, and content sexually. Using all of your powers of recall and visualization, re-create your feelings just as you felt them then.

In your imagination, bring those feelings forward, making them so real and so vivid that you can actually experience those feelings now, and remember how it feels in every muscle and sinew of your body. It is that sense of confidence, satisfaction, and of being in control that you want to project outward in everything you do.

Let that remembered feeling flow through your body, influencing the way you stand, the way you walk, the way you talk, the way you shake hands, the way you make eye contact, the way you focus your attention, and in every way you interact with other people it is there, just below the surface, present in everything you do.

In the future, whenever you want to recall this feeling and be at your most confident and project your most charismatic personality, all you have to do is press your thumb and middle finger together, and you will immediately feel the confidence, satisfaction, and sense of control filling your body and mind, and radiating outward from you.

This does not mean that you try to be openly flirtatious or seductive. If you are charismatic, you do not have to "come on" to another person in order for that person to pick up on your confidence and personal magnetism. You don't even have to try. Just by knowing in the back of your mind what it feels like when you are at your most powerful and persuasive, you give off subtle signals. Keeping the picture of yourself at your most powerful and persuasive in the back of your mind will make you *feel* powerful and persuasive. And when you feel that confidence inside, it radiates from you.

CHARISMA AND A PLEASING PERSONALITY

In most of his works Napoleon Hill wrote about the subject of charisma as part of his commentary on the importance of developing a pleasing personality if you wish to succeed in any aspect of life. Although having a pleasing personality is listed as one of Hill's seventeen principles of success, and it is the title of a chapter in *Law of Success* as well as at least two of his other books, in *Think and Grow Rich* Hill chose to incorporate the information within other chapters.

"You are what your habits make you."

By reviewing each of the chapters in *Think and Grow Rich: The 21st-Century Edition,* and by drawing upon material from *Law of Success* and other works written by Hill, the editors of this workbook have assembled the following material in order to provide a more focused overview than what appears in the book.

THE ELEMENTS OF A PLEASING PERSONALITY

Below each of the qualities listed, there is space for you to grade yourself and make notes about how that quality relates to your personality.

1. Good showmanship. A showman is someone who appeals to people through their imagination and keeps them interested through curiosity. A good showman is quick to recognize and to capitalize on other people's likes and dislikes at the right psychological moment.

1 2 3 4 5 6 7 8 9 10 _____

_____

_____

2. Harmony with yourself. You cannot have a pleasing personality without first developing harmony and control within your own mind.

1 2 3 4 5 6 7 8 9 10 _____

_____

_____

3. Definiteness of purpose. The procrastinator who drifts through life without a plan or a purpose does not have a very pleasing personality.

1 2 3 4 5 6 7 8 9 10 _____

_____

_____

4. Appropriateness of style and clothing. First impressions are lasting. The person with a pleasing personality dresses in clothing appropriate to the situation.

1 2 3 4 5 6 7 8 9 10_____

_____

_____

5. Posture and carriage of the body. Everyone judges others by their body language: the way they walk and the general posture of their bodies.

1 2 3 4 5 6 7 8 9 10_____

_____

_____

6. Voice. The tone, volume, pitch, and general emotional coloring of a person's voice constitute important factors of a pleasing personality.

1 2 3 4 5 6 7 8 9 10_____

_____

_____

7. Sincerity of purpose. This quality needs little explanation, but having it is essential if you want to gain the confidence of others.

1 2 3 4 5 6 7 8 9 10_____

_____

_____

8. Choice of language. The person with a pleasing personality is comfortable talking in everyday language or speaking formally, and he or she knows which to use when.

1 2 3 4 5 6 7 8 9 10_____

_____

_____

9. Poise. Poise is a quality that comes naturally when you have self-confidence and self-control.

1 2 3 4 5 6 7 8 9 10_____

_____

_____

10. A good sense of humor. Perhaps no other quality is more essential than this.

1 2 3 4 5 6 7 8 9 10_____

_____

_____

11. Unselfishness. Selfishness and a pleasing personality are never found together.

1 2 3 4 5 6 7 8 9 10_____

_____

_____

12. Facial expression. This is an accurate medium for the interpretation of your moods and thoughts. You can have a big smile, a crooked grin, or it may be as subtle as a twinkle in the eye, but you can always tell if it is sincere.

1 2 3 4 5 6 7 8 9 10_____

_____

_____

13. Positive thought. The vibrations of your thoughts are picked up by others. To be pleasing, you must be radiating good feelings and pleasant thoughts.

1 2 3 4 5 6 7 8 9 10_____

_____

_____

14. Enthusiasm. People who lack enthusiasm cannot inspire others. Enthusiasm is also an essential factor in all forms of salesmanship.

1 2 3 4 5 6 7 8 9 10_____

_____

_____

15. A sound body. Poor health does not attract people. You are unlikely to project a pleasing personality without health and vigor.

1 2 3 4 5 6 7 8 9 10_____

_____

_____

16. Imagination. This is one of the most essential factors of a pleasing personality.

1 2 3 4 5 6 7 8 9 10_____

_____

_____

17. Tact. Lack of this quality has cost many people their positions. Lack of tact is usually expressed through insensitivity to others and loose conversation.

1 2 3 4 5 6 7 8 9 10_____

_____

_____

18. Versatility. A general knowledge of the important subjects of current interest, as well as of the deeper problems of life and living, is a quality conducive to a pleasing personality.

1 2 3 4 5 6 7 8 9 10_____

_____

_____

19. The art of being a good listener. Train yourself to listen attentively when other people are speaking.

1 2 3 4 5 6 7 8 9 10 _____

_____

_____

20. The art of forceful speech. Forceful speech can only be acquired by practice. Have something to say worth listening to, then say it with all the enthusiasm at your command.

1 2 3 4 5 6 7 8 9 10 _____

_____

_____

21. Personal magnetism or charisma. It is a manifestation of sexuality, it is the major asset of every great leader, and it is the factor of a pleasing personality that is the hardest to teach. You must discover your own charismatic qualities, then make the most of what you have.

1 2 3 4 5 6 7 8 9 10 _____

_____

_____

THE ELEMENTS OF A NEGATIVE PERSONALITY

Below each of these qualities listed, there is space for you to grade yourself and make notes about how that quality relates to your personality.

1. Disloyalty. There is no substitute for loyalty! And the person who lacks loyalty cannot possibly market personal services effectively.

1 2 3 4 5 6 7 8 9 10 _____

_____

_____

2. Dishonesty. There is no substitute for honesty! It is the keystone to character. Without sound character, no person can market their services effectively.

1 2 3 4 5 6 7 8 9 10_____

_____

_____

3. Greed. A person who is cursed by greed cannot keep it under cover.

1 2 3 4 5 6 7 8 9 10_____

_____

_____

4. Envy and hatred. These qualities make a pleasing personality impossible. Remember that like attracts like.

1 2 3 4 5 6 7 8 9 10_____

_____

_____

5. Jealousy. This is a mild form of insanity. It is fatal to a pleasing personality.

1 2 3 4 5 6 7 8 9 10_____

_____

_____

6. Anger. Whether passive or active in form, this is a quality that arouses antagonism and makes one disliked by others.

1 2 3 4 5 6 7 8 9 10_____

_____

_____

7. Fear. There are six basic fears against which every person must guard. These are negative states of mind that must be eliminated before one can develop a pleasing personality.

1 2 3 4 5 6 7 8 9 10_____

_____

_____

8. Revenge. A vengeful person cannot be pleasing to anyone.

1 2 3 4 5 6 7 8 9 10_____

_____

_____

9. Fault-finding. The person who has the habit of finding fault with others might more profitably spend time looking within for faults.

1 2 3 4 5 6 7 8 9 10_____

_____

_____

10. Gossiping about scandal. People may listen to the scandalmonger, but they will not like the person. And you cannot trust them.

1 2 3 4 5 6 7 8 9 10_____

_____

_____

11. Uncontrolled enthusiasm. Too much enthusiasm is as bad as none.

1 2 3 4 5 6 7 8 9 10_____

_____

_____

12. Excuses. It is better to take responsibility for mistakes you did not make than to develop the habit of trying to place responsibility for these mistakes on others.

1 2 3 4 5 6 7 8 9 10 _____

_____

_____

13. Exaggeration. It is better to understate a truth than to overstate it. Exaggeration causes loss of confidence.

1 2 3 4 5 6 7 8 9 10 _____

_____

_____

14. Egotism. Self-confidence is one of the most desirable and necessary traits, but it must be controlled and directed to definite ends. All forms of self-praise are easily recognized as evidences of inferiority complexes, therefore your motto should be "Deeds, not words."

1 2 3 4 5 6 7 8 9 10 _____

_____

_____

15. Obstinacy and stubbornness. A certain amount of determination and the ability to stand by your opinions is essential, but these qualities should not become a blanket policy.

1 2 3 4 5 6 7 8 9 10 _____

_____

_____

16. Selfishness. A selfish person cannot be trusted.

1 2 3 4 5 6 7 8 9 10 _____

_____

_____

NOTES & COMMENTS
_____
_____
_____
_____
_____
_____
_____
_____
_____
_____
_____
_____
_____
_____
_____
_____
_____
_____
_____
_____
_____

THE GOLDEN RULE AND CHARISMA

The following segment is excerpted and adapted from _Law of Success: The 21st-Century Edition,_ Volume III, Lesson Ten:

Here is a Golden Rule exercise that is guaranteed to improve your character and your personality. Find at least one person each day in whom you see some good quality that is worthy of praise—and praise them for it. Remember, however, that this praise must not be cheap, insincere flattery; it must be genuine. Speak your words of praise with such earnestness that they will impress those to whom you speak.

Then watch what happens. You will have rendered those whom you praise a benefit of great value to them, and you will have gone just one more step in the direction of developing the habit of looking for and finding the good qualities in others.

I cannot overemphasize the far-reaching effects of this habit of praising, openly and enthusiastically, the good qualities in others, for this habit will soon reward you with a feeling of self-respect and manifestation of gratitude from others that will modify your entire personality. Here, again, the law of attraction enters, and those whom you praise will see in you the qualities that you see in them. Your success in the application of this formula will be in exact proportion to your faith in its soundness.

I do not merely believe that it is sound—I know that it is—and the reason I know is that I have used it successfully and I have also taught others how to use it successfully. I promise you that you can use it with equal success.

Furthermore, you can, with the aid of this formula, develop a pleasing personality so quickly that you will surprise all whom know you. The development of such a personality is entirely within your own control, which gives you a tremendous advantage and at the same time places the responsibility on you if you fail to exercise your privilege.

GENIUS AND CREATIVITY

Following the section on sexuality and its connection with charisma and personality, Napoleon Hill turns his attention to sexuality and its connection with creativity. He reminds the reader that, in his philosophy, what some people call the sixth sense is actually your creative imagination at work.

Hill uses the subject of creativity and opening your mind to your creative imagination to introduce the idea that you can learn certain thinking techniques used by geniuses. Hill then offers a very brief description of the technique developed by Dr. Elmer R. Gates.

Because Elmer Gates was such a brilliant thinker but is so little known today, the editors of this workbook have included a more complete explanation of his technique below. In it you will also find that Gates' experiments confirm Hill's theory that exercising the mind can literally increase brain size and, therefore, increases your capacity for creative thought.

THINKING INSIDE AND OUTSIDE THE BOX

At the beginning of the twentieth century, Elmer Gates (1859–1923) was one of the most famous and successful inventors in America, and he operated the largest private laboratory in the country. Although he invented and patented hundreds of successful devices and processes, he described himself not as an inventor but as a psychologist. In fact, his inventions were almost an afterthought of what he considered his real work. His inventions were an offshoot of his research into how the creative mind worked. In order to study what made his mind creative, he had to think creatively, and when he thought creatively he came up with very successful inventions.

In the early years of his career, the newspapers and the popular press loved writing about Elmer Gates. He was getting so much media exposure, one of the major breakfast cereal companies tried to get him to endorse their products. His research and his methods were so groundbreaking the press couldn't get enough of him, and in almost every article the writer just had to tell about Gates' isolation chamber. How could you go wrong writing about a guy who locked himself in an isolation chamber to come up with ideas?

The fact is, as much as the newsmen loved to write about Gates' "ideas chamber," it was only one of a number of experiments he had devised to find the optimum environment to promote creativity in thinking. What Gates was doing was so much more than sitting in a room thinking, but it was also so complex and demanding that few writers even tried to explain it. It was easier to write about idea booths.

ELMER GATES TAUGHT HIMSELF TO BE A GENIUS

Elmer Gates was first and foremost a psychologist, and while sitting in his isolation chamber he was perfecting what he considered to be an improved scientific method for discovering new information about a given subject. He called his method *psychurgy,* meaning the art of mind-using. The basic premise is that the mind and the thinking process are directly related to the physical brain, and the more brain cells that you can bring to work on a particular problem, the better and more creative the ideas will be that come to your mind. In simple terms, the mind-brain is like a muscle that gets bigger and works better with exercise.

It was known to science that certain kinds of learning happen in certain areas of the brain. Gates wanted to prove that by increasing a certain kind of learning, it would physically alter the corresponding part of the brain. Using animal experiments similar to those that would later be made famous by B. F. Skinner, and by inventing new devices and techniques to analyze the results of the learning experiments, Gates was able to prove that, as he predicted, the neural structure of that particular part of the brain had been increased. In short, more information makes more brain-mass, and more brain-mass gives the mind more capacity with which to create.

The principle technique that Elmer Gates used to expand the mind's capacity he dubbed *psychotaxis: psycho* meaning *of the mind,* and *taxis* meaning *arrangement or order.* It is a way to use each of the senses to systematically break down and classify a particular object or concept so that you can then reassemble in your mind a complete image of the thing.

First Gates would use each of his senses to examine every piece of data about the subject at hand. He would look at it, he would smell it, he would taste it, he would listen to it, and he would feel it.

Then he would re-create in absolute detail each of those sensations in his mind. He would repeat the process over and over, until he knew and could instantly recall all that his senses could tell him about the subject.

Next, in his mind, he would apply the same degree of focused learning and review to every verifiable fact about the subject that he could confirm. No opinion or theories—just proven facts.

Finally, and again in his mind, he would work his way through a series of mental exercises that he designed to intellectually experience every aspect and facet of the subject.

By repeating this process over and over it stimulated specific areas of the brain, and just as happened with the experimental animals, the increased neural structure in turn increased his creativity.

IT TOOK 33 YEARS TO LEARN JUST ONE CATEGORY

This was not just learning or memorizing or recalling or analyzing or reminiscing or introspection, but it was all of that and much more. The psychotaxis review of even a minor concept would take Gates months of daily effort to complete. It took Elmer Gates thirty-three years to complete his psychotaxis review of the arts and sciences. It took him twelve years to organize the feelings, emotions, and subconscious processes. Then it took him seven years to review the industrial arts.

One way to visualize what he was doing is to think of him first selecting a subject, finding the part of the brain that takes in information about that subject, then constantly putting facts into that part of the brain and taking them out to examine them over and over. It would be similar to going in and out of a warehouse where you knew every nook and cranny and exactly where to find what you want.

When Gates posed a question to himself, it was immediately connected with a vast complex of conscious and unconscious bits of information about that subject. With so many bits of information looking for ways to fit together, it is little wonder that when he decided to "think" about something, the results were often brilliant and original ideas that could be turned into commercially successful inventions.

The version of the Gates method presented here is far too sketchy for you to put into practice and, in truth, how Gates actually used his mind is probably too demanding for most readers to even attempt. However, if you would like to learn more, we suggest that you visit the Web site at http://www.elmergates.com.

There you will find more biographical information, links to reprints of all Elmer Gates' books, lectures, papers, and articles, and reference to the biography *Elmer Gates and the Art of Mind-Using*, written by his son Donald Edson Gates.

THE IMPORTANCE OF LOVE

Napoleon Hill closes this chapter with a rather long dissertation on success after forty, how wisdom comes with age, and the importance of love as a moderating influence. This overly romantic section seems a little out of place until you take into account the circumstances in which it was written.

At the time Hill wrote *Think and Grow Rich* he was fifty-four years of age and had been married to his second wife, Rosa Lee, for only a few months. He had been pushing himself and his new bride to finish this latest book and he was writing day and night, as Rosa Lee was editing and typing the manuscript.

So if this section seems a little overboard in the hearts-and-flowers department, it's just Napoleon Hill being his usual irrepressible self. Never one to do things in half-measures, Hill was completely smitten by his new bride, and even though he was well beyond middle-age by the standards of the day, he was full of enthusiasm and confidence, so he did what he always did: he wrote about how, even at fifty-four, you can find new love, new hope, and new worlds to conquer.

THE SUBCONSCIOUS MIND

13

CHAPTER 13: OVERVIEW AND ANALYSIS

THE CONNECTING LINK

This chapter opens with a recap of what has been established about the subconscious in previous chapters:

- Your subconscious mind receives the same information that your conscious mind receives, but it does not evaluate the information; it just stores it.

- Through autosuggestion you can burn your aim or desire into your subconscious.

- Your subconscious mind will help turn your desire into a reality by opening a connection to Infinite Intelligence, which may provide you with hunches, flashes of insight, and inspiration.

HOW TO ENERGIZE YOUR SUBCONSCIOUS

The subconscious can turn desires into reality, but for it to happen you must believe it is possible and that you have the right stuff to do it.

"Every day all kinds of thought impulses are reaching your subconscious mind without your knowledge. Some of these impulses are negative, some are positive. Right now you should be specifically trying to shut off the flow of nega-tive impulses, and actively working to influence your subconscious mind through positive impulses."

EDITOR'S COMMENTARY

Your subconscious acts as both the connection to Infinite Intelligence and as a storehouse of all the information you have ever received.

Hypnosis is used in therapy to unlock repressed memories, and the police use it to help victims and witnesses recall details.

When planting an idea in your subconscious, strong emotion creates an impact similar to a traumatic experience and your planted idea will be burned deep into your subconscious.

When you try to come up with a creative idea, it reawakens bits and pieces of forgotten information stored in your subconscious, and the chain reaction of old information sparked by new ideas can produce sudden flashes of creativity or insight.

You can make yourself "money-conscious" by burning your aim or purpose deep into your subconscious mind so that it will become your natural habit to be conscious of your aim or purpose in every aspect of your life.

HOW TO ENERGIZE YOUR SUBCONSCIOUS (continued)

Because your subconscious is always working, you must focus on giving it positive thoughts to work with. If you don't, then just like a garden that gets overgrown with weeds, your subconscious mind will pick up negatives because nothing else is available.

MAKE YOUR POSITIVE EMOTIONS WORK FOR YOU

The subconscious responds to emotion more than to reason or logic. Hill lists the seven most powerful positive emotions and the seven most destructive negative emotions. One or the other must dominate, and it is up to you to train yourself by working with the positive emotions so that they become your habit.

EDITOR'S COMMENTARY

The editors explain the difficulty of keeping negativity from infecting your mind, and they introduce the concept of repeating creative affir-mations as a way to combat negativity by imprinting positive concepts into your subconscious mind. The editors offer six rules to follow when writing a positive affirmation.

THE SECRET OF EFFECTIVE PRAYER

Hill draws the comparison between prayer and the process of burning your aim or purpose into your subconscious. He cites the way in which radio signals are broadcast to illustrate how desire is sent to Infinite Intelligence.

Hill concludes the chapter by reiterating the need to inject emotion into your desire and passion into your prayer if you want it to transmit from the mind of man to Infinite Intelligence.

CHAPTER 13: THE WORKBOOK

Readers may find it curious that Napoleon Hill chose to include this chapter about the subconscious mind and place it this far into the book when the subject matter is so closely related to the material presented earlier in chapter 5, Autosuggestion. Although it may seem more logical to have presented this material all in one place as a part of chapter 5, it is likely that Hill was simply following his own advice that an idea has to be repeated over and over in order for it to become embedded in the subconscious.

To put Hill's success system to work in your life it is imperative that you understand and accept the theory of autosuggestion and that you understand and accept the concept of the subconscious mind. The more often you hear or read about a new or unusual idea, the more accepting you will become of that idea. In effect, by going over these concepts often, and spacing the references throughout the book, Napoleon Hill is actually using the technique of autosuggestion to influence your subconscious to accept the theories that underlie autosuggestion and the subconscious.

"It is your responsibility to make sure it is positive emotions that constitute the dominating influence of your mind.

Form the habit of applying and using positive emotions, and eventually they will dominate your mind so completely that the negatives cannot enter it."

NOTES & COMMENTS

WORKING WITH YOUR SUBCONSCIOUS MIND

Following is an overview of everything you have learned about the subconscious, presented in point form for quick reference:

- The human body consists of billions of living, intelligent, individual cells that carry on the work of building and maintaining your body.

- Every movement of the human body is controlled by either the conscious mind or the subconscious mind. Not a muscle can be moved until an order to do so has been sent out by one or the other of these two sections of the mind.

- The conscious mind receives outside information through the five senses: sight, hearing, touch, taste, and smell.

- The subconscious mind also receives the same information through those five senses.

- Your subconscious mind does not judge whether the information it receives is good or bad, right or wrong; it just takes in everything and stores it as raw data.

- If the information the subconscious receives is in the form of an order or a direction, the subconscious will not question but will try to carry out the order or follow the direction given.

- You can give your subconscious orders or directions by using the method of autosuggestion, which is the process of intentionally planting an idea in your subconscious through repetition.

- The stronger the emotion you feel toward the idea that you want to plant in your subconscious, the stronger the impression it will make on your subconscious.

- The subconscious is your internal storehouse of ideas and information, and it is also your access to ideas from Infinite Intelligence that exist outside your normal thinking.

- As your internal storehouse of ideas and information, when an idea is planted in your subconscious it connects with other thoughts, ideas, and bits of forgotten information, and you fit them together in your mind to form new ideas or solutions.

- As your access to Infinite Intelligence, when an idea is planted in your subconscious, sometimes the pull of the idea is so strong that it attracts ideas coming from outside your own subconscious mind. These ideas come from what Hill calls Infinite Intelligence, and these are the ideas that flash into your creative imagination as hunches, intuitions, sudden insights, and foreknowledge.

- Your subconscious is going to work whether or not you want it to. It is constantly receiving information and it is constantly processing that information, even when you are asleep.

- If you don't intentionally put your subconscious to work for you by planting what you want it to concentrate on, you can be sure that other thoughts and ideas that you don't want will find their way in.

The editors of this workbook recognize that although Napoleon Hill has gone to great lengths to explain the capabilities of the subconscious mind, some readers will still have reservations about attempting the techniques. It's not that these readers don't believe they have a subconscious mind, it's just that even if they understand it intellectually, it is still an intangible. They would feel much more comfortable working with it if they could see proof that it exists. The following will convince you that your subconscious does in fact exist.

WHERE IS YOUR MIND?

Although the mind is not an organ or a muscle or any other specific part of the body, when we refer to the mind what we generally mean is some combination of the central nervous system and the autonomic nervous system.

WHAT IS THE CENTRAL NERVOUS SYSTEM?

The central nervous system is the way in which you consciously control your body. It includes your brain and your spinal cord.

WHAT IS THE AUTONOMIC NERVOUS SYSTEM?

The autonomic nervous system operates on a subconscious level and is the system that controls such things as breathing, digestion, heart rate, and other bodily activities that you don't have to think about.

WHAT IS THE SUBCONSCIOUS MIND?

As Napoleon Hill uses the term, it means the activity that goes on in your mind that is below the level of consciousness. It is a sort of inner mind, like a mind inside your mind.

As you work with autosuggestion and other techniques, it may be helpful to establish your own mental image of what you think your subconscious mind is like. Perhaps it's a large warehouse with shelf upon shelf of stored information, or maybe you'd prefer some kind of synapse-zapping supercomputer, or, to go in another direction, maybe it's a dusty old ornate book filled with handwritten entries of everything you know.

WHAT DO YOU KNOW ABOUT YOUR SUBCONSIOUS MIND?

Let's begin with what you know about your subconscious from your own experience. Start with the fact that you do not have to think about breathing, keeping your heart beating, or making your stomach digest food. These and many other body functions are controlled by the autonomic nervous system, which works without any conscious thought on your part. It doesn't matter if you are wide awake or knocked unconscious, these processes just continue on doing what they do. They are not under your conscious control, so you don't have to think about doing them. They just happen.

Next, for most people reading this, you don't have to consciously think about sitting up, holding this book, or getting up and walking across the room. There was a time when you did have to think about doing those things, but once you mastered each skill it became routine and now you just do it subconsciously. The same is true with more complicated actions such as typing, playing the piano, driving a car, and other job functions that are now done by rote. You don't have to consciously think about performing each function because your subconscious takes care of that for you.

Now take it a step further. Even if you have turned over some activity to your subconscious, you can still use your conscious mind to improve such skills as your typing or piano-playing simply by bringing them back into your conscious mind and modifying the way you do it, or by practicing until you can perform the skill better.

It is also possible, with proper training, to affect the subconscious activities controlled by your autonomic nervous system. By using biofeedback you can learn to affect your blood pressure, raise or lower your body temperature, slow your breathing, and even change the rate at which your heart beats.

To recap, we know that your subconscious mind plays a role in your everyday life. Although you may not have thought of it in this way, you actually have a good deal of personal experience using your subconscious mind. You do things all the time that you don't consciously think about. This means that even though you may have had reservations about the subconscious, you had been relying on it anyway.

YOU CAN COMMUNICATE WITH YOUR SUBCONSCIOUS

Explanations and examples can go a long way toward making a convincing argument, but nothing is as convincing as seeing it for yourself. The following will let you do just that.

SUBCONSCIOUS MOVEMENTS

This method involves the scientific principle known as the ideomotor response. This response is your body's unconscious physical reaction to your thoughts. Ideomotor responses are physical cues and movements that happen subconsciously. They can be measured by EEG, PET, and MRI scans, but they are so tiny that you are not aware you are making them.

For our purposes here, the important information in the preceding paragraph is to know that your subconscious mind can control muscular movements.

If your subconscious can control muscular movements, then it is possible that if you set up a special code, your subconscious could send you messages by twitching certain muscles.

It's not only a possibility, but it really works!

SENDING SIGNALS

Here is how you can actually see your subconscious talking to you. Your subconscious may not be able to speak out loud, but it can send you signals. Your subconscious can cause small movements in certain muscle groups. These movements are very tiny, but they are enough to create quite pronounced movement in the right thing. The right thing is a pendulum.

If you take something like a key or a ring, tie it to the end of a piece of thread or light string, and holding it between your thumb and forefinger let it dangle like a pendulum, your subconscious can make it move enough that it can send you signals.

In order to succeed with this method, you must make your subconscious mind aware that it is able to move the muscles that will make the pendulum move. That's it. You've done it. The moment you finished reading the preceding sentence, your subconscious had been informed that it can make the pendulum move. That's all there is to it.

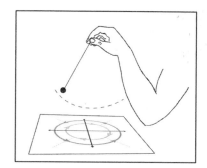

You don't need to be concerned that you have to learn something special to make it work. You just learned it. And there is no need to believe in something special either. This is not a question of faith. The ideomotor response is a scientific fact that has been known and studied since French scientist Michel Eugene Chevreul published a paper on it in 1833. He called it "the body's answer to a thought or an idea."

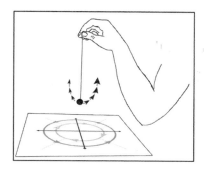

Once your subconscious has been made aware that it has this ability, then it remains only to identify what the movements are that it can make and what each movement will mean. On the right side of this page are some illustrations that will save us a thousand words. As you can see, there are four drawings of a person holding a pendulum over what looks somewhat like a compass. In the first drawing the pendulum is moving vertically (as in a north–south direction), in the second drawing it is moving horizontally (as in an east–west direction), in the third the pendulum is rotating in a clockwise direction, and in the fourth it is rotating counterclockwise. Those are the four different movements that your subconscious mind, working through ideomotor response, can cause the pendulum to make.

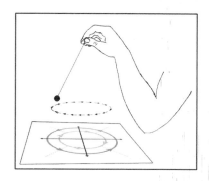

Now that you know your subconscious can make the pendulum move in four different directions, your subconscious can use those movements to send you four different signals. If you were to ask your subconscious a question, it could give you an answer by making the pendulum move in a way that would send you a signal.

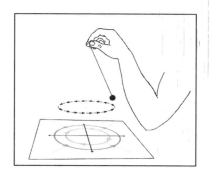

The reason we have gone through all of this in such a methodical, step-by-step explanation is so that by reading this your subconscious mind has been exposed to all the information it needs, but we have

NOTES & COMMENTS

avoided dictating what your actions should be. We have not given it any preconceived instructions about which way the pendulum should move to signal any of the four possible answers.

THE FINAL PREPARATIONS

The next step in the process is to decide what each of the movements means, and it will be most convincing if we do not make the choice, and you do not consciously make the choice, but you leave it up to your subconscious to tell you what each of the movements means.

To do this we are now going to list the four possible answers, but we wish to make it emphatically clear that there is no preconceived significance to the order of the possible answers. Specifically, the order of this list is not intended to coincide with the order of the previous list of four possible movements. It is possible that your subconscious may choose that order if it wishes, but it will be entirely up to your subconscious to select which movement indicates which answer.

The four possible answers are:

1. Yes
2. No
3. I don't know
4. I don't wish to answer

Although you could continue reading and come back to this exercise later, we strongly recommend that you stop and test it for yourself right now. For one thing, it will certainly satisfy any questions you may have about the existence of the subconscious, and secondly, if you do it now, before reading further, there is less chance that the result might be influenced, and the less chance there is of corruption, the greater the chance that you will be convinced.

The first step is to create your pendulum. There is nothing mystical, magical, or spiritual about this device, and there is nothing special about what you use to make it. All you will need is a piece of thread, string, or a thin necklace or chain, and some kind of weight to attach to the end. The weight can be anything that is easy to attach, such as a ring, a key, a medallion, or even a couple of paperclips will do if they are heavy enough to keep the thread taut when hanging freely.

At the back of this workbook you will find an illustration that looks something like a compass. There is nothing mystical, magical, or spiritual about this drawing either. It's really nothing more than a couple of circles and two lines that cross at the centre. We have provided you with one that can be easily removed from this book and placed on a flat surface, because some people find that suspending the pendulum over an illustration that indicates possible directions makes it work faster. We assure you that just as there is nothing special about the pendulum, there is nothing special about this illustration. Your subconscious will make the pendulum move and it won't matter whether you use the illustration.

DO IT NOW AND CONVINCE YOURSELF

Rest your elbow gently on a table or desk, with the pendulum held between your thumb and forefinger. The pendulum is positioned over the centre of the circle.

You are going to give your subconscious mind what amounts to a short training session. Basically, you are just reminding your subconscious that it can move the pendulum through the ideomotor response, and you are giving yourself a sense of what it feels like when the pendulum swings.

- We are going to begin this part of the exercise by again mentioning the possible movements, but to make sure that the editors aren't influencing your subconscious to follow our set pattern, this time we will change the order of the possible movements. We will begin with the horizontal movement. You can remind yourself of the possible movements by thinking it to yourself in your mind, or you can speak out loud. Some people find that speaking the words aloud makes a stronger impression.

- As you tell your subconscious that it is able to move the pendulum horizontally, you intentionally swing the pendulum very gently left to right a couple of times, then stop it from swinging.

- Next, tell your subconscious it is possible to move it vertically, and you swing it vertically up and down a few times to get the feel of it, then stop it from swinging.

- Tell your subconscious it is possible to move the pendulum in a counterclockwise circle, and move it in the counterclockwise circle, then stop it from moving.

- Tell your subconscious it is possible to move it around in a clockwise circle, and move it in the circle, then stop it from moving.

- Now that you have stopped the pendulum from swinging, let it rest while suspended over the centre of the circle. From now on you will not move the pendulum. You will just hold the thread still, and the pendulum will move itself.

- It is also important that you avoid trying to use your conscious mind to influence the direction of movement. Just let your subconscious choose what to do on its own. Otherwise you will never be confident that it was your subconscious creating the movement.

- One final point before starting the process. The main reason for teaching you this technique is to provide you with concrete evidence of the existence of your subconscious. To increase your confidence we have taken steps to avoid giving information that might appear to influence the outcome of the exercise. To make it even more convincing, you might want to have another person assist you with the exercise. Having an assistant will allow you to close your eyes or turn your head away when you ask your subconscious to select the movements. That way, when your assistant tells you which movement was selected, it will be a complete surprise to you and, again, proof-positive that it is your subconscious mind at work.

LETTING YOUR SUBCONSCIOUS CHOOSE

Now you are ready to proceed with the exercise and establish which movements your unconscious mind wants to use to indicate the four responses. We will begin with the response *yes*. The first step is to decide the best way for you to ask your subconscious which movement it wants to use to signify the answer *yes*.

- For some people it requires nothing more than just thinking of *yes*, turning the word over in their mind a few times, and the pendulum will begin to move in one of the four possible directions.

- Rather than just thinking the words to yourself, sometimes speaking the words aloud will make the pendulum react faster.

- Some people feel the need to literally plot out a question that they will pose in their mind, such as: "I am asking my subconscious to select one of the four possible movements to signify the answer *yes* in response to my questions."

- Some people use visualization to picture what the idea of *yes* means to them, and they create a visual symbol for *yes*, such as a person nodding their head, a hand holding a red felt-tipped marker and writing a checkmark over and over, or two hands giving the thumbs-up signal.

- It may also help to exaggerate the idea of *yes*. Make it huge in your mind, like a giant billboard flashing *YES . . . YES . . . YES.*

NOTES & COMMENTS

Once the pendulum begins to move (and once it is working it will do so very clearly), and you have established the movement that will signal *yes,* you then do the same for each of the other three responses. You ask your subconscious to select the movement it wishes to use to signify *no,* then ask which movement it will use to indicate *I don't know,* and finally ask it to show you the movement indicating *I don't want to answer.* Once your subconscious has selected the movement for each answer, it is very likely that it will maintain the same choices in any future sessions.

As stated earlier, our purpose in teaching this technique is to overcome any skepticism you might have about the subconscious mind. But as most readers will have deduced, Chevreul's pendulum method has other uses. It is primarily a diagnostic technique used by many psychiatrists and therapists to help patients discover the root causes of phobias, fixations, compulsions, and other emotional difficulties.

Because your subconscious mind is like a storehouse of everything you ever learned or experienced, and because, as you now know, your subconscious mind can communicate with you by answering certain kinds of questions, if you ask your subconscious a carefully planned set of questions, you can learn a great deal about specific events that had a significant impact on your development.

Although the psychological application of the ideomotor response is fascinating, it is not the focus of *Think and Grow Rich,* and having used it to make our point about the subconscious, this workbook will return to more directly related material. However, if you wish to investigate further, we suggest that you go on the Internet and search *ideomotor response,* which will produce a wealth of references and related Web sites. The editors also suggest that you look up author and clinical psychologist Leslie M. LeCron and author David Cheek, M.D., both of whom have written extensively about the use of the technique.

MAKE YOUR POSITIVE EMOTIONS WORK FOR YOU

Now that you have seen proof that your subconscious mind can actually affect things in the real world, you should find it easier to accept that if you burn an idea into your subconscious mind, your subconscious will use that idea to change how you think and, therefore, what you do.

The next lesson for you to learn is the best way to burn an idea into your subconscious mind. The subconscious responds to emotion more than to logic. You must inject emotion and feeling into your desire if you want it to stick.

Following are the seven most powerful positive emotions that you should tap into when you are trying to burn your desire into your subconscious. Remember, it's the emotion that makes your desire more than just a wish or a daydream.

THE SEVEN POSITIVE EMOTIONS

A negative emotion and a positive emotion cannot occupy your mind at the same time. One must dominate, and it is up to you to train yourself by working with the positive emotions so often that they become your habit. In the following list of positive emotions, after each emotion listed there is space for you to write your own aim or purpose and a brief statement of how the emotion relates to it.

1. **THE EMOTION OF DESIRE:** In Napoleon Hill's philosophy, an aim or purpose is something you set your sights on. What is the desire behind your objective? What is it that you really desire—is it money, fame, independence, glory, acceptance, dominance, revenge, admiration —or is there another secret desire that is really behind what you say is the reason you want something?

2. **THE EMOTION OF FAITH:** In Napoleon Hill's philosophy, faith is not reliance on a divine outside force. Faith is unwavering belief that you are capable of accomplishing your aim or purpose. Faith is principle, a commitment; it's something you hold to be real and true. Why and how can you bring your faith to your aim or purpose?

_____

_____

_____

3. **THE EMOTION OF LOVE:** The emotion of love can be a deep affectionate concern for a person or persons, such as your mate or your family, or you can love an object such as your home, or a painting, or you can love an ideal such as liberty, mankind, or your country. It often manifests as a joyous compulsion to do something for someone. How can your love for someone or something be used to motivate you to accomplish your aim or purpose?

_____

_____

_____

5. **THE EMOTION OF ROMANCE:** The emotion of romance is a passionate spiritual connection between two people that is part love and part sexual attraction. Unlike love, which may be aesthetic, or idealized, romance is a state of ecstasy directed toward the one you love. Unlike sexuality, which is a biological drive, romance is an emotional yearning that is idealistic, ardent, and passionate. How does the emotion of romance fit into your aim or purpose?

_____

_____

_____

4. **THE EMOTION OF SEX:** Traditionally, much of man's sexuality was involved with the admiration earned from being the provider and protector of his family. Similarly, woman's sexuality involved attracting the best mate as provider, and with nurturing her children. In western society the push toward equality of the sexes has altered the traditional roles and

the role that sex plays as a motivator to succeed. Does your sexuality still make you want to succeed so you will be admired? Do you think you will be more sexually attractive if you are a success? Can you use your sexual signals to get what you want? Does sex still make you want to impress your mate by triumphing over your rivals? How can your desire for sexual fulfillment be redirected toward trying to accomplish something?

_____

_____

_____

6. **THE EMOTION OF ENTHUSIASM:** The emotion of enthusiasm is not the act of pretending to be excited about something. Real enthusiasm starts with a sincere interest in something that turns into such a powerful desire to share your fascination and pleasure in it, that your appreciation for its value or importance becomes contagious. What is it about your aim or purpose you believe in so much that you can "sell" it to somebody without even trying?

_____

_____

_____

7. **THE EMOTION OF HOPE:** The emotion of hope is the feeling that what you desire can happen; that it is a possibility. It is confidence that your aim or purpose will work out for the best. It is the belief that you have good reason for feeling the way you do. Does your aim or purpose give you hope? Does it offer hope to others? Does your aim or purpose serve a greater purpose? Can this be your salvation? Does it benefit the greater good?

_____

_____

_____

There are other positive emotions, but these are the ones most commonly used in creative effort. Master these seven positive emotions and they will help you to develop a "money-consciousness" by filling your mind with positive emotions.

THE SEVEN MAJOR NEGATIVE EMOTIONS

1. The emotion of fear
2. The emotion of jealousy
3. The emotion of hatred
4. The emotion of revenge
5. The emotion of greed
6. The emotion of superstition
7. The emotion of anger

In reading the preceding list it should be very clear why you must avoid feeling these emotions when you are trying to plant an aim or purpose in your subconscious.

It is a basic psychological truth that you cannot hold a positive and a negative in your mind at the same time. One has to dominate. Any one of the emotions on the list is such a powerful negative force that it would overwhelm your positive aim or purpose.

It is your responsibility to make sure that positive emotions constitute the dominating influence of your mind. That is where the law of habit will help you. Form the habit of applying and using the positive emotions. Eventually they will dominate your mind so completely that the negatives cannot enter it.

THE CHAIN OF NEGATIVES

The following is adapted from *Law of Success: The 21st-Century Edition*, Volume Two, Lesson Seven, Enthusiasm:

> If you fill your mind with fear, hatred, revenge, jealousy, superstition, selfishness, and greed, your subconscious mind will not germinate the seed of your aim or purpose, nor will Infinite Intelligence translate it into physical reality. These negative, destructive thoughts will choke out the seed of your definite aim or purpose.

One of the most interesting aspects of the human mind is that the thoughts, ideas, information, and experiences it receives are stored together in related groups. The negative impressions are stored away, all in one portion of the brain, while the positive impressions are stored in another portion. When one of these impressions (or past experiences) is called into the conscious mind, there is a tendency to recall with it all other thoughts and memories of a similar nature, just as the raising of one link of a chain brings up other links with it.

Take the feeling of fear, for example. The moment you permit a single emotion that is related to fear to reach your conscious mind, it starts dredging up all of the other things that make you fearful. Like attracts like, even when it is negative. Every thought has a tendency to draw to it other thoughts of a similar nature.

A feeling of courage cannot claim the attention of your mind while a feeling of fear is there. One or the other must dominate. The negative power of fear will trump the positive power of your desire to be courageous. This principle applies to and controls every sense impression that is lodged in the human mind.

THE HARDER YOU TRY, THE MORE YOU FAIL

In hypnotherapy the susceptibility of the subconscious to negative emotions is known as the law of reversed effect. This law states that if you force your willpower to overcome an idea that you have built up in your imagination, it can backfire because the subconscious becomes obsessed with defending its established idea. When there are conflicting desires, something vividly imagined (such as a severe fear or phobia) will always overpower your logical but less emotional

NOTES & COMMENTS

willpower. The point here is that if you want to overcome one of those negative emotions, you better be prepared to make your aim or purpose even more emotional.

The following explanation of the law of reversed effect provides a more detailed explanation than what is offered in the book.

THE LAW OF REVERSED EFFECT

The law of reversed effect states that whenever there is a conflict between imagination and willpower, the imagination wins.

The example often used to illustrate this concept is as follows: If you take a sturdy six-inch by six-inch beam that is twelve feet long and place it on the ground, you will be able to easily walk along the beam without falling off. Raise the beam a foot off the ground, and you can probably still walk the beam without much problem. But raise that beam thirty feet off the ground, and despite the fact that you know you can walk a six-inch beam, you will not be able to do it because your subconscious already harbors a built-in imagined fear that is greater than your willpower to walk the beam.

Another aspect of the law of reversed effect is that when you attempt to plant what you consider to be a positive idea, if the subconscious already harbors a negative, trying to force the new idea has the reverse effect and the negative becomes even more firmly planted. That is because, when you try to force something on your subconscious, the subconscious becomes obsessed with defending its already established idea. In effect, it digs in its heels. The harder you "try" to do something, the more the subconscious resists and the more difficult it becomes.

In *Think and Grow Rich: The 21st-Century Edition,* the explanation of the negative connotation of the word "try" leads into the subject of creating positive affirmations. In this workbook, positive affirmations are already covered in great detail in chapter 5, Autosuggestion.

THE SECRET OF EFFECTIVE PRAYER

When Andrew Carnegie gave Napoleon Hill the task of formalizing his philosophy of personal achievement, he advised Hill to make sure that it could be accepted and used by anyone of any religion or creed. Hill took Carnegie's advice so much to heart that a few sentences at the end of this chapter are the only place in *Think and Grow Rich* where he deals directly with a religious concept. Even so, his comments here are about the practice of praying in general and not about the prayers of a particular religion.

Hill begins by drawing a parallel between the practice of appealing to a deity through prayer and the practice of tapping into Infinite Intelligence through autosuggestion. He points out that both in praying for an outcome and in planting a desire in your subconscious, the emotion with which you approach it, and the degree of faith you have that it can actually happen, are crucial to the outcome.

Hill says that if you approach either with fear of failure, the chances are that it is your doubts or fears that will be foremost in your mind, and it will be those doubts or fears that are conveyed most powerfully —not the thought behind the prayer or the statement of your desire.

Whether offering a prayer for a particular outcome, or using autosuggestion to imprint your desire, if you do so with all of your emotion, conviction, and belief that it can happen, you will receive an answer, an idea, a plan, or a solution.

That does not mean you will get a miracle. In fact, you may not even like the answer you get, and nowhere does it say the answer to your prayer will be *yes.* But if it is a *yes,* it won't be the kind of *yes* that suddenly appears in your driveway or your bank account. It will appear in your imagination. Then it will be up to you to make it happen.

Hill then steps away from a parallel to prayer, and uses the concept of sending a radio signal to illustrate the steps in the process.

NOTES & COMMENTS

The most important point to be taken from this is that it is the subconscious mind which translates the desire into terms that Infinite Intelligence can answer. Likewise, it is the subconscious mind that translates the prayer into terms the deity can answer.

The subconscious is at the very heart of things because that is where the emotion is added. A memorized prayer is just words. A self-suggestion is just words. Words, in and of themselves, have no emotion. To be powerful, the words must convey emotion. The emotion of a word happens at a subconscious level.

Hill concludes the chapter by stating that once you understand what the subconscious does, it should be clear why just repeating words has little effect. Without a burning desire and complete faith that what you can conceive and believe you really can achieve, your words are just sounds that vibrate off into emptiness, because without emotion they convey no meaning.

THE
BRAIN

14

CHAPTER 14: OVERVIEW AND ANALYSIS

A BROADCASTING AND RECEIVING STATION FOR THOUGHT

Napoleon Hill refers to his comparison between radio broadcasting and the way in which you communicate with Infinite Intelligence. He says he came up with the analogy when he was working with the famed inventors Dr. Alexander Graham Bell and Dr. Elmer Gates.

Hill recaps the concept that through Infinite Intelligence you receive ideas that appear in your creative imagination as hunches or flashes of insight.

EDITOR'S COMMENTARY

This Commentary presents an eight-point recap of the subconscious mind:

1. The brain is both a broadcaster and a receiver.

2. You can send and receive better under the influence of emotion.

"In the past we have depended too much on our physical senses and have limited our knowledge to the physical things that we could see, touch, weigh, and measure."

"It has been determined that there are from 10 billion to 14 billion nerve cells in the human cerebral cortex, and we know that these are arranged in definite patterns."

3. The thoughts you send are those that you want to burn into your subconscious.

4. The thoughts you receive appear in your creative imagination.

5. Your subconscious mind is both a storehouse of information and the way you connect with Infinite Intelligence.

6. Because everything in the universe is all a part of the same basic energy, the energy of your subconscious mind shares a connection with the energy of other subconscious minds.

7. Under certain circumstances, the energy of an idea that is outside your mind can, through Infinite Intelligence, become a part of your subconscious mind.

8. When such ideas come to you, they flash into your creative imagination as hunches, intuitions, flashes of insight, or inspirations.

THE GREATEST FORCES ARE INTANGIBLE

People may doubt that a connection between minds is possible because it depends on an intangible force that they don't understand. However, there are many intangibles, such as gravity, that we rely on all the time. With the enormous capacity of the human brain, it is foolish to discount a phenomenon just because it is not fully understood.

EDITOR'S COMMENTARY

Although scientific knowledge has advanced much since Hill wrote the book, we still have no better theory than Hill's explanation about how we get hunches or premonitions.

The Commentary explains the work of Einstein, Pribram, and other scientists who have investigated the interconnectedness of all things.

The editors use the example of the folds and bumps in a tablecloth as an illustration of interconnectedness, and offer another example using the fingers on your hand to show that just because you can't see the connection, that doesn't mean it isn't there.

Even if we don't know *how* Infinite Intelligence works, our experience and common sense tells us that it *does* work, so we can use Hill's methods to put it to work for us.

WHAT IS TELEPATHY?

Hill quotes an article that appeared in the *New York Times* about the work being done on extrasensory perception by Dr. J. B. Rhine and his associates at Duke University.

The Editor's Commentary that follows provides background and information about the continuing studies being done by the Rhine Research Institute.

HOW TO JOIN MINDS IN TEAMWORK

Hill ends this chapter by explaining how he and the members of his staff have regular meetings to blend their minds together to come up with solutions to business problems. Hill notes that this is a practical application of the Master Mind.

CHAPTER 14: THE WORKBOOK

YOUR BRAIN AND WHAT IT DOES

The human brain is the most complex organ in the human body. It weighs approximately three pounds and looks somewhat like the two halves of a walnut joined in the middle. The two halves are called hemispheres, and on the surface they appear to be made of convoluted gray matter. The connection between the two halves is made up of millions of fibers and is called the corpus callosum.

The brain contains over one hundred billion neurons or nerve cells. Each neuron is connected to thousands of neural networks that are similar to electrical circuits. It sends and receives electrical and chemical signals throughout the body, which is how it controls both the central nervous system (which consciously directs behavior and

"It is inconceivable to me that such a network of intricate machinery should be in existence for the sole purpose of carrying on the physical functions connected with the growth and maintenance of the physical body."

NOTES & COMMENTS

action) and the autonomic nervous system (which controls such things as breathing, heart rate, and digestion).

The brain also has a central role in higher mental activity such as thinking, memory, language, conceptualizing, reasoning, creativity, and problem-solving. It is these activities that are the focus of this chapter of the workbook, and they are dealt with at length following this description of the brain.

The two halves of the brain communicate with the nervous system in a way that the left hemisphere of the brain controls the right side of the body, and the right hemisphere controls the left. If you know someone who has had a stroke or damage to one side of the brain, you have probably observed that it is the opposite side of the body that shows the effects the most.

LEFT BRAIN, RIGHT BRAIN

Beginning in the 1960s, a team of scientists at Caltech conducted a project called the split-brain study. It began with a patient who suffered from severe epileptic seizures. To relieve the seizures, neurosurgeons Joseph Bogen and Philip Vogel performed the first operation that severed a human corpus callosum, thereby separating the two hemispheres of the patient's brain. The surgery alleviated the seizures, but it produced an extraordinary result. They found that, when separated, the two sides of the brain could no longer communicate with each other, but the patient was still able to function even though he then had what amounted to two minds operating inside one person.

Following the surgery, a second team, led by psychobiologist Roger W. Sperry along with his students Michael Gazzaniga, Jerre Levy, and Colwyn Trevarthen, began working with this patient. The results of their studies with this patient, as well as a number of other patients who later received the split-brain surgery, has led to knowledge that revolutionized our understanding of how the brain works.

They found that in the healthy human brain, each side of the brain specialized in different modes of thinking. It is as though inside our heads we have two halves of a brain, and each half tends to handle information in a different way, so that, in effect, we have two ways of knowing and understanding.

Although the two sides of the brain appear to be almost mirror images, since the 1850s science has identified the left side of the brain as the dominant major hemisphere because that is where the functions of language and speech are centered. Until the split-brain studies, it was assumed that the left was dominant because the right side was not as evolved or developed. Now we know it's not that the right isn't as advanced as the left, it is simply that it deals differently with the information it receives.

THE ANALYTICAL LEFT OR THE INTUITIVE RIGHT

We have said that the two sides of the brain operate in a way that gives us two ways of knowing things. The popular but overly simplified explanation is to think of the left side of your brain as being the intellectual and thinking side, and the right side as the intuitive and feeling side. That is misleading because there are many activities that could be handled by either side; it's just that one side is either faster at it or likes doing it better than the other side does. The fact is that both sides of the brain have some role to play in almost all functions.

Under normal circumstances, both sides work together. Tasks are often divided between the two halves, with each handling the part that it is best suited to. However, the left side, being the dominant side, will often try to take over to get things organized, which can tend to limit your creativity. And sometimes we limit our options by consciously making the decision to use one side or the other out of habit, not out of which is best suited.

THE TENDENCIES OF THE TWO SIDES OF THE HUMAN BRAIN

The left-hemisphere way of knowing is:

- to verbalize
- to see things in words or numbers
- to interpret literally
- to plot and plan how things come out
- to examine and analyze and see details
- to deal with things in order, one at a time
- to be objective and rational
- to come to logical conclusions

The right-hemisphere way of knowing is:

- to visualize
- to see things in images or metaphors
- to interpret creatively
- to imagine how things come together
- to get the big picture and see patterns
- to juggle many things at once
- to dream up ideas
- to have leaps of logic and insight

NOTES & COMMENTS

LEFT, RIGHT, AND CENTER

It should be remembered that these characterizations are tendencies, not hard-and-fast divisions. It does not mean that your left brain cannot come up with a fantasy, nor does it mean that your right brain cannot keep a schedule. However, if you are writing something, it is your right brain that will likely take the lead in coming up with the imagery, emotion, and metaphors, but you will need the left to find the words that express what you want to say. If you are trying to design and construct something, it is your left brain that will be most helpful in calculating the best sequence and plotting the plan of assembly, but it will likely be the right side of your brain that has the insights that make it a creative and original solution.

HOW DOES LEFT OR RIGHT BRAIN AFFECT HILL'S THEORY?

First let us restate Napoleon Hill's basic theory: By using autosuggestion techniques such as affirmations and visualizations, you can imprint your aim or purpose into your subconscious mind. Your subconscious mind is your storehouse of information and ideas, and it is also your connection to Infinite Intelligence. It is from Infinite Intelligence that your brain picks up ideas that appear in your creative imagination as hunches, intuitions, and flashes of insight.

The dual brain research confirms that certain kinds of ideas that occur in your mind are associated with one or the other side of your brain. When you affect the physical brain it has an effect upon the thoughts in your mind. Therefore, it has been scientifically proven that to some degree your brain does control your thoughts.

HOW CAN YOU USE LEFT BRAIN, RIGHT BRAIN?

This will not be the most important tip that you will learn from this workbook, but it will prove helpful when you are imprinting your aim or purpose on your subconscious.

Most people develop a kind of personal symbolism for their visualizations. For instance, when they are planting an idea in their subconscious, the mind that they visualize might have the feeling of a slightly mysterious, closed, secret hiding place, but when they are trying to come up with an idea, their mind might become a vast library.

Now that you know that the left and right sides of your brain have different tendencies, you should use that knowledge when you work with visualization. Very simply, if you are trying to impress an aim or purpose that tends toward the logical, analytical, or intellectual, as you create your visualization, mentally locate your vision of your mind on the left side of your head. Or, if your aim or purpose is more creative, intuitive, or fanciful, visualize the mind that receives it as being on the right side of your head.

ENERGY, MATTER, AND SENDING IDEAS

When Hill developed his theories about the similarity between radio waves and human thought, he did so in consultation with three of the most brilliant minds in the field: Thomas Edison, who, in addition to

NOTES & COMMENTS

NOTES & COMMENTS

inventing the electric light bulb, was also the inventor of the phonograph, the motion-picture camera, and movie projector; Dr. Alexander Graham Bell, inventor of the telephone and numerous other hearing-related devices; and Dr. Elmer Gates, mentioned in previous chapters for his extraordinary thinking process, but who also invented numerous acoustic and electronic devices.

It is no coincidence that many of the inventions perfected by these three men involved the use and manipulation of sound waves and electricity. It was because of their deep understanding of these areas of scientific research that Hill sought their advice and counsel. He was hoping they could develop experiments that would confirm his theory that the brain operates like a radio sending and receiving station. Although they could not provide Hill with conclusive scientific proof to back up his theory, all three men held views similar to Hill's, as is clear from the books and materials they published about their work.

To this day, science has still not been able to produce irrefutable proof, but as you will learn later, the most recent scientific evidence comes ever closer to corroborating the theory shared by Napoleon Hill, Alexander Graham Bell, Elmer Gates, and Thomas A. Edison.

VIBRATING MATTER

Whether you are looking at the Empire State Building, a grain of sand, a glass of water, or your right hand, what you are seeing is an organized collection of molecules. Molecules are made up of atoms. Atoms are made up of protons and neutrons, with electrons orbiting around at close to the speed of light. In between is empty space. In fact, almost 99 percent of each atom is space.

Things that appear to be solid and separate from one another are really just collections of atoms which are mostly empty space. The hardest piece of steel is in fact particles within particles revolving around other particles. So is your hand. So is your brain. So is a nerve cell.

WAVES OF ENERGY

In the human brain there are approximately 100 billion neurons or nerve cells. Each neuron is connected to thousands of neural networks which are sort of like electrical circuits that in turn control the mental processes and physical functions.

- When neurons communicate they send electrical pulses.
- Electrical impulses radiate waves of energy.
- Waves of energy have an effect on the objects they run into.

HOW WAVES OF ENERGY CAN AFFECT OTHER THINGS

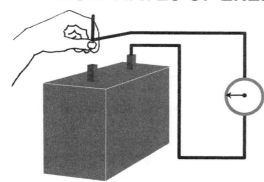

1. Connect a voltmeter to two lengths of wire that can be attached to the two terminals of a battery. One end of the wire is connected to the negative terminal, the other end of the wire is unattached.

2. A second voltmeter is connected to a loop of wire, as shown in the illustration below right.

3. When the loose end of the wire is touched to the positive terminal of the battery, a pulse of electricity passes through the wire, which registers on its voltmeter. As the electricity pulses through the wire, it also causes a wave of energy to travel outward into the air.

4. Each pulse sends out a wave of energy, and as each wave hits the other loop of wire, the electrons in the wire loop react to the wave of enery, causing the electrons to flow in the wire, which registers on its voltmeter.

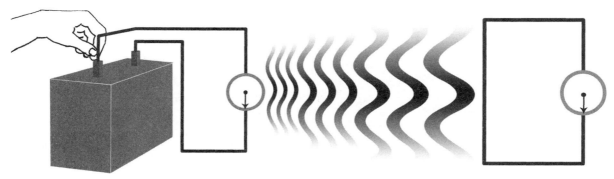

SENDING AND RECEIVING THOUGHT WAVES OF ENERGY

Hill's concept of how you receive a hunch or an intuitive thought is very similar to the way the second loop of wire picks up the radiating waves of energy being sent out from the wire attached to the battery.

- Electromagnetic waves are waves of energy that are able to travel through space, air, and solid materials.

- Science has categorized waves by the term *frequency,* which refers to the number of waves per second.

- As the chart below illustrates, the lowest frequency waves are radio waves. As the waves get faster they become microwaves, then infrared waves, then visible light waves, then invisible ultraviolet light waves, followed by x-rays, and finally gamma rays.

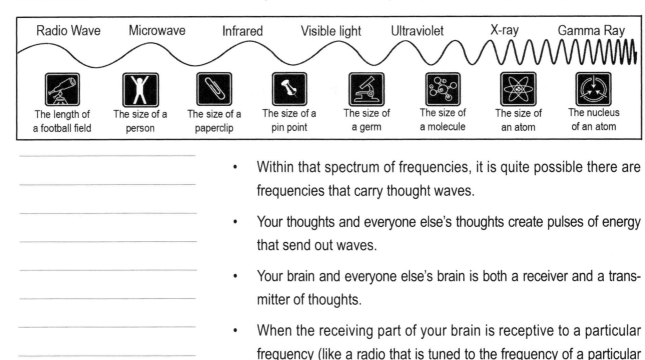

Radio Wave	Microwave	Infrared	Visible light	Ultraviolet	X-ray	Gamma Ray
The length of a football field	The size of a person	The size of a paperclip	The size of a pin point	The size of a germ	The size of a molecule	The size of an atom	The nucleus of an atom

- Within that spectrum of frequencies, it is quite possible there are frequencies that carry thought waves.

- Your thoughts and everyone else's thoughts create pulses of energy that send out waves.

- Your brain and everyone else's brain is both a receiver and a transmitter of thoughts.

- When the receiving part of your brain is receptive to a particular frequency (like a radio that is tuned to the frequency of a particular station), your brain can "pick up" thoughts that are causing waves of energy to radiate at that particular frequency.

NAPOLEON HILL AND ALEXANDER GRAHAM BELL

As mentioned above, there are many wavelengths that could be carrying thought waves. Following is how Napoleon Hill explained it in *Law of Success*, Volume One, Lesson One, Introduction to the Master Mind:

> It is my belief that all vibrations that produce energy are simply varying forms of the same thing; the difference is in the rate of vibration. The difference between light and sound is only the rate of vibration. Thoughts, too, are energy. Therefore, the only difference between thought, sound, heat, or light is the number of vibrations per second.
>
> Sound waves are floating around us at all times, but these waves cannot be detected, beyond a short distance from their source, except by the aid of a properly tuned radio receiver.
>
> Now, it seems reasonable to suppose that thought, being the most highly organized form of energy known, is also constantly sending waves, but these waves, like those of sound, can only be detected and correctly interpreted by a properly attuned mind.

The following is how Alexander Graham Bell wrote about the concept of waves of energy being generated by human thinking:

> It has occurred to me that there must be a great deal to be learned about the effect of those vibrations in the great gap where the ordinary human senses are unable to hear, see, or feel the movement . . . It seems to me that in this gap lie the vibrations that we have assumed to be given off by our brains and nerve cells when we think.
>
> We may assume that the brain cells act as a battery and that the current produced flows along the nerves. But does

it end there? Does it not pass out of the body in waves that flow around the world unperceived by our senses, just as wireless (radio) waves passed unperceived before Hertz and others discovered their existence?

This is what Hill wrote about Elmer Gates' explanation of how brain or thought waves relate to Gates' method of "sitting for ideas":

It was more than twenty years ago that I first talked with Dr. Gates on this subject. Since that time, through the discovery of radio, we have a reasonable hypothesis through which to explain the results of these "sittings."

I have not a doubt that when Dr. Gates sat down in a room and placed himself in a quiet, passive state of mind, the dominating thoughts in his mind served as a force that attracted the similar thought waves of others.

It may be that by the act of focusing your mind on a given subject you send out thought waves that reach and blend with those of a related or similar nature, thereby establishing a line of communication between the one doing the concentrating and the thoughts of a similar nature that have been previously set into motion.

IS IT YOUR BRAIN OR YOUR MIND?

At the beginning of this chapter on the brain, Napoleon Hill states his belief that the brain is a sending and receiving station for thoughts. What is very significant in that sentence is the implication that the brain and the mind are the same thing. In fact, throughout the chapter Hill uses the two words _brain_ and _mind_ interchangeably. It is his assumption that the mind and the brain are either one and the same, or at least that the mind is housed in the brain.

Napoleon Hill is often quoted as saying that your mind is like a muscle; the more you use it, the stronger it becomes and the better it works. Although that was not the conventional belief at the time, Hill was supported in his theory by the work of Elmer Gates—who *was* one of the most respected scientists of the day. As was explained in the section on Gates in chapter 13, Dr. Gates theorized that learning or training in a particular subject will actually alter a specific area of the brain. Using animal experiments, Gates was able to scientifically test the theory in his laboratory. The results were just as he predicted: the neural structure of the targeted part of the brain had been increased. As previously noted, more information makes more brain-mass, and more brain-mass gives the mind more capacity with which to create.

In the years since Hill wrote about his own theory and Dr. Gates' experiments, medical science has come to accept what was considered their unconventional view of the way the adult brain works. By the beginning of the twenty-first century, numerous research programs including those at Harvard Medical School, the University of California at San Diego, UCLA, and the University of Wisconsin have concluded that the adult brain has an ability that is now being called *neuroplasticity,* which means it changes its structure and function in response to experience. In layman's terms, that means Hill and Gates were right—it's like a muscle that gets stronger the more you use it.

Before moving on, we want to point out the implication of the results achieved by Gates and now reaffirmed almost one hundred years later by modern science: the brain, which is a physical thing, was physically altered by thinking, which is something the mind did.

Starting in the 1930s and 1940s, famed neurosurgeon Dr. Wilder Penfield expanded our knowledge of the brain tremendously by creating a map of the surface of the brain showing which areas governed which muscular actions and bodily responses. He was able to determine which area of the brain governed which part of the body by applying mild electrical stimulation to various parts of the cortex while it was exposed during brain surgery. It was during this procedure that Penfield found that by stimulating the temporal lobes in the front of the brain, it would cause the patient to recall vividly detailed memories.

As Penfield stimulated patients' brains, it produced memories so real that patients could smell flowers or feel textures. But there was an even more surprising result. Although these patients' brains were making them experience completely realistic memories, when Dr. Penfield asked the patients where they were, they knew that they were not in the memories; they knew they were in the hospital.

One patient was so involved in her realistic memory of a birthday-party picnic that she could smell the daisies and taste the cake. But when Dr. Penfield asked, "Are you at the picnic?" she said, "No, I'm in the operating room."

Who, then, was the person who was in the memory, and who was the person who said "no"?

Penfield concluded that although he could tweak the brain to make it believe hallucinations that are indistinguishable from reality, there is still a separate mind stepped back from and outside the brain that knows what is going on. This is how he described it:

> "I cannot find the choice-maker. I cannot find the interpreter. All I can measure are the effects of the choices, the interpretations, and the decisions once they are already made. Then I can localize them in the brain. But I can't localize this person, the choice-maker who is making those choices."

More recently, the development of the EEG, CAT scans, PET scans, and functional MRI scans now allow us to literally watch the brain as it is working. By using these scanning techniques, trained medical professionals can observe various areas of the brain lighting up to reveal when you are thinking, what part of your brain you are using to think with, how well you are thinking, if the thought you are thinking is true or false, and, to some degree, even what the thought is that you are thinking.

But the one thing the scans do not tell is where the mind is that is thinking the thoughts that light up the scans.

MIND WAVES INTO BRAIN WAVES

Another extraordinary example of modern science and brain research is the work being done with computer interfaces that can translate thoughts into action. There are a number of successful projects in which people with disabilities are taught how to manipulate the cursor on a computer monitor using nothing but their thoughts. Most of these projects use sensors that detect electroencephalograph signals generated by the neurons in the brain. A computer program translates those brain waves into electronic signals that operate the computer and move the cursor.

The most significant aspect for our purposes is that it is the patient's thought that sets everything in motion. A thought that the patient chooses to think of in his mind somehow stimulates an area of the physical brain, which causes the brain to send out a brain wave, which is picked up by the EEG machine.

Again, we can track the effects in reverse from the moving cursor back to the EEG sensors, back to the brain wave and the specific place in the brain where it originated, and there we come to an abrupt halt.

Where is the mind that thought the thought?

BEING WITHIN IS NOT THE SAME AS BEING INSIDE

Where the mind resides is one of the most challenging scientific questions. There are some scientists who believe that your mind is, in fact, the three or four pounds of matter and the one hundred billion neurons inside your cranium, and it can all be explained biologically.

However, that has become the minority view among scientists. With the advancements in scanning technology, the research into energy emissions, the work being done not just with brain waves but with thought waves, the holographic brain/body theory, and the concept of consciousness as biochemical messengers that link all of our systems and organs—joined with the greater understanding that on a subatomic level everything is energy—all come together to produce a conception of the mind not as a thing but as energy without form.

Brain surgeries have proved there is no doubt that the mind has a connection to the brain, but it is not as though the mind is sitting inside the brain working the controls. The mind is indeed in the brain, but it is there in the same way that magnetism is in a magnet, or a positive charge is in an electron. It is not a thing *inside* the brain, it is energy *within* the brain. Most modern scientists envision the mind as something like waves of energy, and they see the brain as a kind of physical transmitter that conveys information.

To illustrate the concept, Deepak Chopra likens it to listening to Beethoven on a radio and then tearing the radio apart hoping to find Beethoven inside. You won't find him there because he really isn't there. As you pull out the parts and wires, just like probing the cortex of the brain, reception will be affected and the sound will sputter in and out until it finally quits. But you won't find Beethoven inside the pieces of the radio, and you won't find your mind inside the pieces of your brain.

As we near the end of the first decade of the twenty-first century, most scientists no longer conceive of the mind as a thing. Some don't even use the word *mind,* because it is a noun and a noun is a thing. They believe that rather than using *mind* we should use the verb *minding,* which means *paying attention,* and that better conveys the idea.

Unlike a brain that is a thing that exists at some place in time and space, a mind is timeless and occupies no space. And a thought or idea is just a ripple of energy.

SO WHAT DOES IT MEAN TO YOU?

It means you can believe in Napoleon Hill's theory. It also sheds some light on the concept of the Master Mind. The following explanation is excerpted and adapted from *Law of Success: The 21st-Century Edition,* Volume One, Lesson One, Introduction to the Master Mind:

It is a fact that some minds clash the moment they come into contact with each other, while other minds show a natural affinity for each other.

It's quite probable that the mind is made up of energy, and when two minds come close enough to form a contact the mixing sets up a chemical reaction and starts vibrations that affect the two individuals pleasantly or unpleasantly.

That the reaction takes place gives us a starting point from which we may show what is meant by the term *Master Mind.*

A Master Mind may be created through the bringing together or blending, in a spirit of perfect harmony, of two or more minds. Out of this blending, the chemistry of the mind creates a third mind which may be used by one or all of the individual minds. This Master Mind will remain available as long as the friendly, harmonious alliance between the individual minds exists.

THE SIXTH SENSE 15

CHAPTER 15: OVERVIEW AND ANALYSIS

THE DOOR TO THE TEMPLE OF WISDOM

This chapter opens with Napoleon Hill announcing that this is the final principle in his philosophy of success. This chapter is about your creative imagination, which Hill describes as the receiving set of the mind, through which you receive thoughts, plans, and ideas. If you develop this ability you will have a surprising sensitivity both to what is happening and to what is going to happen.

MIRACLES OF THE SIXTH SENSE

Hill notes that this ability is generally referred to as some kind of mysterious sixth sense, but he says he is far too experienced to believe that nature's laws can be broken in that way. He says it is no miracle and it is no accident that you get hunches or intuitions. We may mistake them for miracles, but they are just a part of nature's law and the human thinking process that Hill identifies as creative intelligence. And because

"No matter who you are, or what may have been your purpose in reading this book, you can profit by it even if you don't fully understand how or why the principle described in this chapter works. This is especially true if your major purpose is that of accumulation of money or other material things."

it is a law of nature, you can work with it just as you work with gravity, electricity, radiation, or horticulture to achieve your aim or desire.

LET GREAT PEOPLE SHAPE YOUR LIFE

Hill opens this section by confessing that he has always been in awe of certain historical figures. He tells about the technique he developed to shed some of his backwoods ways and improve his character by emulating the great men of history, in the hope of catching some of what made them great.

Hill chose the nine men whose lives and work had impressed him most. He researched and studied their histories and accomplishments until he felt he understood them well enough to know how they might think and act. Then before going to sleep each night, he would imagine that he sat at the head of a table surrounded by these nine men, and he would conduct an imaginary council meeting in which they would give him advice on how to handle problems that he faced in his real life.

Hill says that he knows his counselors only existed in his imagination, but he believes by creating each one in such detail he was able to tap into certain ideas and information which resided in parts of his subconscious that he could not have reached in any other way.

EDITOR'S COMMENTARY

The editors explain that Hill's experience with his imaginary counselors is very similar to what happens with authors who find that their fictional characters begin to suggest dialogue and plot points. A similar thing also happens in therapy sessions when people "role play" so effectively that they get flashes of insight into someone else's experience and emotions.

TAPPING THE SOURCE OF INSPIRATION

There is no doubt that somewhere in the mind there is something that receives hunches and intuitions. Even if we can't control it, we would be foolish not to at least leave ourselves open to it. Hill says that by keeping his mind open to the possibility, he has had flashes of intuition and insight that may have actually saved him from being injured.

Hill concludes the chapter with the statement that neither complete understanding nor devout belief is necessary to test the technique. It will work for you if you can give it the benefit of the doubt and just believe enough to accept that it is a possibility.

CHAPTER 15: THE WORKBOOK

There are five senses through which you perceive things:

1. sight
2. touch
3. hearing
4. smell
5. taste

The term *sixth sense* refers to yet another way of perceiving or knowing that we have all experienced but which cannot be attributed to the usual senses. This so-called sixth sense includes all of the forms of intuition and insight, such as hunches, gut feelings, instincts, mother's intuition, premonitions, first impressions, the eureka response, sudden inspiration, empathy, instant dislikes, suspicions, mistrust, and even love at first sight.

IT'S NOT YOUR SIXTH SENSE, IT'S CREATIVE IMAGINATION

It is Napoleon Hill's position that this way of knowing is not an additional "sixth" sense; he says it is just your creative imagination doing exactly what it is supposed to do. The following will walk you through the steps that led to Hill's conclusion:

Where do the ideas come from that appear in your creative imagination?

The ideas come from your subconscious, and you are not consciously aware of them until they appear in your creative imagination.

Where does your subconscious information come from?

- From everything you ever learned through your five senses, which stays in your subconscious as unfiltered data.

- From information that your conscious mind has forgotten or had set aside as not applicable at the time.

- From the ideas you have intentionally burned into your subconscious through self-suggestion.

- From bits of information that have come to you through Infinite Intelligence from outside sources.

How do you get information from Infinite Intelligence?

- Pulses of energy are generated when other people think thoughts and create ideas.

- The pulses of energy created by an idea send waves radiating outward from the thinker, similar to broadcasting radio waves radiating from an antenna.

- Like the radio waves that are part of the electromagnetic spectrum which is traveling around us and within us at all times, thought waves are part of the Infinite Intelligence that is also around us and within us at all times.

- Sometimes your mind-brain becomes attuned to pick up certain frequencies.

- If another thinker's idea is sending pulses of energy at the same frequency that your mind-brain is attuned to, it receives that idea from Infinite Intelligence. When your physical brain intercepts these waves, the information the waves are carrying becomes a part of your subconscious.

- Ideas and information received from Infinite Intelligence become a part of the store of ideas in your subconscious mind.

How does your subconscious come up with the creative ideas?

- When you try to come up with an idea, you flip through your memory, you collect new data, and you try to fit the pieces together into something that seems right to you.

- At the subconscious level, all the bits and pieces of forgotten ideas and information are constantly interconnecting with each other, sometimes fitting together in new ways to create ideas that weren't there before.

- Also at the subconscious level, the new data from your conscious mind is interacting with the forgotten information plus the new ideas that just put themselves together out of bits and pieces of other old ideas, all combining to produce yet another level of new creative ideas.

- A more specialized kind of creative idea is produced when you have burned an aim or purpose into your subconscious and it influences only the bits and pieces of information that are related to your aim or purpose, bringing them together into new ideas that specifically support your desire.

What role does Infinite Intelligence play in creative imagination?

When any of the above-listed kinds of ideas come to you in your creative imagination you may experience a charge of excitement and satisfaction, but it always feels like it was perfectly logical that you should come up with the idea or solution. It always feels like it is the natural result of the thinking and research you put into it.

NOTES & COMMENTS

However, when the information that enters your subconscious mind from Infinite Intelligence appears in your creative imagination, it feels unusual and you don't know why you thought of it. It doesn't feel like it is the logical result of what you know.

Whether you call it a gut feeling, an instinct, mother's intuition, premonition, the eureka response, sudden inspiration, empathy, first impression, instant dislike, suspicion, mistrust, or love at first sight, Hill says the reason you don't know "where on earth that idea came from" is very simply that it doesn't come from your experience. It's not your idea. It's a random thought wave rippling through Infinite Intelligence, which happened to be of the right frequency to become part of your subconscious. When your conscious mind turned to thoughts of a similar nature, the idea naturally popped into your creative imagination, and because it doesn't feel familiar you call it a hunch, a premonition, or one of the other terms for an intuitive feeling.

What if it isn't unusual after all?

Although most people tend to look upon these intuitive events as unusual phenomena, Napoleon Hill asks you to consider an alternative approach. What if these aren't just wild ideas that sometimes happen? What if it isn't unusual after all? What if intuitive ideas are just as much a natural part of the thinking process as making a decision, or remembering, or imagining, or any of the other processes that you use all the time? What if it isn't some strange sixth sense, but just one of the laws of natural science working exactly the way it's supposed to?

Hill came to this theory from his observation of the regularity of the cause-and-effect relationship that is evident in every aspect of life. Hill concluded that there is a grand scheme of things that follows the laws of science and nature. As he often observed, acorns always grow into oak trees and never carrots because it is a law of nature, and it is no accident that water runs downhill instead of up, because that too is a law of nature. Why should this be any different? What if it is no accident that you get hunches or intuitions about some person or some thing that turns out to be true? What if that is a law of nature too?

But if it *is* a law of natural science, why is it so hit and miss?

Hill's response to that is to question the assumption that intuition is hit and miss.

What if these intuitive ideas are only supposed to happen to you some of the time and only under certain circumstances? After all, you don't always recall the right answer, you don't always get the joke, and you don't always know exactly what you want to say. If those parts of your thinking process don't always work perfectly, why should you expect these intuitive ideas to be any more regular or controllable?

So what does it matter if it is part of natural law?

Intuitive thinking has often been unfairly lumped in with such things as fortunetelling or communing with spirits. But by developing a straightforward, observation-based theory, Napoleon Hill has gotten rid of all the hocus-pocus and the new-agey psychobabble.

First, based on science, he found a reasonable explanation of how intuitive thoughts get into your mind. It's no more mysterious than the way that radio works.

Next, he came up with a reasonable explanation as to why these ideas seem to come at random times. It's simply that your mind isn't always 100 percent right 100 percent of the time.

The most important aspect of Hill's theory is that if these intuitive ideas are working according to natural law, then you can work with that law of nature just as you work with any of the other laws of science or nature, and through them you can better accomplish your aim.

But what if it's not true? What if intuitive thinking isn't responding to a law of natural science? As Hill has explained in other chapters, as unusual as it sounds, if you believe that it is a law, and if you treat it as though it is a law, it will work like a law. What you can conceive and believe, you can achieve. Try it, and you will convince yourself.

Why was Napoleon Hill so sure of his theory?

The whole point of this book is to teach you how to *think* and grow rich, and everything Hill learned from his research convinced him that although this kind of thinking cannot be completely controlled, you can nurture it and develop it so that you get better at it. The most persuasive evidence was that five hundred of the most successful men in the world told him to pay attention to his hunches.

TRUST YOUR HUNCHES, GO WITH YOUR INSTINCTS

When Napoleon Hill finally wrote *Think and Grow Rich,* there was no doubt in his mind that his principles of success worked. He had spent thirty years studying how and why some people are successful while other people aren't, and his research was not just a comparison of statistics and business practices. Hill got his information firsthand from the most important and successful men in America, and he was able to do this because Andrew Carnegie, the person who opened the door for him, was the biggest and most successful of them all.

When Carnegie asked Wall Street bankers to spend time with his protégé Napoleon Hill, they not only opened their office doors but they invited him into their homes and they took him into their confidences —not once but many times over a period of years.

When Andrew Carnegie suggested to the captains of industry that it would be helpful if they would explain to his young author-friend how their businesses worked, they were only too happy to meet with Hill to explain to him how they learned the tricks of their trades.

And so it went with famous scientists and inventors; the heads of universities; the most talented writers, authors, and performers; businessmen; entrepreneurs; international statesmen; labor leaders;

innovators in transportation and communications; political leaders; and even presidents of the United States.

In addition to his personal interviews, during that same period Hill devised a questionnaire for identifying success characteristics that was administered to approximately 25,000 individuals.

The focus of this chapter is Hill's finding that most high-powered and successful people listen to their gut feelings and pay attention to their hunches. Not all the time, and not with all things, but successful people believe that a good part of their success is because they trust their hunches, intuitions, and premonitions.

The editors would also point out that if you go on the Internet and search the phrase "scientific studies of hunches and intuition in success," you will find that in recent times there have been numerous studies done with high achievers, and in most of these modern studies the results agree with Hill's conclusions.

CAN YOU REALLY RELY ON IT?

The key to making your intuition and insight a part of your thinking process is to treat your hunches and gut reactions just as you would any other information that you use to make decisions. First you must realize that it is a fact that many successes have come from flashes of insight or intuition. Then you must acknowledge to yourself that you are prepared to believe it is possible that you too may receive valuable ideas in this way.

If you do believe it is *possible,* then you have at least opened the door. Now you must encourage it to happen. That does not mean you immediately accept everything that pops into your mind, but it does mean you treat everything that pops into your mind as a possibility. You evaluate it, you give it serious consideration, and you weigh the consequences of acting on it.

Sometimes you will have a hunch that turns out to be brilliant. The next time it could be dead wrong. It doesn't always work the way you want it to, and it doesn't always work when you want it to either. But you can increase the likelihood of creating more and better ideas by the simple act of acknowledging to yourself that you believe your creative imagination can help you solve problems.

As you work to improve your ability with this technique, it will help to keep in mind that your intuition isn't something outside trying to get your attention. Your intuition is really just you making yourself known. Your intuition is what you know that is buried just below your consciousness. So your intuition is really you telling yourself something. When you pay attention to your intuition it is you trusting yourself, and who knows you better than yourself?

The key is to keep an open mind and approach each intuition or insight with an attitude of open expectation. It cannot hurt to begin with a positive point of view. If it doesn't work, you can always be sensible later. But if you don't even give it chance, if you start out negative and reject all those crazy off-the-wall ideas, you will never know if it might have been the big winner you were hoping for.

HILL'S INVISIBLE COUNSELORS

Napoleon Hill developed a very specific method for tapping into this intuitive way of knowing. He called the method his "invisible counselors." It is a variation on creative visualization, and he describes his first use of it as a way to improve his character.

This development in Hill's methodology began after he had conducted a searching self-analysis and concluded that he lacked certain qualities which he wanted to incorporate into his personality. He settled on nine specific qualities and then chose nine men—each famous as a symbol of one of those qualities. He delved into each man's history until he knew almost as much about them as he knew about himself.

But Hill intended to do more than just mimic the way these men acted. His intention was to actually incorporate their way of thinking into his own thinking.

To do this, he would visualize himself seated at the head of a table, conducting a meeting attended by his nine famous counselors. In his mind Hill would visualize himself posing questions or presenting problems and he would then visualize his counselors offering solutions, with each one's comments representing the quality or point of view for which he was noted.

This is a very demanding and sophisticated mental exercise. In effect, what Hill did was divide his mind into nine channels, each one having its own special focus and being attuned to a particular aspect of human nature. By mentally posing a question and then answering that question from those nine separate viewpoints, Hill was offering multiple opportunities for his subconscious and his creative imagination to send him intuitive solutions.

By filling his mind with so much information about each of these counselors, Hill was pumping reams of knowledge into his mind, much of which was going into the nooks and crannies of his subconscious. The probability of intuitive thoughts was greatly increased by making the nine channels so vivid and unique, and by creating each one in such detail, he was able to tap into certain ideas and information that resided in parts of his subconscious which he could not have reached in any other way. His counselors may have been imaginary, but the ideas Hill got from them provided solid solutions to real problems.

IS THERE SCIENTIFIC PROOF?

In the previous chapter, The Brain, we commented on the breakthrough work done by Dr. Wilder Penfield in mapping the areas of the cerebral cortex, and his discoveries of the separation between the human brain and the human mind. Dr. Penfield found that, separate from the kind of "knowing" that takes place in the physical brain, there is another kind of knowing that takes place in your nonphysical mind: it is *a part of* your mind, but also *apart from* your mind. In some way your mind has a part that can stand back and either observe itself or exert control over itself without the rest of itself knowing it's doing it.

This unusual part of the mind that Wilder Penfield communicated with during his open-brain surgeries was encountered in quite a different way by Ernest Hilgard, Professor Emeritus of Psychology at Stanford University and one of the most respected psychologists in America.

Ernest Hilgard and his wife, Josephine, headed the highly regarded Laboratory of Hypnosis Research at Stanford University. In 1975 they launched a scientific study into hypnosis and pain control. They developed a series of experiments to determine if a person who had been hypnotized and told not to feel pain could actually feel the pain.

They began each session by confirming that the subject could indeed feel pain. They would then hypnotize him and instruct him that he would *not* feel the pain. They would test again to ensure that it was working and that he was feeling no pain.

They asked the subject to give them a signal by raising one finger if there was some part of his inner self that knew he was in pain even though his hypnotized self couldn't feel it. He raised his finger.

The Hilgards then asked if there was a way to communicate with the part that knew there was pain. They found that they could actually speak to that part of his mind, and that it could answer by speaking through him. It could tell them what was really going on, even though the subject was hypnotized and not aware of the pain.

The Hilgards published the results of their research in numerous papers and books in which they refer to this part of the subconscious as the "hidden observer" or the "silent witness." Their research showed that while the hidden observer knows of its own existence and the existence and experience of the patient, the hypnotized subject knows nothing of the hidden observer.

Just as Wilder Penfield found with the patient who was convinced she was at her birthday picnic but whose silent witness knew that she was in the hospital having a hallucination—and as the Hilgard's hidden observer knew the subject was having pain even though he could not feel it—Napoleon Hill's mind could send him intuitive ideas through an imaginary counselor.

When Hill would visualize his roundtable meetings, his imaginary counselors would present him with intuitive ideas that did not seem to come from anything he was aware that he knew. And although he knew in reality that the ideas originated from within his own mind, it was as though they came from someone else.

If there is a part of the mind that can observe itself and comment on itself, it is likely that it is the same part of the mind that could stand apart from Hill's normal thinking and provide him with flashes of insight or intuitive ideas through his imaginary counselors.

TAPPING INTO OTHER DIVISIONS OF YOUR MIND

In *Think and Grow Rich: The 21st-Century Edition,* the editors note the similarity between Napoleon Hill's imaginary counselors and what happens to authors and their fictional characters, and also to people who immerse themselves in role-playing therapy.

In this workbook we will introduce two other examples that share some common principles with Hill's imaginary counselors. First is a thinking and problem-solving technique by Dr. Edward de Bono called Six Thinking Hats, and the other is the personal-growth therapy known as Neuro-Linguistic Programming.

NOTES & COMMENTS

Six Thinking Hats

The inspiration for Dr. Edward de Bono's Six Thinking Hats is the old expression people often use when they have to solve a problem or come up with an idea, and they say that they have to put on their thinking hat. Suppose it wasn't just one thinking hat but six different thinking hats, and each hat represented a different kind of thinking. Imagine how thoroughly you would have thought about a problem or an idea if you put on the thinking hats one after the other, and each time you put on a different one of the hats, you focused on thinking about the problem just from that one point of view.

No doubt you have already recognized the similarity between using six thinking hats and using nine advisers to prompt you to think more creatively. Edward de Bono suggests that the thinking hats also help to unscramble your thinking so you can use one mode at a time instead of trying to take care of emotions, logic, information, hope, and creativity all at the same time.

Each of the thinking hats is a different color, and each color has a different style of thinking:

1. **White Hat** (think of a blank sheet—objective): Just the facts ma'am, just the facts. No opinions, no interpretations, no rationalizations, just the facts. Information, reports, facts, and figures. With white-hat thinking you focus on pulling together and reviewing all the available data. This tells you not only what you know but also helps you figure out what you don't know.

2. **Red Hat** (think of fire—subjective): The red hat represents emotional thinking and emotional intelligence. It's not what you think, it's what you feel. It doesn't have to be logical and you don't have to rationalize it. It's opinion, emotions, intuition, and empathy. It's also the kind of thinking

you do when you try to understand the responses of others, and when you think how other people will react emotionally to your ideas.

3. **Black Hat** (think of a judge's robe—objective): The black-hat thinker looks for the faults, the errors, what is wrong and negative about the subject. This is critical and judgmental thinking. Using black-hat thinking, you look at all the bad points, the risks and dangers, and try to see why it might not work. This is important because it highlights the weak points in a plan and prompts you to prepare contingency plans.

4. **Yellow Hat** (think of the sun—objective): The yellow hat represents positive thinking, sunshine, brightness, praise, and enthusiasm. It is the optimistic viewpoint that helps you to see all the benefits of the decision, the value in it, and why it will work. However, yellow-hat thinking is not naïve. It's very constructive and it produces concrete ideas and suggestions.

5. **Green Hat** (think of plants—speculative and creative): The green hat is the hat for creative thinking. This is a freewheeling, everything-goes way of thinking in which there is little criticism of ideas. This is the kind of thinking usually referred to as thinking outside the box, or pushing the envelope, and it places the highest value on coming up with alternative ideas and new approaches.

6. **Blue Hat** (think of the sky—overview): The blue hat is the control hat or the conductor hat. The blue hat represents the big picture, looking at the overall process from all the viewpoints. It monitors all the other thinking that will be needed to explore the subject, and it is the blue hat that suggests when you should try on a different hat to get some better ideas. This is the hat worn for running things and for chairing meetings, for compiling summaries, overviews, and conclusions.

To give you some idea of how you could use the Thinking Hats technique, you might start by trying to come up with an idea or solution to a problem you're having by "putting on" the blue hat to first sort out in your mind what your goals and objectives are.

You could put on your white hat to gather all the data you can find and review everything you already know about the problem.

Then you might move to red-hat thinking in order to ask yourself how you really feel about it, and to project how others might react to the problem.

Next you might move on to the yellow hat and then the green hat, in order to generate positive ideas and possible creative solutions.

You might also move between white-hat thinking as a part of developing information, and black-hat thinking to develop criticisms of the solution.

Although not as creatively vivid or as intellectually demanding as learning everything possible about nine famous people, the Six Thinking Hats technique will definitely push you to consider ideas you would not have thought of otherwise. And the more avenues you open into your thinking, the more likely the possibility of your creative imagination producing ideas from Infinite Intelligence.

Neuro-Linguistic Programming

In the early 1970s, John Grinder, a professor of linguistics at the University of California at Santa Cruz, and Richard Bandler, a student leading a Gestalt therapy group there, developed a self-improvement method they called Neuro-Linguistic Programming.

It is a method for identifying what it is about yourself that is keeping you from being as successful as you wish to be, and then changing who you are by systematically adopting the language, beliefs, and behaviors of those people who have achieved the kind of success and excellence you want for yourself.

In short, your thoughts, gestures, and words create your world and who you are in that world. NLP can change that perception by teaching you to use new thoughts, gestures, and words that will make you successful. These new thoughts and words are guaranteed to work because they are copied from people who are proven successes.

Readers of *Think and Grow Rich* will immediately recognize NLP as a version of Napoleon Hill's imaginary advisers, backed up by more current scientific research and some of the techniques made popular by the human potential movement. However, unlike Hill's mental round-table, which he invented as his own personal way to improve certain things about himself, NLP is a formal system with its own extensive vocabulary of unique terminology, and very specific techniques and practices. Its founders and followers consider it to be a superior form of therapy for solving psychological problems, and they believe NLP will replace the traditional therapeutic methods.

Starting from the premise that people become successful because of the way they think, act, and speak, Bandler and Grinder set out to analyze the thoughts, actions, and speech of three people who were extremely successful communicators. They chose three highly respected therapists: Milton Erickson, the father of hypnotherapy; Fritz Perls, the founder of Gestalt therapy; and Virginia Satir, the noted family therapist. They analyzed in minute detail every aspect of the style, language, and methods used by these three individuals.

Their research revealed certain patterns from which they created "models." Their theory is that these models can be used by anyone to remake themselves, and by remaking themselves patterned after these models they will improve their ability to communicate, which in turn will help them achieve their desires. The three models they developed from their study of Perls, Satir, and Erickson are the basis from which the entire NLP technique was constructed.

NOTES & COMMENTS

By studying the NLP models, you learn first what you want to change about yourself, and second you learn specific techniques for adopting the style and language of someone else who has already succeeded in what you wish to accomplish.

The idea is that if someone has excelled at something, you can learn how that person did it by observing the details of their behavior and then copying them right down to the smallest detail. When you are modeling another person, you must suspend your own beliefs and adopt everything about the model, from the way they carry themselves, to their personal style, to the way they use language. You must study all you can about their thoughts, feelings, and beliefs, until you can imitate their every thought and movement. In every way you must act as if *you* are your model. The more realistically you act as if you are the model, the more your brain begins to learn the model's patterns and eventually the patterns adapt to you so that you are no longer "acting as if"—you have actually become your version of the pattern.

NLP has had its greatest success in the areas of motivation, counseling, coaching, peak performance, sales training, and dealing with personal issues ranging from changing negative beliefs to overcoming fears and phobias, depression, and addiction.

As noted earlier, Neuro-Linguistic Programming involves much more than Hill's method for improving his character and coming up with intuitive ideas, but the bloodlines are clear. The basic idea of studying and copying someone so that you can tap into what makes them a success is a direct line to Hill's imaginary counselors.

The amount of detail that has been provided on the Six Thinking Hats and Neuro-Linguistic Programming is enough to show the similarities between these methods and Napoleon Hill's invisible counselors, and perhaps even enough for readers to experiment in a minor way with the Six Thinking Hats. However, if you are serious about attempting the techniques, you will need much more detailed explanations, especially for NLP.

If you wish to learn more, the editors suggest reading *Six Thinking Hats* by Edward de Bono, which you will find available through most booksellers.

To learn more about Neuro-Linguistic Programming, we suggest you might start with the first book by Bandler and Grinder, *Frogs Into Princes*, or *Neuro-Linguistic Programming, Volume I,* by Dilts, Grinder, Bandler, and DeLozier, or just search NLP on the Internet.

THE
SIX GHOSTS
OF FEAR

16

CHAPTER 16: OVERVIEW AND ANALYSIS

HOW MANY ARE STANDING IN YOUR WAY?

This chapter opens with Hill's statement that before you can use his philosophy you must get rid of indecision, doubt, and fear. Indecision crystallizes into doubt, which turns into fear. This chapter describes the causes and cures of the six basic fears.

THE SIX BASIC FEARS

Hill lists these six fears, noting that there are other fears too but they are all variations on one of the six basics. All fears start with thought impulses, and because your thoughts are the one thing over which you have complete control, if you choose to, you can control your fears.

FIRST BASIC FEAR: THE FEAR OF POVERTY

Napoleon Hill says fear of poverty is the most destructive fear because it can drive you to harm others in an effort to get what you want.

"Before you can put any portion of this philosophy into successful use, your mind must be prepared to receive it. The preparation is not difficult. It begins with study, analysis, and understanding of three enemies that you shall have to clear out: indecision, doubt, and fear."

He lists many of the ways that the fear of poverty can affect your character and destroy your ambition, and he follows that with a list of the symptoms of the fear of poverty.

Hill closes this section by reprinting an essay by Westbrook Pegler which points out what can happen when a person becomes beaten into hopelessness by poverty.

SECOND BASIC FEAR: THE FEAR OF CRITICISM

Hill says this is the fear that robs you of initiative and destroys your ambition. He says that to criticize is the one thing everyone seems to think they have a right to do. He also comments on how harmful it can be when parents criticize their children.

This section closes with a list of the symptoms of the fear of criticism.

THIRD BASIC FEAR: THE FEAR OF ILL HEALTH

This fear is associated with the fear of old age and it is also based on the fear of the economic toll it can take.

Hill comments on hypochondria and how the fear of ill health can end up *creating* ill health.

The section closes with the symptoms of this fear.

FOURTH BASIC FEAR: THE FEAR OF LOSS OF LOVE

This can be the most painful fear of all, and Hill calls jealousy a form of mental illness.

The section closes with the symptoms of the fear of loss of love.

FIFTH BASIC FEAR: THE FEAR OF OLD AGE

Hill says this fear is the result of the fear of poverty, the fear of losing control of your life, and the fear of what is on the other side.

The section closes with a list of symptoms of the fear of old age.

SIXTH BASIC FEAR: THE FEAR OF DEATH

This last fear is closely tied to the fear of pain and to the fear of the unknown, caused by certain religious beliefs.

Hill believes that everything in the universe is either matter or energy, and because death is just a transformation of matter into energy, life cannot be destroyed.

The section closes with a list of symptoms of the fear of death.

THE DISASTER OF WORRY AND DESTRUCTIVE THINKING

Worry is a state of mind based on fear. Worry is sustained fear caused by indecision. Because worry is a state of mind, it can be controlled.

Hill uses the story of a death-row prisoner to illustrate that decision gives peace of mind; *in*decision turns all six fears into worry.

He says that if you have fear in your mind, it gives off the sense of a loser and people pick up on it. But because fear is also a state of mind, it can be controlled by you.

THE DEVIL'S WORKSHOP

By this Hill means the susceptibility to any kind of negative influences —from bad associates to people who depress you to a dependence on drugs. Your only defense is your willpower.

SELF-ANALYSIS QUESTIONS

In this section Hill lists sixty questions that will help you to see yourself as you really are.

THE ONE THING OVER WHICH YOU HAVE ABSOLUTE CONTROL

Hill restates his warning that you must protect your thoughts and not let others influence you. You either control your mind or it controls you.

FIFTY-FIVE FAMOUS ALIBIS BY OLD MAN "IF"

Hill suggests that you go over this list of fifty-five excuses people use to explain their failures to see which ones you also use. He notes that, if you follow his philosophy, all of the alibis are obsolete.

Napoleon Hill closes with a restatement of his basic philosophy and the promise that if you put it to use, the rewards are well worth the effort.

"To protect yourself against negative influences, whether of your own making or the result of negative people around you, recognize that your willpower is your defense. You must put it into constant use until it builds a wall of immunity against all the negative influences in your own mind."

CHAPTER 16: THE WORKBOOK

REAL FEAR, AND WHAT-IF FEAR

Fear is a natural and reasonable response to the threat of danger, pain, or evil. If you are faced with a situation that presents the possibility you can suffer harm, fear is a perfectly reasonable response. In fact, fear as a response to danger is hard-wired into your brain. It is called the fight-or-flight response, which describes the way your respiration increases, your adrenaline floods into your blood stream, your immune system mobilizes, and you become prepared physically and psychologically to attack or escape.

The kind of fear that prompts the fight-or-flight response is real and immediate. Something happens, you respond. But there is another kind of fear that might be called imagined or anticipatory fear, and it is these what-if fears that Napoleon Hill writes about under the heading The Six Ghosts of Fear:

- the fear of poverty
- the fear of criticism
- the fear of ill health
- the fear of loss of love of someone
- the fear of old age
- the fear of death

If you suffer from one of these what-if fears, there is only one way to get rid of it: stop dwelling on your fear. That may sound too simplistic, but this is exactly what you must do. There is no other answer.

Fears are nothing more than states of mind. Nature has endowed human beings with absolute control over only one thing, and that one thing is thought. This fact, coupled with the additional fact that everything we create begins in the form of a thought, leads us to the principle by which fear may be mastered.

Hill has three constant messages that pertain to managing these fears:

1. The only thing over which you have complete control is your mind.

2. Your mind will attract whatever it dwells upon.

3. You cannot hold both a positive and a negative in your mind at the same time.

You either believe that you will achieve your aim or purpose, or you fear that you will not achieve it. It must be one or the other. It is up to you to stop dwelling on the fear of what *might* happen, and stay focused on accomplishing your aim or purpose.

FIRST BASIC FEAR: THE FEAR OF POVERTY

Every person reading this workbook must face the fact that it is possible you could find yourself out on the street, living hand-to-mouth.

For some readers, the fear of poverty can be a motivating force that pushes you to succeed so it will never happen to you. For others, the fear of poverty has just the opposite effect. For them the fear of poverty keeps them from pushing themselves to succeed because the fear of losing what they have is more real than the possibility of success.

The fear of poverty can kill your adventurous spirit and turn you into a timid, overly cautious do-nothing. If you allow yourself to fear poverty, you will dwell on the fear and never see the other side. It has to be put into perspective. You must strike a balance.

What that means is that you accept poverty as one possibility, but you also recognize that riches are a possibility too. If you change from fearing poverty to desiring wealth, you will have done it.

Knowledge of what could happen and fear of what could happen are two different things. When you have knowledge you act. When you have fear you react.

FEAR OF POVERTY

As you read through each of the following symptoms of the fear of poverty, give yourself a grade from one to ten and make a note explaining why you feel that way.

Return in three months to see if you think your grade has improved. Then come back again at the end of six months and grade yourself once more.

1. **Indifference.** Expressed through lack of ambition, willingness to tolerate poverty and accept whatever life hands you. Also laziness, lack of initiative, imagination, and self-control.

1 2 3 4 5 6 7 8 9 10 _____

_____

_____

2. **Doubt.** Generally expressed through excuses designed to cover up or apologize for your failures. Sometimes expressed as envy of those who are successful, or by criticizing them.

1 2 3 4 5 6 7 8 9 10 _____

_____

_____

3. **Worry.** Usually expressed by finding fault with others, a tendency to spend beyond your income, neglect of personal appearance, nervousness, lack of poise, self-consciousness, and often the use of alcohol or drugs.

1 2 3 4 5 6 7 8 9 10 _____

_____

_____

4. **Indecision.** The habit of permitting others to do your thinking; sitting on the fence.

1 2 3 4 5 6 7 8 9 10 _____

_____

_____

5. **Overcaution.** The habit of looking for the negative side of every circumstance. Knowing all the roads to disaster but never searching for the plans to avoid failure. Always waiting for "the right time" to begin, instead of getting started now.

1 2 3 4 5 6 7 8 9 10 _____

_____

_____

6. **Procrastination.** This symptom is closely related to overcaution, doubt, and worry. Spending more time in creating excuses than it would take to do the job. Refusal to accept responsibility. Willingness to compromise with difficulties instead of using them as steppingstones to advancement. Bargaining with life for a penny instead of demanding prosperity, opulence, riches, contentment, and happiness. Associating with those who accept poverty instead of seeking the company of those who demand and receive riches.

1 2 3 4 5 6 7 8 9 10 _____

_____

_____

SECOND BASIC FEAR:
THE FEAR OF CRITICISM

Fear of criticism manifests itself in a thousand different ways. People are afraid to be criticized for everything, from whether they wear the right clothes and have the right sneakers to whether they belong to the right group, gang, clique, club, or organization. You can be criticized because you don't speak with the right accent, have the right skin color, the right religion, the right political beliefs, or even whether you are the right gender, height, or weight. Whether it's called peer pressure or keeping up with the Joneses, it is a fear of being criticized.

The criticism doesn't even have to actually happen to you for the fear to set in. Just watch a few other people get criticized, and that's usually enough to keep you from giving it a try.

Faith in yourself and in your abilities is the only thing that will overcome fear of criticism. Self-esteem is *self* esteem, not something you have given to you; it is how *you* feel.

That is why the fear of criticism becomes less important as you get older. Over time you have more experience with who you really are, and you care less about what other people think, but you care more about what *you* think about yourself.

Here's your opportunity to gain that knowledge right now, no matter how old you are. Ask yourself, what's the worst that could happen if I attempt something and someone criticizes me? The worst thing is that you might get your feelings hurt for a bit.

Now ask yourself what's the best thing that could happen? If the best thing that could happen is that you accomplish your goal, it's a no-brainer.

If the worst is that you get your feelings hurt, and the best is that you succeed, it doesn't take a genius to know that you are better off if you give it a try.

FEAR OF CRITICISM

As you read through each of the following symptoms of the fear of criticism, give yourself a grade from one to ten and make a note explaining why you feel that way.

Return in three months to see if you think your grade has improved. Then come back again at the end of six months and grade yourself once more.

1. **Self-consciousness.** Generally expressed through nervousness, timidity in conversation and in meeting strangers, awkward movements, and shifting of the eyes.

1 2 3 4 5 6 7 8 9 10_____

_____

_____

2. **Lack of poise.** Expressed through lack of voice control, nervousness in the presence of others, poor posture, poor memory.

1 2 3 4 5 6 7 8 9 10_____

_____

_____

3. **Indecision.** Lacking in firmness and the ability to express opinions definitely. The habit of sidestepping issues instead of meeting them squarely. Agreeing with others without careful examination of their opinions.

1 2 3 4 5 6 7 8 9 10_____

_____

_____

4. **Inferiority complex.** The habit of expressing your own self-approval as a means of covering up your feelings of inferiority. Using "big words" to impress others (often without knowing the actual meaning of the words). Imitating others in dress, speech, and manners. Boasting of imaginary achievements and "acting superior" to cover up the fact that you feel inferior.

1 2 3 4 5 6 7 8 9 10_____

_____

_____

5. **Mental and physical laziness.** The lack of self-assertion, slowness in reaching decisions, being too easily influenced, the habit of accepting defeat without protest or quitting an undertaking when opposed by others.

1 2 3 4 5 6 7 8 9 10_____

_____

_____

6. **The habit of criticizing others** behind their backs and flattering them to their faces; suspicion of other people without cause; unwillingness to accept the blame for mistakes.

1 2 3 4 5 6 7 8 9 10_____

_____

_____

7. **Extravagance.** The habit of trying to "keep up with the Joneses" and spending beyond your income.

1 2 3 4 5 6 7 8 9 10_____

_____

_____

8. **Lack of initiative.** Failure to embrace opportunities for self-advancement, lack of confidence in your own ideas, hesitancy of manner and speech, deceit in both words and deeds.

1 2 3 4 5 6 7 8 9 10_____

_____

_____

NOTES & COMMENTS

_____

_____

_____

_____

_____

_____

_____

_____

THIRD BASIC FEAR: THE LOSS OF LOVE

No one wants to lose the love of someone they care for, but there is a big difference between a natural and normal concern, and living in fear that it will happen. The real issue is why you think it is a possibility that you will lose the love of the person you desire.

If you are afraid that someone won't love you, it may mean that you are dependent on the love of some person (or group) to help define your self-image and make you feel successful and complete.

Fearing the loss of love can also be a signal that at some level you know something about yourself that makes you believe you are not worthy of their love. You are worried that you cannot live up to their expectations. Your fear is not just that you will lose love; it is also the fear that your secret weakness or failing will be exposed.

The greatest danger in fearing the loss of love is that it can also erode your faith by eating away at your self-image and self-confidence. If you don't believe that you deserve to be loved, if you are constantly worried that you aren't good enough, it is hard to maintain a healthy self-respect. And if you do not respect yourself, you cannot have faith in yourself.

FEAR OF THE LOSS OF LOVE

As you read through each of the following symptoms of the fear of the loss of love, give yourself a grade from one to ten and make a note explaining why you feel that way.

Return in three months to see if you think your grade has improved. Then come back again at the end of six months and grade yourself once more.

1. **Jealousy.** The habit of being suspicious of friends and loved ones. The habit of accusing your wife or husband of infidelity without grounds. General suspicion of everyone and absolute faith in no one.

1 2 3 4 5 6 7 8 9 10 _____

_____

_____

2. **Fault-finding.** The habit of finding fault with friends, relatives, business associates, and loved ones upon the slightest provocation, or without any cause whatsoever.

1 2 3 4 5 6 7 8 9 10 _____

_____

_____

3. **Gambling.** The habit of gambling, stealing, cheating, and otherwise taking hazardous chances to provide money for loved ones in the belief that love can be bought. The habit of spending beyond your means or incurring debts to provide gifts for loved ones in order to make a good impression. Other symptoms include insomnia, nervousness, lack of persistence, weakness of will, lack of self-control, lack of self-reliance, bad temper.

1 2 3 4 5 6 7 8 9 10_____

_____

_____

FOURTH BASIC FEAR: THE FEAR OF ILL HEALTH

The fear of ill health manifests itself in worrying about your aches and pains, your diet and weight, and every other fluctuation in your bodily functions. If your mind can't stay focused on your chief aim because it is being distracted by your fear for your health, then it is your fear that you are focusing on, and what you focus on is what burns itself into your subconscious.

By dwelling on the fear of ill health, it may plant the suggestion in your subconscious to the degree that through autosuggestion you develop hypochondria, a condition in which your imagination produces the physical symptoms of the very disease that you fear. Or, because of all the stress and anxiety caused by your fear, your natural resistance becomes lowered, which makes you susceptible to real disease.

FEAR OF ILL HEALTH

As you read through the following pages about each of the symptoms of the fear of ill health, give yourself a grade from one to ten and make a note explaining why you feel that way.

Return in three months to see if you think your grade has improved. Then come back again at the end of six months and grade yourself once more.

1. **Negative use of self-suggestion.** This can result in looking for, and expecting to find, symptoms of all kinds of disease; "enjoying" your imaginary illness and speaking of it as being real; the habit of trying fads and "isms" and home remedies recommended by others; talking to others about operations, accidents, and other forms of illness; experimenting with diets, exercises, and weight-loss systems without professional guidance.

1 2 3 4 5 6 7 8 9 10_____

_____

_____

2. **Hypochondria.** The habit of excessively talking about illness, and by concentrating the mind on disease you begin to expect it to happen to you. This is brought on by negative thinking, and nothing but positive thought can cure it.

1 2 3 4 5 6 7 8 9 10_____

_____

_____

3. **Lack of exercise.** Fear of ill health interferes with exercise and may result in weight gain.

1 2 3 4 5 6 7 8 9 10_____

_____

_____

4. **Susceptibility.** Fear of ill health breaks down your natural resistance, which makes you susceptible to real disease. The fear of ill health is often related to the fear of poverty, especially in the case of the hypochondriac who constantly worries about the possibility of having to pay doctors' bills, hospital bills, etc. This type of person spends much time preparing for sickness, talking about death, saving money for cemetery plots, burial expenses, and such.

1 2 3 4 5 6 7 8 9 10_____

_____

_____

5. **Self-coddling.** Seeking sympathy and feigning illness to cover a lack of ambition.

1   2   3   4   5   6   7   8   9   10 _____

_____

_____

6. **Intemperance.** Using alcohol or drugs to destroy pain instead of eliminating the cause.

1   2   3   4   5   6   7   8   9   10 _____

_____

_____

NOTES & COMMENTS

_____

_____

_____

_____

_____

_____

_____

_____

FIFTH BASIC FEAR: THE FEAR OF OLD AGE

The fear of old age is actually one of the easiest fears to deal with because it doesn't matter whether you fear getting older or not; you are still going to get older. That does not mean you shouldn't do what you can to keep on top of things, maintain your health, and stay as youthful as possible, but being fearful won't do any good.

Having fear about growing older probably means that you believe your success is directly tied to your youthfulness and that somehow your success will diminish as you age. If you dwell on that fear it will erode your faith in your abilities and you just might lose your grip. Or you could look at all the people just like you who are making a difference in the world, and you could just keep doing what you do. Only now you'll do it better, because you've got the experience that comes with age.

FEAR OF OLD AGE

As you read through the following pages about each of the symptoms of the fear of old age, give yourself a grade from one to ten and make a note explaining why you feel that way.

Return in three months to see if you think your grade has improved. Then come back again at the end of six months and grade yourself once more.

1. **Lack of enthusiasm.** The tendency to slow down and develop an inferiority complex, falsely believing you are "slipping" because of age. The habit of killing off initiative, imagination, and self-reliance by falsely believing you are too old to have these qualities.

1 2 3 4 5 6 7 8 9 10 _____

_____

_____

2. **Self-consciousness of speech.** The habit of speaking apologetically of yourself as "being old" merely because you have reached the age of perhaps fifty, instead of reversing the rule and expressing gratitude for having reached an age of wisdom and understanding.

1 2 3 4 5 6 7 8 9 10 _____

_____

_____

3. **Inappropriate dress and action.** Trying to appear much younger than your age by going overboard in your attempt to keep up with the style and mannerisms of youth.

1 2 3 4 5 6 7 8 9 10 _____

_____

_____

SIXTH BASIC FEAR: THE FEAR OF DYING

The fear of death is very similar to the fear of getting older. It does not matter how much or how little you fear death, you are still going to die. Naturally you should take reasonable precautions to protect your life, but living in fear of dying is the ultimate oxymoron.

Napoleon Hill acknowledges that various religions have played on people's fear of what awaits them on the other side, but in keeping with Andrew Carnegie's advice to avoid any religious bias, Hill's philosophy focuses on the here-and-now rather than the hereafter.

NOTES & COMMENTS

_____

_____

_____

Hill says that if you wish, you can come to terms with your mortality through the laws of natural science. The entire world is made up of matter or energy. Matter cannot be destroyed; it just converts to energy. Today you are matter. When you die you will become another form of energy.

FEAR OF DYING

As you read through each of the following symptoms of the fear of dying, give yourself a grade from one to ten and make a note explaining why you feel that way.

Return in three months to see if you think your grade has improved. Then come back again at the end of six months and grade yourself once more.

1. The habit of thinking about dying instead of making the most of life. This is generally due to lack of purpose or lack of a suitable occupation. This fear is more prevalent among the aged, but sometimes the more youthful are victims of it too. The greatest of all remedies for the fear of death is a burning desire for achievement, backed by useful service to others. A busy person seldom has time to think about dying. A busy person finds life too thrilling to worry about death.

1 2 3 4 5 6 7 8 9 10_____

_____

_____

_____

2. Sometimes the fear of dying is closely associated with the fear of poverty, where death would leave loved ones poverty-stricken.

1 2 3 4 5 6 7 8 9 10_____

_____

_____

_____

3. In other cases the fear of death is caused by illness and the breakdown of physical body resistance.

1 2 3 4 5 6 7 8 9 10_____

_____

_____

4. The most common causes of the fear of death are ill health, poverty, lack of appropriate occupation, disappointment over love, or religious fanaticism.

1 2 3 4 5 6 7 8 9 10_____

_____

_____

FEAR, WORRY, AND NEGATIVE INFLUENCES

Relieve yourself forever of the fear of dying by reaching a decision to accept death as an inescapable event. Eliminate the fear of old age by acepting it not as a handicap but as a blessing that carries with it wisdom, self-control, and understanding. Master the fear of loss of love by reaching a decision to get along without love, if that is necessary. Defeat the fear of criticism by deciding not to worry about what other people think. Overcome the fear of ill health by the decision to forget symptoms. And whip the fear of poverty by reaching a decision to get along with whatever wealth you can accumulate without worry.

In addition to the six basic fears, there is another kind of evil that Hill refers to as susceptibility to negative influences. If you really wish to succeed with this philosophy, you must examine yourself very carefully to determine whether you are susceptible to negative influences.

Make your analysis searching. As you read the questions on the following pages, be tough on yourself. You must deal with your own faults as you would deal with a real and serious enemy.

SELF-ANALYSIS QUESTIONNAIRE

The following list of questions is designed to help you see yourself as you really are. You should read through the list now, making notes as you go.

You should also set aside another day when you can give adequate time to go through the list again, and this time you should have your journal handy so you will have adequate space to answer those questions that require more elaboration. When you do this, it would be best if you read the questions and state your answers aloud so that you can hear your own voice. This will make it easier for you to be truthful with yourself.

1. Do you complain often of "feeling bad" and, if so, what is the cause?

_____

_____

_____

2. Do you find fault with other people at the slightest provocation?

_____

_____

_____

3. Do you frequently make mistakes in your work and, if so, why?

_____

_____

_____

4. Are you sarcastic and offensive in your conversation?

_____

_____

_____

5. Do you deliberately avoid associating with anyone and, if so, why?

_____

_____

_____

6. Do you suffer frequently with indigestion? If so, what is the cause?

_____

_____

_____

7. Does life seem futile and the future hopeless to you?

_____

_____

_____

8. Do you like your occupation? If not, why not?

_____

_____

_____

9. Do you often feel self-pity and, if so, why?

_____

_____

_____

10. Are you envious of those who excel you?

_____

_____

_____

11. To which do you devote the most time—thinking of success or of failure?

_____

_____

_____

12. Are you gaining or losing self-confidence as you grow older?

_____

_____

_____

13. Do you learn something of value from all mistakes?

_____

_____

_____

14. Are you permitting some relative or acquaintance to worry you? If so, why?

_____

_____

_____

15. Are you sometimes excited about life, and at other times in the depths of despondency?

_____

_____

_____

16. Who has the most inspiring influence on you, and for what reason?

_____

_____

_____

17. Do you tolerate negative or discouraging influences that you could avoid?

_____

_____

_____

18. Are you careless of your personal appearance? If so, when and why?

_____

_____

_____

19. Have you learned to ignore your troubles by being too busy to be annoyed by them?

_____

_____

_____

20. Does anyone "nag" you and, if so, for what reason?

_____

_____

_____

21. How many preventible disturbances annoy you, and why do you tolerate them?

_____

_____

_____

22. Are you easily influenced by others, against your own judgment?

_____

_____

_____

23. Would you call yourself a "spineless weakling" if you permitted others to do your thinking for you?

_____

_____

_____

24. Do you use autosuggestion to make your mind positive?

_____

_____

_____

25. Do you suffer from any of the six basic fears? If so, which ones?

_____

_____

_____

26. Have you developed a method to shield yourself against the negative influences of others?

_____

_____

_____

27. Do you have a definite major purpose and, if so, what is it and what plan do you have for achieving it?

_____

_____

_____

28. Which do you value most, your material possessions or your privilege of controlling your own thoughts?

_____

_____

_____

29. Do you resort to alcohol, drugs, cigarettes, or other compulsions to "quiet your nerves"? If so, why do you not try willpower instead?

_____

_____

_____

30. Has today added anything of value to your stock of knowledge or your state of mind?

_____

_____

_____

31. Do you face squarely the circumstances that make you unhappy, or do you sidestep the responsibility?

_____

_____

_____

32. Can you name three of your most damaging weaknesses? What are you doing to correct them?

_____

_____

_____

33. Do you analyze all mistakes and failures and try to profit by them, or do you take the attitude that this is not your duty?

_____

_____

_____

34. Do you encourage other people to bring their worries to you for sympathy?

_____

_____

_____

35. Do you choose, from your daily experiences, lessons or influences that aid in your personal advancement?

_____

_____

_____

36. When others offer you free, unsolicited advice do you accept it without question or do you analyze their motive?

_____

_____

_____

37. What habits of other people annoy you most?

_____

_____

_____

38. Do you form your own opinions, or do you permit yourself to be influenced by other people?

_____

_____

_____

39. Have you learned how to create a mental state of mind with which you can shield yourself against all discouraging influences?

_____

_____

_____

40. Does your occupation inspire you with faith and hope?

_____

_____

_____

41. Are you conscious of possessing spiritual forces of sufficient power to enable you to keep your mind free from all forms of fear?

_____

_____

_____

42. Does your religion help to keep your mind positive?

_____

_____

_____

43. Do you feel it your duty to share other people's worries? If so, why?

_____

_____

_____

44. If you believe that "birds of a feather flock together," what have you learned about your-self by studying the friends you attract?

_____

_____

_____

45. What connection, if any, do you see between the people with whom you associate most closely and any unhappiness you may experience?

_____

_____

_____

46. Is it possible that some person whom you consider to be a friend is, in reality, your worst enemy because of his or her negative influence on your mind?

_____

_____

_____

47. By what rules do you judge who is helpful and who is damaging to you?

_____

_____

_____

48. Are your intimate associates mentally superior or inferior to you?

_____

_____

_____

49. How much time out of every twenty-four hours do you devote to:

- your occupation_____
- sleep_____
- play and relaxation_____
- acquiring useful knowledge_____
- plain wasted time_____

50. Who among your acquaintances:

- encourages you most_____
- cautions you most_____
- discourages you most_____

51. Does your presence have a negative influence on other people as a rule?

_____

_____

_____

52. Whom do you believe to be the greatest person living? In what respect is this person superior to yourself?

_____

_____

_____

53. What is your greatest worry? Why do you tolerate it?

_____

_____

_____

54. Do you usually finish everything you begin?

_____

_____

_____

55. Are you easily impressed by other people's business titles, college degrees, or wealth?

_____

_____

_____

56. Do you cater to people because of their social or financial status?

_____

_____

_____

57. Are you easily influenced by what other people think or say about you?

_____

_____

_____

58. Do you change your mind often? If so, why?

_____

_____

_____

59. What, above all else, do you most desire? Are you willing to subordinate all other desires for this one, and how much time daily do you devote to acquiring it?

_____

_____

_____

60. How much time have you devoted to studying and answering these questions? (At least one day is necessary for the analysis and the answering of the entire list.)

_____

_____

_____

If you have answered all of these questions truthfully, you now know more about yourself than the majority of people know about themselves. Once you have completed your second review, and have further elaborated on all of the questions, come back to them once each week for several months and be surprised at the amount of additional knowledge of great value to yourself you will have gained by the simple method of answering these questions truthfully.

If you are not certain about the answers to some of the questions, seek the counsel of those who know you well, especially those who have no motive in flattering you, and see yourself through their eyes. The experience will be both revealing and rewarding.

ADDITIONAL NOTES & COMMENTS

_____

_____

_____

_____

_____

FIFTY-FIVE FAMOUS ALIBIS BY OLD MAN "IF"

People who do not succeed have one distinguishing trait in common. They know all the reasons for failure, and have what they believe to be airtight alibis to explain away their own lack of achievement.

Some of these alibis are clever and a few of them are justifiable by the facts. But alibis cannot be used for money. The world wants to know only one thing: Have you achieved success?

A character analyst compiled a list of the most commonly used alibis. As you read the list, examine yourself carefully and determine how many of these alibis you use. Remember, the philosophy presented in this book makes every one of these alibis obsolete.

If I didn't have a wife and family . . .

If I had enough "pull" . . .

If I had money . . .

If I had a good education . . .

If I could get a job . . .

If I had good health . . .

If I only had time . . .

If times were better . . .

If other people understood me . . .

If conditions around me were only different . . .

If I could live my life over again . . .

If I did not fear what "they" would say . . .

If I had been given a chance . . .

If I now had a chance . . .

If other people didn't "have it in for me" . . .

If nothing happens to stop me . . .

If I were only younger . . .

If I could only do what I want . . .

If I had been born rich . . .

If I could meet "the right people" . . .

If I had the talent that some people have . . .

If I dared to assert myself . . .

If only I had embraced past opportunities . . .

If people didn't get on my nerves . . .

If I didn't have to keep house and look after the children . . .

If I could save some money . . .

If the boss only appreciated me . . .

If I only had somebody to help me . . .

If my family understood me . . .

If I lived in a big city . . .

If I could just get started . . .

If I were only free . . .

If I had the personality of some people . . .

If I were not so fat . . .

If my real talents were known . . .

If I could just get a "break" . . .

If I could only get out of debt . . .

If I hadn't failed . . .

If I only knew how . . .

NOTES & COMMENTS

NOTES & COMMENTS

If everybody wasn't against me . . .

If I didn't have so many worries . . .

If I could marry the right person . . .

If people weren't so dumb . . .

If my family were not so extravagant . . .

If I were sure of myself . . .

If luck were not against me . . .

If I had not been born under the wrong star . . .

If it were not true that "what is to be will be" . . .

If I did not have to work so hard . . .

If I hadn't lost my money . . .

If I lived in a different neighborhood . . .

If I didn't have a "past" . . .

If I only had a business of my own . . .

If other people would only listen to me . . .

If—and this is the greatest of them all—I had the courage to see myself as I really am, I would find out what is wrong with me and correct it. And I know that something must be wrong with the way I have done things, or I would already have the success that I desire. I recognize that something must be wrong with me, otherwise I would have spent more time analyzing my weaknesses and less time building alibis to cover them.

ADDITIONAL COPY OF THE
SELF-INVENTORY QUESTIONNAIRE

(as explained on page 189)

SELF-INVENTORY QUESTIONNAIRE

1. Have I attained the goal that I established as my objective for this year? (You should work with a definite yearly objective to be attained as a part of your major life objective.)

1 2 3 4 5 6 7 8 9 10 _____

_____

_____

_____

2. Have I delivered service of the best possible quality of which I was capable, or could I have improved any part of this service?

1 2 3 4 5 6 7 8 9 10 _____

_____

_____

_____

3. Have I delivered service in the greatest possible quantity of which I was capable?

1 2 3 4 5 6 7 8 9 10 _____

_____

_____

_____

4. Has the spirit of my conduct been harmonious and cooperative at all times?

1 2 3 4 5 6 7 8 9 10 _____

_____

_____

_____

5. Have I permitted procrastination to decrease my efficiency and, if so, to what extent?

1 2 3 4 5 6 7 8 9 10 _____

_____

_____

_____

6. Have I improved my personality and, if so, in what ways?

1 2 3 4 5 6 7 8 9 10 _____

_____

_____

_____

7. Have I been persistent in following my plans through to completion?

1 2 3 4 5 6 7 8 9 10 _____

_____

_____

_____

8. Have I reached decisions promptly and definitely on all occasions?

1 2 3 4 5 6 7 8 9 10 _____

_____

_____

_____

9. Have I permitted any of the six basic fears to decrease my efficiency?

1 2 3 4 5 6 7 8 9 10 _____

_____

_____

_____

10. Have I been either overcautious or undercautious?

1 2 3 4 5 6 7 8 9 10 _____

_____

_____

_____

11. Has my relationship with my associates at work been pleasant or unpleasant? If it has been unpleasant, has the fault been partly or wholly mine?

1 2 3 4 5 6 7 8 9 10 _____

_____

_____

_____

12. Have I dissipated any of my energy through lack of concentration of effort?

1 2 3 4 5 6 7 8 9 10 _____

_____

_____

_____

13. Have I been open-minded and tolerant in connection with all subjects?

1 2 3 4 5 6 7 8 9 10_____

_____

_____

_____

14. In what ways have I improved my ability to render service?

1 2 3 4 5 6 7 8 9 10_____

_____

_____

_____

15. Have I been intemperate in any of my personal habits?

1 2 3 4 5 6 7 8 9 10_____

_____

_____

_____

16. Have I expressed, either openly or secretly, any form of egotism?

1 2 3 4 5 6 7 8 9 10_____

_____

_____

_____

17. Has my conduct toward my associates been such that they respect me?

1 2 3 4 5 6 7 8 9 10_____

_____

_____

_____

18. Have my opinions and decisions been based on guesswork, or on accuracy of analysis and thought?

1 2 3 4 5 6 7 8 9 10_____

_____

_____

_____

19. Have I followed the habit of budgeting my time, my expenses, and my income, and have I been conservative in these budgets?

1 2 3 4 5 6 7 8 9 10_____

_____

_____

_____

20. How much time have I devoted to unprofitable effort, which I might have used to better advantage?

1 2 3 4 5 6 7 8 9 10_____

_____

_____

_____

21. How may I rebudget my time and change my habits so that I will be more efficient during the coming year?

1 2 3 4 5 6 7 8 9 10 _____

_____

_____

_____

22. Have I been guilty of any conduct that was not approved by my own conscience?

1 2 3 4 5 6 7 8 9 10 _____

_____

_____

_____

23. In what ways have I rendered more service and better service than I was paid to render?

1 2 3 4 5 6 7 8 9 10 _____

_____

_____

_____

24. Have I been unfair to anyone and, if so, in what way?

1 2 3 4 5 6 7 8 9 10 _____

_____

_____

_____

25. If I had been the purchaser of my own services for the year, would I be satisfied with my purchase?

1 2 3 4 5 6 7 8 9 10_____

_____

_____

_____

26. Am I in the right vocation and, if not, why not?

1 2 3 4 5 6 7 8 9 10_____

_____

_____

_____

27. Has the purchaser of my services been satisfied with the service I have rendered and, if not, why not?

1 2 3 4 5 6 7 8 9 10_____

_____

_____

_____

28. What is my present rating on the fundamental principles of success? (Make this rating fairly and frankly, and have it checked by someone who is courageous enough to do that for you accurately.)

1 2 3 4 5 6 7 8 9 10_____

_____

_____

_____

IDEOMOTOR ILLUSTRATION
(as referenced on page 289)

The Four Possible Movements:

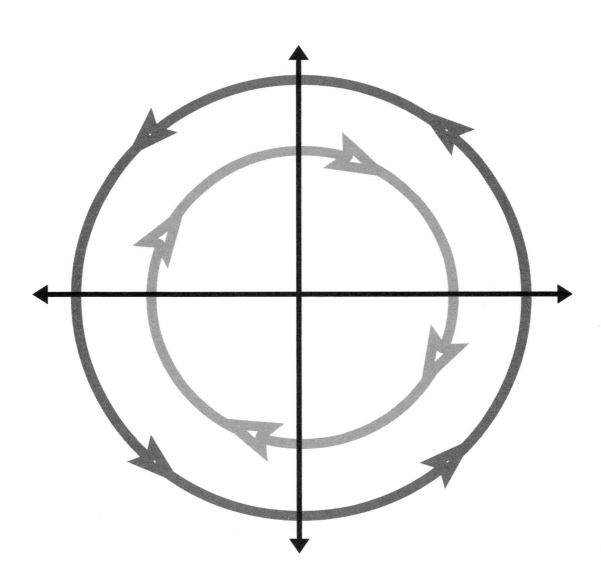

Highroads Media, Inc. is the publisher of more books and audiobooks
by Napoleon Hill than any other publisher in the world. Other titles available:

NEW BOOKS FROM HIGHROADS MEDIA

Napoleon Hill's First Editions (hardcover)

Selling You! (trade paperback)

REVISED & UPDATED BOOKS

Think and Grow Rich: The 21st-Century Edition (hardcover)

Law of Success: The 21st-Century Edition (trade paperback)

LEATHER-BOUND, GILT-EDGED COLLECTOR'S EDITIONS

Think and Grow Rich (single volume)

Law of Success (available in four volumes)

AUDIOBOOKS AVAILABLE ON CD

Selling You! (abridged audiobook)

Selling You! (unabridged audiobook)

Think and Grow Rich (unabridged and abridged audiobook editions)

Think and Grow Rich: Instant Motivator (original audiobook)

Law of Success (four-volume unabridged audiobook set)

Your Right to Be Rich (unabridged audiobook)

Napoleon Hill's Keys to Success (unabridged and abridged audiobooks)

Believe and Achieve (abridged audiobook)

The Richest Man in Babylon & The Magic Story (original audiobook)

A Lifetime of Riches: The Biography of Napoleon Hill (abridged audiobook)

For more information about Napoleon Hill books and audiobooks, contact:
Highroads Media, Inc., 6 Commerce Way, Arden, NC 28704
telephone: (323) 822-2676
fax: (323) 822-2686
email: highroadsmedia@sbcglobal.net
visit us at our website: www.highroadsmedia.com